MW00781215

Shakespeare's Artists

Shakespeare's Artists

The Painters, Sculptors, Poets and Musicians in his Plays and Poems

B.J. Sokol

Bloomsbury Arden Shakespeare
An imprint of Bloomsbury Publishing Plc

BLOOMSBURY
LONDON · OXFORD · NEW YORK · NEW DELHI · SYDNEY

Bloomsbury Arden Shakespeare

An imprint of Bloomsbury Publishing Plc

Imprint previously known as Arden Shakespeare

50 Bedford Square	1385 Broadway
London	New York
WC1B 3DP	NY 10018
UK	USA

www.bloomsbury.com

BLOOMSBURY, THE ARDEN SHAKESPEARE and the Diana logo are trademarks of Bloomsbury Publishing Plc

First published 2018

© B.J. Sokol, 2018

British Library Cataloguing-in-Publication Data
A catalogue record for this book is available from the British Library.

ISBN:	HB:	978-1-350-02193-8
	ePDF:	978-1-350-02195-2
	eBook:	978-1-350-02194-5

Library of Congress Cataloging-in-Publication Data
A catalogue record for this book is available from the Library of Congress.

Cover design: Irene Martinez Costa
Cover image: Signed self-portrait of Catherina van Hemessen, aged 20 (1548).
© ART Collection/Alamy Stock Photo

Typeset by RefineCatch Limited, Bungay, Suffolk
Printed and bound in Great Britain

To find out more about our authors and books visit www.bloomsbury.com. Here you will find extracts, author interviews, details of forthcoming events and the option to sign up for our newsletters.

For Mary: 'beauty is love'

CONTENTS

LIST OF
ILLUSTRATIONS

LIST OF ABBREVIATIONS

In the notes, Shakespeare plays and poems will be indicated by the use of the following abbreviations:

AC	*Antony and Cleopatra*
AW	*All's Well That Ends Well*
AYL	*As You Like It*
CE	*The Comedy of Errors*
Cor	*Coriolanus*
Cym	*Cymbeline*
Ham	*Hamlet*
1H4	*Henry IV, Part 1*
2H4	*Henry IV, Part 2*
H5	*Henry V*
1H6	*Henry VI, Part 1*
2H6	*Henry VI, Part 2*
3H6	*Henry VI, Part 3*
H8	*All Is True (Henry VIII)*
JC	*Julius Caesar*
KJ	*King John*
LC	*A Lover's Complaint*
LLL	*Love's Labour's Lost*
LRF	*The Tragedy of King Lear* (Folio)
LRQ	*The History of King Lear* (Quarto)
Luc	*The Rape of Lucrece*
MA	*Much Ado About Nothing*
Mac	*Macbeth*

MM	*Measure for Measure*
MND	*Midsummer Night's Dream*
MV	*The Merchant of Venice*
MW	*The Merry Wives of Windsor*
Oth	*Othello*
Per	*Pericles, Prince of Tyre*
R2	*Richard II*
R3	*Richard III*
RJ	*Romeo and Juliet*
Son	*Sonnets*
STM	*Sir Thomas More*
TC	*Troilus and Cressida*
Tem	*The Tempest*
TGV	*The Two Gentlemen of Verona*
Tim	*Timon of Athens*
Tit	*Titus Andronicus*
TN	*Twelfth Night*
TNK	*The Two Noble Kinsmen*
TS	*The Taming of the Shrew*
VA	*Venus and Adonis*
WT	*The Winter's Tale*

ACKNOWLEDGMENTS

Many friends and colleagues, some of whom are sadly no longer with us, have shown great generosity and offered invaluable help. I am particularly grateful to several scholars who have allowed me advanced viewing of not yet published work, and to others who, in the spirit of collaborative truth seeking, have provided invaluable encouragement, information, guidance or correction. These include an anonymous reader for the press, Anne Barton, David Black, Ronald Britton, Martin Butler, David Crystal, Armand D'Angour, Heather Dubrow, Gabriel Egan, Sean Elliott, Inga-Stina Ewbank, Roy Foster, Andrew Hadfield, Lisa Hopkins, Clark Hulse, Jay Kennedy, Roger Kennedy, Rosie Keep, Ros King, Jane Kingsley-Smith, Harry Keyishian, Russ McDonald, Willy Maley, Gail Kern Paster, Simon Reynolds, Sarah Richmond, Anthony Rooley, Carol Rutter, Armelle Sabatier, Lucie Skeaping, Quentin Skinner, Tiffany Stern, Richard Strier, Gary Taylor, Grenville Weltch, Christopher Wilson and Henry Woudhuysen. I owe my greatest debt to my wife, for her support, assistance and expertise. All errors are of course my own.

I am also grateful to my former students and colleagues at Goldsmith's College, and to the numerous librarians and archivists who have helped me, especially Paul Taylor at the Warburg Institute. I also wish to thank Mark Ford and René Weis who supported the arrangement of an honorary research association providing me access to the excellent research materials at University College London.

Many scholars have led the way on the various paths that I have followed. My notes indicate my great indebtedness to them, both where I have and where I have not wholly corroborated their stimulating conjectures or conclusions.

ACKNOWLEDGMENTS

Introduction

The scheme overall

To open new perspectives, this book will attempt a literary critical experiment. It will focus on Shakespeare's musicians, poets, painters and sculptors – artist figures who crop up more often than one might imagine in Shakespeare's plays and poems. Shakespeare exhibits a particular fascination with them, often portraying them with great sensitivity and insight.

I will attempt to understand the nature of Shakespeare's artists' activities and what they apparently think and feel, as well as to locate their roles within fictional and contextual frameworks. The hope is that investigating Shakespeare's artists will yield some increments of knowledge, the principle being that understanding literary complexity requires multiple and diverse approaches no one of which can offer a totalizing 'final word'.

One question that arises immediately is whether Shakespeare actually possessed a notion of an 'artist', either as a practical matter or as an intellectual category? Thinking practically, one social historian denies that the Renaissance actually had 'our category of fine art' and 'our ideal of the autonomous artist', holding that 'the dominant meaning of the terms "art" and "artist" in the Renaissance remained distinctly premodern'.[1] That historian's position on Shakespeare and his work is out of keeping with important recent views,[2] but on the other hand he is correct in stating that the *words* 'art' and 'artist' were not used in Shakespeare's time as they are now. Questions of terminology and categorization will occupy this introduction at some length.

Another question is whether Shakespeare thought coherently about aesthetics, an issue on which scholars have diverged widely.[3] Shakespeare never offers statements about (what we call) art or artists *in propria persona*, but his humanly fallible fictional characters or not-fully-reliable narrators do make statements of that sort. Yet we must look beyond Shakespeare's often ironically framed set pieces on, for instance, music being the food of love, or poets being lunatics, or a statue being a 'painted idol, image dull and dead', because his works often go beyond making statements at all. Instead, they often address important questions via resonant thematic, characterological or verbal structures. Such fictional, poetic, or gestural expressions may also involve allusions to other artworks made by Shakespeare himself or his contemporaries.

The word 'contemporary' is important here because all of Shakespeare's portrayals of artists are inflected by contemporary cultural conditions. As Richard Wollheim put it in *Art and its Objects*, 'art is essentially historical'.[4] For instance, writers in Shakespeare's time addressed exclusively anthropomorphic topics (such as human thoughts, sensations, emotions, desires, social interactions).[5] Thus it would have been impossible then to assimilate a recent turn in criticism that aims to connect art with notions of the post-human.[6] Wollheim also subtly argued that 'art is a form of life'.[7] Here this will be aligned with a recently revived doctrine that among Shakespeare's main achievements was the creation of lifelike virtual personages by means of multi-layered, vital-seeming, characterizations.[8]

A false dichotomy

If the chapters of this book are compared with one another, a dichotomy might seem to emerge between observation of details and interpretation of patterns. But rigidly making a split between these two is false because observation cannot become meaningful without the intervention of some interpretation, and interpretation not based on sound observation is worthless. Nevertheless, emphases may vary, and indeed Chapters One, Three and Five involve more numerous and diverse observations across a wider range of Shakespeare works than do Chapters Two, Four and Six,[9] while the even-numbered chapters offer interpretative readings that are more broadly thematic and sometimes more speculative than the odd-numbered ones. Speculative interpretation is identified as such and plausibility will be argued for in terms of unification and applicability, and therefore on the basis of corroborative or inductive evidence rather than strict rationale. Other elucidations offered here are more factually based, with less extrapolation. I believe that there is a need for both kinds of approach, the hypothetical and the fact-finding, in literary studies.

Transactions

Shakespeare's depictions imply that an artwork is not essentially a thing but is, rather, a transaction. Or at least, that it is an invitation to a transaction, the parties to which are an artist, an audience and a culture. This aligns with Ernst Gombrich's idea (applied in following chapters) that the appreciation of visual art requires viewers to provide an imaginative 'beholder's share'. Asserting a requirement of that sort is not equivalent to claiming that there is no essential difference between perception and imagination (a claim suggested by some cognitive scientists and resisted by some philosophers of mind). Quite the contrary, in order to provide Gombrich's beholder's share a viewer must be aware that they are responding to an artwork and not just to a parcel of immediate sensory impressions. However, the necessity of *making* sense of sensations, of *giving* them meaning, does apply more widely than in artistic encounters alone.

Another kind of transaction is required of us here: the integration of opposing positions regarding art in relation to the material world versus art in relation to the aesthetic and intellectual realm. On one hand, Andrzej Jankowski claims that an artist's task is always essentially 'intellectual', and rightly warns:

> The poet 'gives to airy nothing a local habitation and a name'; whether that nothing becomes something depends on the recipient. If he is unwilling to cooperate with the author, a work of art is reduced to the medium or the material substratum of the intellectual object which it is intended to be. A stage is but a stage, words are but words, a painting is but a canvas covered with paint, the greatest poem is but a certain number of black lines.[10]

We must avoid reductive materialism. Yet at the same time, Shakespeare's own artistic profession, similar to those of other Elizabethan artists, was deeply rooted in a network of patrons, publics, playhouses, printing shops, booksellers, a court, a city and a stage of civilization. Therefore, the following chapters must interpret Shakespeare's depictions of artists in terms of an intersection of ideas or ideals with particular economic, social and cultural circumstances.

Would Shakespeare have understood the terms 'art' and 'artist'?

The sense of the word *artist* commonly used today (as in our title) was at best only barely nascent in Shakespeare's time. Thus the *OED* adds a proviso to its definition of a sub-meaning of an 'artist' as 'A person skilled in one of the creative or fine arts'. The proviso is 'Formerly also: a person who cultivates any of the arts presided over by the Muses, i.e. history, poetry, comedy, tragedy, music, dancing and astronomy'.[11] So history and astronomy are added, and the arts of painting and sculpture are subtracted.[12]

The most usual meaning of the term *artist* in Shakespeare's time was: 'One who follows any pursuit or employment in which skill or proficiency is attainable by study or practice,'[13] or 'A person skilled or proficient at a particular task or occupation; an expert.'[14] Shakespeare himself used 'the artist' to refer to anyone literate, and 'the artists' to refer to medical doctors.[15] The 'faulse Art' deprecated in Sonnet 68 is wig-making, recalling Campion's sparkling song of 1601 containing the lines 'Nature art disdaineth, / Her beauty is her own'.[16] When an actual artistic grandee is named as 'that rare Italian master Giulio Romano' in *The Winter's Tale*, the word 'artist' is not used (5.2.96). In a rare possible exception to the rule, King Simonides in *Pericles* says, 'In framing artists art hath thus decreed, / To make some good, but others to exceed' (7.13–14). But it is not certain whether he refers here only to the 'art' of ceremonial tilting, or also to the mixed-media art (graphic and literary) of heraldic *imprese* (on which see Chapter Two).

Overall it seems most likely that Shakespeare simply lacked our term *artist*, but the lack of a term in a culture need not necessarily mean the lack of a corresponding concept.[17] Indeed, many in Shakespeare's age perceived close affinities between the arts of design and poetry and music.[18]

Shakespeare's age also engaged with a long-established idea of a special variety of artificer working under the influence of divine inspiration who might be seen as some kind of equivalent to our 'artist'. Notions of such figures trace back through Renaissance criticism to Plato's *Ion* (533d–534e), *Meno* (99b–d) and *Phadrus* (245a), and also to a remark in Aristotle's *Poetics* (1455a). Nearer to Shakespeare's time, a similar notion is expressed by whoever prepared the apparatus for Edmund Spenser's highly influential *Shepheardes Calender* (1579, and repeatedly reissued). Thus, the headnote to the 'October Eclogue' sharply distinguishes between inspired creativity and skills attainable through study or training:

[Poetry] having bene in all ages, and even amongst the most barbarous alwayes of singular and accompt and honor, and

being indede so worthy and commendable an arte : or rather
no arte, but a divine gift and heavenly instinct not to bee
gotten by laboure and learning, but adorned with both: and
poured into the witte by a certaine [*Enthousiasmos*] and
celestiall inspiration.[19]

So poetry is no mere 'arte' to be got by 'laboure and learning';
calling it a mere 'arte' actually depreciates its inspired status.

However, the reception of such a notion does not necessarily
solve our problem. For in Shakespeare's time, and in
Shakespeare's own usage, a backlash set in against the ancient
idea that artists are characterized by frenzied possession or
divine inspiration. Margot and Rudolf Wittkower tell the
fascinating story of that change of attitude. They begin by
describing an early Renaissance transfer of the mythological
guardianship of artists from Mercury to Saturn, deities that
were also planets, so that the transfer represented a change in
astrological/humoural influences. Originally, Mercury had been
the tutelary deity over 'artists', at a time when the term 'artist'
bracketed all those possessed of assiduously learned skills:[20]

Mercury's Greek equivalent, Hermes, was venerated as the
god of commerce and as the inventor of the sciences, of
music and the arts. It is for this reason that his 'children' are
industrious and devoted to study; they are watch-makers,
organ-builders, sculptors and painters.

But, say the Wittkowers, this was changed during the Italian
Renaissance when Neoplatonic inspirational 'madness' became
the distinguishing feature of fine artists, who were therefore
prone to obsession, eccentricity and melancholy. This
Renaissance concept of artistic inspiration also absorbed
Aristotle's idea that a bilious, melancholic, or saturnine
temperament could signal genius.[21] So, according to the
Wittkowers, a 'shift of "patronage" – from Mercury to
Saturn – came about' for the 'exalted creators' of Renaissance
high art (or philosophy): 'in Ficino's re-assessment of the

Aristotelian position, men endowed with genius have a saturnine rather than a mercurial temperament and Saturn must therefore be claimed as their planet'.[22]

However, a further change took place by Shakespeare's time, when, according to the Wittkowers, 'quite a few writers began to grow rather critical of melancholy' as a correlative to genius.[23] In the same period, advanced medical thinking held that melancholy was a disease rather than a blessing,[24] and Shakespeare reflects this in numerous places.[25] Theseus in *A Midsummer Night's Dream* intoning 'The lunatic, the lover, and the poet / Are of imagination all compact' should not be taken out of context. In context, Theseus is actually dismissing poets as unreliable fantasists, thereby showing himself blind to, and actually deriding of, Hippolyta's sensitive perception of the poetic magic of the green world in the Athenian woods (5.1.2–22).

Among the writers named by the Wittkowers as being dubious about the artist's dependence on a saturnine temperament is Timothy Bright, who 'was no longer in sympathy with the melancholic humour'.[26] We may note that 'the first suggestion' that Bright's 1586 *A Treatise of Melancholie* 'was connected with *Hamlet* occurred in 1853'.[27] And indeed, although a poet, playwright and musician,[28] Hamlet is not the essential melancholic artist-hero possessed of a saturnine, atrabilious temperament conducive to genius; his melancholy derives from harsh experience and his frenzies, pretended or otherwise, are not Neoplatonic. Neither are any of the often unhappy poet-narrators frequently met in Shakespeare's Sonnets half-mad, gloomy, saturnine artists.[29] When characters such as Orsino or Jaques adopt a melancholy pose as a fashionable accessory to their identity, they are satirized, and artistically sterile. And although Shakespeare mentions or alludes to a number of mythological figures in relation to the arts (detailed in Chapter Six), his numerous references to Saturn are only as a frigid old deity ill-matched with Venus or April,[30] or as a scheming and malevolent god or planetary influence.[31]

Saturnine gloom and madness do not particularly characterize Shakespeare's artists, but this does not mean that they are immune to the deeper and sometimes darker elements of the human psyche revealed also in the constitution of Shakespearean non-artists. In terms of cultural history, they do not particularly incline to neo-classical ideals of artistic restraint, but neither do they indulge in *Sturm und Drang* or Romantic agony. Rather, in Shakespeare's worlds artists are typically naturalized (far more than they are now); artistic activities are seen as part and parcel of ordinary life at all levels of society. When, on occasion, Shakespeare's artists are seen to be marginalized or even destroyed, that in itself may be essential to the portrayal of senseless waste in a tragedy. In those terms, Shakespeare's artists are distinctive features of, even bellwethers of, the social fabric.

The business end of this Introduction

To keep this study within bounds, several topics will be excluded from consideration. Artist-like figures not addressed here include Ariel in *The Tempest*, whose ontological status is certainly not entirely wholly immaterial,[32] and Shakespeare's King Richard II who may be seen as speaking verse in the 'fourth voice of poetry' as well as the 'third' (as defined in Chapter Three).[33] Shakespeare's many allusions to actual artists (Virgil, Ovid, Gower, Chaucer, Petrarch, Mantuan, Wyatt, Sidney, Spenser, Marlowe, Ben Jonson) demonstrate his deep interest in art and its makers, but we will not consider these in detail because they are not Shakespeare characters. We will also largely overlook Shakespeare's portrayals or descriptions of theatrical artists (as seen in the Sonnets, *A Midsummer's Night Dream, The Taming of the Shrew, Hamlet, The Winter's Tale* and *Two Noble Kinsman*). This exclusion is for want of space, and also because there have been many valuable studies of Shakespeare's actors, dancers, directors, theatrical interludes and meta-theatre generally, but far fewer that focus on his painters, sculptors, poets and musicians. Again where there are many excellent studies, we will not focus on Elizabethan playhouse practices, except where they impact directly on how Shakespeare's artists are portrayed or interpreted.

We will use 'Elizabethan' as shorthand to indicate Shakespeare's working lifetime. When early texts are cited in original spelling substitutions of 'v' for 'u' and 'j' for 'i' are made silently, as these are merely typographical rather than substantive changes. Because modernization may be misleading, Shakespeare's Sonnets are always cited from the 1609 edition, and some plays are cited from early texts as well. When facsimile editions of early texts are used, references will be made by citing 'through line numbers', called 'tln'. Where not otherwise specified, Shakespeare texts will be cited from the *Oxford Electronic Shakespeare* and Ben Jonson texts from the *New Cambridge Online Edition of Ben Jonson*.

1

Painters and Sculptors in Shakespeare's Poems

Prospectus

This first chapter will set out several broad notions that will be pertinent throughout this book, illustrating them in relation to descriptions of visual art in Shakespeare's poetry. Concepts explored will include: that art is effective only when artists and their audiences actively collaborate; that the Renaissance compared diverse art forms and perceived a hierarchy-transcending commonality between them; that from the Renaissance onwards the individuality of artists was assessed in relation to their distinctive styles; that artists producing sharply illusory verisimilitude were dispraised by the knowing, and those conveying impressions of liveliness and interiority were seen as excellent.

Allusiveness and elusiveness

Shakespeare's work contains dozens of references to painters or paintings, and at least a dozen to sculptors or statues. Several of these references appear in figures of speech but are nonetheless informed by observations of the personal and professional lives of actual visual artists of Shakespeare's time.

For example, Sonnet 24 is based on a metaphor of the lover as a painter and begins, 'Mine eye hath play'd the painter and hath steeld, / Thy beauties forme in table of my heart.' The sonnet then mentions the 'trade' of the painter. The painter's profession was then becoming a trade in the sense that it was moving away from a guild system in which anonymous artisans worked largely for religious institutions to one in which highly regarded independent artists offered their services in secular marketplaces to higher- or middling-class customers or patrons.[1] The sonnet goes on to name a metaphorical painter's 'shop', complete with 'windowes': such shops were beginning to be seen in Shakespeare's London.[2]

In *King Lear*, Kent's description of the courtier Oswald, 'A stone-cutter or a painter could not have made him so ill though they had been but two years o' th' trade' (2.2.57), again mentions a 'trade' in the visual arts, and here Kent brackets the 'trade' of an inexperienced 'stone-cutter or a painter' with that of a jobbing 'tailor'. Shakespeare undoubtedly glanced towards the Elizabethan monumental sculptors who produced the relatively crude painted funeral effigies that were used all over England (most of whose workshops were in Southwark, near the Globe theatre). Self-employed artists, and also naive painter-sculptors, will recur as our discussions progress (see Figure 10 on p. 88).

The above examples from Sonnet 24 and *King Lear* display in an extreme form Shakespeare's tendency only to allude to visual artists, and not to present them to be seen or heard. Compared with poets and musicians, relatively few visual artists have speaking roles or appear onstage. Similarly, whereas visual artworks are rarely made visible on Shakespeare's stage, poems and music are often recited or played there. Even when some of Shakespeare's poems elaborately describe visual artworks there are scant references to their makers.

Shakespeare's allusions to visual artists can be so indistinct that their genders are undetermined (something that is almost never the case with his musicians or poets). One exception occurs when Gower in *Pericles* describes the multi-talented

Marina, who sings, dances and composes 'lays' (poems) to perfection, and moreover 'with her nee'le composes / Nature's own shape' (20.3–8). The kidnapped Marina attains such great fame as an artist that she attracts very well-paying aristocratic students and thereby saves herself from potential prostitution (9–11). In fact, Gower's fantastic account of a financially and socially independent female artist accords with certain realities. Some high-born or wealthy Elizabethan women did produce visual artworks, such as the remarkable embroideries worked by Mary, Queen of Scots and Bess of Hardwick. Among professional Elizabethan artists there was at least one well-paid woman limner (miniature painter), Levina Teerlinc.[3]

Despite the indeterminacy of the personal characteristics of Shakespeare's visual artists, we may be encouraged by the intriguing words of Shakespeare's Sonnet 24: 'through the Painter must you see his skill'. This might signal that visual artists and their work reflect a special liveliness for Shakespeare. Our approach to them will often have to accord with the Biblical injunction 'Ye shall know them by their fruits' (Matthew 7.16). To those fruits we turn next.

Paragoni of the senses and of the arts

> The eye, which is the window of the soul, is the chief organ whereby the understanding can have the most complete and magnificent view of the infinite works of nature.
>
> LEONARDO DA VINCI[4]

The visual arts have long been understood to have a natural primacy over arts that use different sensory channels and physical media. Today this primacy is reflected in the informal use of the word 'artist' to specify a painter or sculptor, but not a musician or poet. 'Art' also denotes visual art in compounds such as art gallery, art museum or art history. We also say that we have 'seen' rather than 'heard' a play or a film. Early modern English writers did exactly the same, for it has been

shown that 'plays were much more commonly thought of as
visual rather than aural experiences in the literary and dramatic
writing of the period'.[5] Ben Jonson, stoutly withstanding this
usage, spoke to the audience of his *Staple of News* through the
Prologue, thus:

> For your own sakes, not his, he bade me say,
> Would you were come to hear, not see, a play.
> Though we his actors must provide for those
> Who are our guests, here, in the way of shows,
> The maker hath not so; he'd have you wise
> Much rather by your ears than by your eyes.

However, Jonson, the advocate for words over images, lost out
in his long quarrel with Inigo Jones who, like many in the
Renaissance, championed the visual arts over the others.

As a champion for painting, Leonardo da Vinci offered
fundamental arguments for the priority of seeing over hearing,
smelling, tasting or touching. These appear in a compilation
from his manuscripts that was copied and circulated from the
mid-sixteenth century and editorially labelled the *paragoni* in
1817.[6] There Leonardo asserts that sight is less prone to error
than all the other senses, and makes several claims to the effect
that 'Animals sustain worse injury by losing their sight than
their hearing for several reasons; first they need their sight to
secure the nourishment indispensable to all animals; secondly
by sight the beauty of created things is perceived, which are the
chief cause of love.'[7] For Leonardo, vision is essential for
individual survival, species survival and also spiritual survival,
and so excels all the other senses.[8]

Nevertheless, there were longstanding beliefs that seeing
may be fallible or deceptive, to which Shakespeare reacted.[9]
Leonardo overlooked such traditions for a particular reason:
he sought to rectify the fact that music and verbal composition
were included among the seven liberal arts of the classical
trivium and *quadrivium*, but painting was not. Therefore,
Leonardo's *paragoni* aimed to elevate the status of painting by

arguing it to be nobler than poetry, music and also (for his own professional reasons) sculpture.[10]

Writers especially important to Elizabethans, including Erasmus and Spenser, repeated (or sometimes complicated) longstanding doctrines that 'visual immediacy' or 'pictorial vividness' should be the model for lively literary expression.[11] Such doctrines evoked Horace's famous dictum *ut pictura poesis*,[12] a much-discussed position that was simply inverted in Ben Jonson's claim in his *Discoveries* that 'Picture took her feigning from poetry'.[13]

The longevity of literary fame was sometimes confused with actual immortality, for instance by the immature King of Navarre in Shakespeare's *Love's Labour's Lost* who hopes to found an academy of the 'heirs of all eternity' (1.1.1–7). The King's fallacy in prohibiting bodily pleasures neatly aligns with body-versus-soul distinctions that featured in some competitive *paragoni* debates. For instance, Leonardo held that compared with painting, sculpting is a dirty, noisy, mechanical, non-cerebral activity.[14] On the contrary, Michelangelo held that the sort of sculpture that removes matter by carving ('*per forza di levare*') is (even more than painting) actually anti-material because it releases ideal forms from gross matter.[15] Michelangelo's Sonnet 83 asserts:[16]

> The greatest artist has no single concept
> Which a rough marble block does not contain
> Already in its core: *that* can attain
> Only the hand that serves the intellect.[17]

In a similar vein, music, and also poetry, were often associated in the Renaissance with the purely intellectual realm. Yet, as we shall see, Shakespeare did not necessarily endorse notions that music and poetry are transcendental (although he does present characters who repeat these commonplaces).

There were reasons to oppose a Hellenizing subordination of the visual realm to *logos* and *melos*. For one, Genesis indicates a provision of goods to attract human vision before the invention of language or music. Humanity having just been created, God prepared for its use 'every tree that is pleasant for *sight* and is good for food' (2.9).[18] Only after this did God arrange for Adam *first* to see and *then* to name all the creatures, initiating language (2.19–20). Later in Genesis, Jubal first devised musical instruments (4.21).

Because Shakespeare frequently juxtaposes the verbal with the visual, he has often been said to allude to the *paragoni* tradition.[19] More than a few critics have been misled into thinking that when Shakespeare specifically mentions verbal and visual materials side by side this must conform to the oppositional or contentious pattern seen in Leonardo's combative *paragoni*. One critic, for instance, argues that Sonnet 16's lines, 'Which this (Times pensel or my pupill pen) / Neither in inward worth nor outward faire / Can make you live your selfe in eies of men', embody a contentious *paragone* between painting's 'pensel' and writing's 'pen', and bases an emendation upon that.[20] However, other critics have shown that these lines (however complex in other ways) actually equate the 'pen' and 'pensel' in terms of their equivalent inabilities.[21] In other places, Shakespeare does reflect *paragoni* contrasts. Sonnet 55, for instance, recalls that the visual artworks of antiquity, as material objects, are subject to the ravages of the 'sluttish time'. The speaker in Sonnet 59, on the contrary, questions whether the poetry of 500 years ago betters today's. It could be argued, therefore, that Shakespeare saw visual artworks as inferior to literary ones on account of their vulnerable materiality.

However, rather than being contentious or combative, in many cases Shakespeare's implied *paragoni* accord with a trend that became dominant in mid-sixteenth century continental treatises in which a contrasting of differing arts or artistic media leads to a conclusion that they are more similar than different, and that they should, ideally, be more cooperative than competitive.[22] A letter from Michelangelo, solicited by Benedetto Varchi to be published together with seven other letters from contemporary painters and sculptors, is one among many Renaissance texts opposing the contentious comparisons of differing arts.

Michelangelo concluded that 'since Painting and Sculpture require similar accomplishments they might be induced to make peace with one another and give up these disputes'.[23] In the same book, published in 1549, Varchi printed two lectures that he had given to the Florentine Academy. In these he contrasted by pairs poetry, painting and sculpture, finding each pairing more equal than opposed and calling one pair 'not only equal, but one and the same'.[24] Similarly, in the 1550 and 1568 editions of his *Lives*, Vasari 'chose not to commit himself as to the relative superiority of the two arts [painting or sculpture]', and rather held that *disegno* 'is the foundation of both of these arts'.[25] Aretino in Ludovico Dolce's 1557 *Dialogo della pittura* asserts that a painter should be 'versed in historical narrative and the tales of poets', while a painter-like 'ability to make designs is extremely useful to a man of letters', thus suggesting that in each 'profession' a knowledge of the other can 'prove most beneficial'.[26] Following the same trend, Richard Haydocke's introduction to his 1598 English translation of Giovanni Lomazzo's *Tracte* on visual arts finds neither painting nor carving 'worthier', and that 'Painting, Carving and Plasticke are all but one and the same art'.[27]

Shakespeare's *paragoni* of the senses, especially in *The Rape of Lucrece*

Dualistic conceptions are seemingly adopted in Ben Jonson's prefatory lines to the masque *Hymenae* (1606), which claim that the text is the soul of theatrical art and spectacle its mere body.[28] Shakespeare's *Pericles*, published in 1609, confutes this divisive *paragoni* position by means of repeated analyses and syntheses of the visual and aural elements of theatrical narrative in the Choruses of the play.[29]

In the first chorus the speaker identifies himself as the Ricardian poet John Gower (who thereby becomes one of only two historical artists whose names and works are alluded to simultaneously by Shakespeare). Gower, as Chorus, refers ten times to visual versus audible channels of communication.[30] During Choruses 2–6, Gower presents four dumb-show interludes: in this way, heard and seen versions of the same stories are presented in separated-out segments. Both Gower's striding rhymes and the dumb shows have a kind of antique charm, but their presentations also focus attention on how, when speech and action are combined by the actors of the play, those formerly disjoined and now united elements produce a palpably more vivid sense of the presence of life. Thus several *paragoni* of visual and verbal communications implicit in *Pericles* emphasize that superior results arise from the merger of the two, rather than from their separation.

Sonnet 23 images an 'unperfect actor on the stage', who forgets his lines. Shakespeare's narrator there hints at another *paragone* between gesture and speech when he commends the 'domb presagers' of a 'speaking brest' over spoken words, and so begs the beloved to 'learne to read what silent love hath writ, / To heare with eies belongs to loves fine wit'. However, a very similar *paragone* involving inarticulateness, which is embedded in a lengthy sequence in *The Rape of Lucrece*, has a much more complex outcome. In the first part of that sequence, after being raped Lucrece fails in an attempt to write to her absent husband Collatine about her ordeal. The poem's description of her struggles to compose that letter will be excruciatingly familiar to anyone who has attempted to convey adequately in writing – to an audience unprepared for the communication – something very strongly felt. Thus Lucrece is described agonizing over revisions, bedevilled by indecision, and finding her search for 'inventions' beset by maddening oscillations between feelings she has over- and under-written:

> What wit sets down is blotted straight with will;
> This is too curious-good, this blunt and ill.
> Much like a press of people at a door
> Throng her inventions, which shall go before.

>   (1299–1302)

Wracked by quandaries, Lucrece gives up on explaining 'her grief's true quality' and instead writes a letter simply saying that she is very unhappy and needs Collatine to return swiftly. The poem tells us that on his return she expects that her 'action' and visible 'sighs and groans and tears' will truly express her emotional state.[31] The poem's narrator then generalizes on this in the mode of a pro-spectacle and anti-text *paragone*:

> To see sad sights moves more than hear them told,
> . . .
> 'Tis but a part of sorrow that we hear;
> Deep sounds make lesser noise than shallow fords,
> And sorrow ebbs, being blown with wind of words.

> (1323–30)

Next, however, matters become much more complex. To help describe this, some special terminology will be convenient.

It will be convenient for this study to use the term *ekphrasis* to denote an account given in a verbal work of art of any emotion-laden visual scene. This accords with the word's origin, meaning a description or 'speaking out'. In practice, *ekphrases* may be divided into four types: verbal descriptions of a real or imagined visual scene, or verbal descriptions of actual or imagined visual artworks. Some commentators choose to use the term *ekphrasis* to denote only the third, or the third and fourth, of these possibilities, restricting its meaning to a description in a written text of a visual artwork. However, there are notable Shakespearean examples of all four types of *ekphrasis*,[32] and moreover (as we shall later see), examples where an instance of one of the four types seems to flow seamlessly into another.

In *Lucrece* 1333–60 a brilliant *ekphrasis* of the first type confutes the narrator's claims, which we have just described, of the superiority of visual over verbal representation. This *ekphrasis* presents in visual close-up a tacit but dynamic interchange between Lucrece and a tongue-tied servant who has been summoned to carry her letter. That 'duteous vassal' is overcome by blushes of shyness in the presence of his mistress and is too awkward to speak. Lucrece, having been raped, projects her own misplaced embarrassment on to this servant's silent colouring, and so glares at him and blushes back. This elicits the servant's even more furious blushing, and so Lucrece imagines that he is aware of the cause of her unwarranted feelings of shame. We are told, however, that the hopelessly 'bashful' servant has no such thoughts. So here visual cues produce a thoroughgoing *mis*communication when 'two red fires in both their faces blazed'.

Displaying a remarkable shift from observation to pontification, Shakespeare's narrator next overlooks Lucrece's misjudgement and comments sententiously on the supposed superiority of the wordless 'groom' over loquacious servants:

Such harmless creatures have a true respect
To talk in deeds, while others saucily
Promise more speed, but do it leisurely.
Even so this pattern of the worn-out age
Pawned honest looks, but laid no words to gage.

(1347–51)

This sudden change of registers, a retreat from describing an unfortunate but lifelike miscommunication to intoning commonplaces, may imply a narrator who is unable to look steadily on the misery of the current situation. Whatever the cause of the narrator's inappropriate response, it prefigures the final misinterpretation in the poem. This is Lucrece's misplaced presumption of having been shamed and her ill-conceived notion of honour, which result in her suicide.

In fact, the narrator of *Lucrece* previously contradicted their own eventual praise of the wordless servant, by remarking on the groom's 'defect / Of spirit, life, and bold audacity' (1345–6).[33] So Shakespeare's complex *paragone* of speech and gesture uncovers potential virtues and demerits on both sides of the verbal-visual divide, showing that communication may fail equally from wordiness or from dumbly relating only through 'deeds'.[34] Had Lucrece's 'groom' been capable of speech, she would have suffered less and his own humanity would have been less degraded. If Lucrece had managed her written communication with her husband, perhaps her demonstrative suicide would have been avoided.

Why do many Shakespeare characters make defective assessments of visual arts?

As surprising as it may seem, according to Martin Kemp before the mid-sixteenth century there was no discussion of the uniquely different styles in the work of particular visual artists. Kemp claims that artists' individual styles, which the Renaissance called their 'touch', became a topic of discussion only after 1550 when Vasari first published his accounts not just of artists' lives, but also of their personal methods and approaches to their work.[35] We might add that in 1557 Dolce's Arentino connected 'the very fact that diversity exists in the complexions and humors of mankind' with the emergence of 'painters of different kinds'.[36] In 1604, Vasari's kind of attention to individual styles was extended to the work of northern Renaissance and mannerist artists in Karel Van Mander's *Book on Picturing*.[37]

To gather an impression of an artist's individuality from their work requires seeing that work, or having it described adequately. For reasons that might be speculated upon,[38] verbal *ekphrases* of visual artworks (*ekphrases* of the third and sometimes in poems the fourth kind) replace their visual display not only in Shakespeare's poems (where this is inevitable), but also very often in his plays. Moreover, many of those *ekphrases* do not convey much of an individuating sense of the authors of those artworks, but often they seem, rather, to stereotype all visual artists. This is because many Shakespearean speakers describe artworks only in terms of their 'excellence', more or less, in conveying illusionary verisimilitude. This places those works on a monolithic scale of value, leaving no room for individuality. If the makers of visual artworks are only more or less 'perfectly' nature's 'ape',[39] further to differentiate them would be pointless. However, it will be argued here, especially in the next chapter, that Shakespeare typically treats speakers of that sort satirically.

There is an implicit defect in valuing artworks on the basis of verisimilitude. This is that an artwork that is perfectly able to 'ape' or 'counterfeit' nature will automatically do all the work of communication, giving its viewers no opportunity or responsibility to provide what Ernst Gombrich calls the 'beholder's share'.[40] The essential necessity of participating imaginatively in a transaction with dramatic art equivalent to the beholder's share is repeatedly urged on the audience by the Chorus in *Pericles*. For instance, Gower urges the play's spectators to 'Be attent, / And time that is so briefly spent / With your fine fancies quaintly eche', and again to 'in imagination hold / This stage the ship'. Thus he says that the play does not actually 'hold the mirror up to nature' except in the spectators' minds.[41]

The connections between mirror-imaging, the visual arts, and other realms of Renaissance culture and thought are manifold and intriguing, but there is little space for discussing them here.[42] We might just mention that in the earlier Renaissance both Leonardo and Alberti suggested that artists use flat mirrors to judge their paintings.[43] A plausible explanation for that is that the poor quality of the only sorts of mirrors that were technologically available then would have increased the blurriness of images, giving more scope for Gombrich's beholder's share. Gombrich also describes the contrary displeasure inflicted by being too 'realistic', in the sense of waxwork-like visual representations. Such images, he states, may appear, beyond 'cheap and vulgar', so 'odious' as to cause painful distaste and revulsion.[44]

We will next consider a Shakespearean treatment of visual art that conveys a realistic sense of vitality without falling prey to such objections.

Three contrasting accounts of visual art in *Venus and Adonis*

> What fine chisel
> Could ever yet cut breath?
>
> (*The Winter's Tale* 5.3.78–9)

Three passages in Shakespeare's first print publication, his 1593 best-selling narrative poem *Venus and Adonis*, describe or allude to three visual artworks: an imagined (and metaphorical) statue, an imagined painting and a famed but purportedly actual ancient painting. We will consider these out of order, because the others that flank it will help us to analyse the by-far longest and most complex (middle) one to appear, the poem's *ekphrastic* description of an imaginary painting of a horse.

The first and third mentions of artworks in *Venus and Adonis* are both concerned with the misconstruing of art: a beholder's share transaction gone wrong. The first comprises a metaphor in which painting and sculpture are associated with 'lifeless' things, such as pagan idols.[45] The view expressed is that artworks are no more than lumps of dead stuff – the speaker utterly refuses to supply the beholder's share that can bring meaning or liveliness into an encounter with them. Thus, angry with Adonis for displaying visual allure but actually being as unresponsive and infertile as a picture or statue, Venus addresses him:

> Fie, lifeless picture, cold and senseless stone,
> Well painted idol, image dull and dead,
> Statue contenting but the eye alone,
> Thing like a man, but of no woman bred.
>
> (211–14)

Here the inert 'statue', pleasing to the eye alone, may resemble a man but has no spirit or sense.[46]

The third mention of a visual artwork in the poem again alleges the non-nurturing aspects of a particular painting. Here the painting is so compellingly illusionistic that the beholder's share has no space in which to operate, and thus no part to play. This painting is described by the poem's narrator in a simile which likens sex-famished Venus' deplorable sexual frustration to starvation: 'Even so poor birds, deceived with painted grapes, / Do surfeit by the eye, and pine the maw' (601–2). Here the narrator alludes to the classical story (retold in Holland's Pliny and other Elizabethan texts) of living birds attempting to eat a bunch of grapes painted in the fifth century BC by the artist Zeuxis of Heraclea.[47] For the reasons advanced above, such supreme skill in conveying an illusion of verisimilitude tends to erase its maker, and indeed Zeuxis is unnamed in Shakespeare's poem.

In this passage, the poem's narrator becomes unreliable in a way that parallels the above-noted swerving to a new agenda on the part of the narrator in *The Rape of Lucrece*. For although the narrator of *Venus and Adonis* surely alludes to the classical admiration of Zeuxis' production of verisimilitude, the narration shifts the focus away from Zeuxis' skill and on to the plight of the deceived birds who, we are told, go hungry. This version is more preposterous than the source stories, which suggest only that Zeuxis displays excellent colouring, shadowing and tonal effects (called in the Renaissance 'perspective of colour' and 'aerial perspective'),[48] producing the illusion of three-dimensional depth (called in the Renaissance 'relief').[49] The sources do not claim that the birds were starved upon seeing Zeuxis' painted grapes; in Pliny's version they are only momentarily deluded. The narrator of *Venus and Adonis* exaggerates in order to compare the birds' plight with that of Venus being allured by Adonis' beauty and likely to die for want of sexual relief. The narrator's rhetorical overshoot overstates the wondrous deceptiveness of *trompe l'oeil* painting, recalling a Renaissance trope seen also in Vasari's reporting on a famed work by Giulio Romano.[50]

Turning now to the second of the three mentions of artworks in *Venus and Adonis*, the one that is the most extensive and significant, we find a description of an imagined painting in which an artist sets out to portray a supreme beauty. This same aim is implied in the story recounted by Alberti in which Zeuxis used five different 'beautiful young girls' for models when he composed an image representing the beauty of the pagan procreation goddess Lucina.[51] A celebration of procreative beauty features as well in the description in *Venus and Adonis* of an imaginary painting of a perfectly formed horse that liberates itself from constraints in order to pursue a sexual objective. Thus the imagined painting of the horse presents a vital natural force which is, quite literally, bestial.[52]

It has been noted that this painting 'is introduced in a stanza exactly in the middle of this episode'.[53] It is indeed true that the painting is *introduced* in the sixth, or central, stanza of the eleven-stanza sequence in the poem devoted exclusively to the horse (lines 289–94 within 259–324), but in fact, the narrator's account of the painting does not end in that central stanza, and neither is the motif of the horse confined to that section of the poem.

The same horse is actually first met near the poem's beginning when the love goddess Venus takes charge of it, lifting young Adonis from his mount:

> . . . desire doth lend her force
> Courageously to pluck him from his horse.
> Over one arm, the lusty courser's rein;
> Under her other was the tender boy,
> Who blushed and pouted in a dull disdain
> With leaden appetite, unapt to toy.

(29–34)

Later in the poem, a horse-riding motif, surely recalling the painter's breeding horse, appears when Venus 'sinketh down . . . on her back' while pulling Adonis on to her, so that:

> Now she is in the very lists of love
> Her champion mounted for the hot encounter.
> All is imaginary she doth prove.
> He will not manage her, although he mount her.

(593–8)

Here riding without good manège images the thwarted sexual connection; this leads directly into the *ekphrasis* involving the starved birds.

In between its two accounts of Venus' unwanted sexual advances, and inverting them deliberately, the poem contains the above-mentioned eleven stanzas devoted to the successful sexual exploits of Adonis' horse. Those stanzas commence just after unhorsed Adonis, who has just wrested himself free from Venus' brawny arms, aims to depart and so 'hasteth to his horse' (258). He then finds that the horse has broken his 'rein',[54] and has run off in pursuit of a nearby 'breeding jennet, lusty, young, and proud' (260). Poor Adonis again has atrocious luck with horsemanship, for the ensuing long sequence contains a description of these animals enacting a full-blown Petrarchan wooing. Thus Adonis' runaway horse first encounters an 'outward strangeness' typical of all 'females' (309–10), next it assumes the role of 'a melancholy malcontent' (309–16), and then, 'His love, perceiving how he was enraged / Grew kinder' (317–18). At the end of the sequence the two animals race off together 'unto the wood', leaving Adonis, the 'testy master' of the runaway horse, distinctly unmasterful (319–24). Rather than merely comically incongruous, this parody is both satiric of and revealing of poetic conventions.

This parody is introduced by a demand that the reader imagine a painter at work:

> Look when a painter would surpass the life
> In limning out a well proportioned steed,
> His art with nature's workmanship at strife,
> As if the dead the living should exceed:
> So did this horse excel a common one
> In shape, in courage, colour, pace, and bone.

(289–94)

The trope of a painter striving to 'exceed' nature is frequently met in Shakespeare's work, as, for instance, when Enobarbus in *Antony and Cleopatra* alludes to the Venus of Appelles when describing Cleopatra in her barge, 'O'er-picturing that Venus where we see / The fancy outwork nature' (2.2.207–8). The instance of this trope in a description of Julio Romano in *The Winter's Tale* will be of particular interest in our next chapter.

To recap, *Venus and Adonis* presents us with a description of Adonis' horse as it might be represented by a painter who 'would surpass the life':

> Round-hoofed, short-jointed, fetlocks shag and long,
> Broad breast, full eye, small head, and nostril wide,
> High crest, short ears, straight legs, and passing strong;
> Thin mane, thick tail, broad buttock, tender hide –
>> Look what a horse should have he did not lack,
>> Save a proud rider on so proud a back.

> (295–300)

But after that *blazon* of the horse's visual aspect, and with no indication that the *ekphrasis* of a painting is terminating, the description of the horse continues with a description of its motion. So an *ekphrasis* of the fourth kind (of an imagined artwork) merges with an *ekphrasis* of the first kind (of an actual scene). Thus the horse 'scuds far off', 'starts at stirring of a feather', 'neighs', 'stamps', and finally runs off with his mistress, 'Outstripping crows' (301–24).

Another way of viewing this is that the imagined painter of the wooing horse in *Venus and Adonis* is so proficient that they can surmount the limitation, often alleged in *paragoni* discussions, that (unlike poetry) painting cannot portray motion. The fact that the painting of the horse is presented in Shakespeare's poem via language (which *can* describe motion) need not mean, however, that Shakespeare is championing poetry over painting, or speech over sight. For the *ekphrasis* of a painting in *Venus and Adonis* showing the vitality of the horse, including even its 'pace' (294), is introduced by the imperative command, 'Look' (289). That imperative implies that gaining the impression of vitality can be achieved by the active contribution of the beholder's share: a transaction that may even allow a static painting to convey motion.

Comparisons can be made between this and Shakespeare's many other accounts of horses and horse-human interactions, including comical word paintings of horses.[55] But for our purposes, in pursuit of understanding a painter, the crucial key to the horse painting in *Venus and Adonis* appears in a 1972 article by Ian Donaldson. Here Donaldson discovers the undoubted source of Shakespeare's narrator making a strange-seeming connection between a painter at work and an image of equine beauty fired by sexual desire. That source is a description of a sexually inspired horse in John Astley's *The Art of Riding* (1584),[56] partly quoted by Donaldson:

> Note when you see a Horsse (saith [Xenophon]) make haste to meet with other Horsses, that be in his view, or mares rather, and then shall you see how nature mooveth him to shew himselfe in his best forme and lustiness of courage, yea, both terrible and beautiful to behold: for then he will set up his crest, bow in his head, prick up his eares, gather up his legs high and nimble, swell in his nostrils, and start out his taile, &c. This is now the patterne that the curious painter with all his skill dooth diligentlie indeuor to imitate, but how much more should the skilfull Rider doo the same?[57]

Donaldson suggests that Astley's painter (not found in Astley's source, Xenophon's *De re equestri*) appears here because 'the rider is an artist, just as the painter is; both rider and painter attempt in their different ways to make the horse appear as he is in his finest and most natural state, which is when he is showing off his paces before a mare'. But Astley's actual text supplies, in addition to the passage quoted by Donaldson, an adjacent marginal note, reading: 'Notes of courage in a horsse upon occasion of what objects.' Here it seems that 'objects' means 'something presented to the sight', or 'something aimed at', or both.[58] Either way, emphasis seems to be thrown on to the perception and volition of the horse, not of the rider. This,

I believe, indicates that the painter's task is to convey the splendid vitality of the horse.

Horses were drawn, engraved or painted by many Renaissance artists, including Veronese, Dürer, Hans Sebald Behem and Achilles Bocchi.[59] Some writers held that depicting animals beautifully was an essential part of an artist's repertoire.[60] Horses could be idealized as in Jacques de Gheyn II's 1603 portrayal of a captured Spanish warhorse, or in Robert Peake the Elder's *Prince Henry on Horseback*, which idealizes the English heir apparent as well as his mount. Or

FIGURE 1 *Giulio Romano, fresco of 'The Horse Morel favorito'. Sala dei Cavalli, Palazzo Te, Mantua. Public domain.*

they could be painted from live models, such as are Giulio
Romano's six portrayals of actual horses in the 'Salla dei
cavalli' in the Palazzo Te that are so lively as to seem to have
motion (Figure 1). Thus the 'strife' and 'workmanship' of the
'painter' mooted in *Venus and Adonis* might be directed
towards either an idealization or a depiction, but either way is
focused on imbuing a painted image, made of mere chemicals,
with a sense of life. This recalls Astley's marginal note, which
suggests that a painter's task is to convey not only the shape
but also the vitality of a horse.

Several Renaissance treatise writers propose that sort of
goal for painters. These hold that the painter should capture
the living qualities of living things and not just produce illusory
simulacra. Thus, 'lifelike' is the culminating term in Alberti's
account of a painter's essential functions: 'to describe' in a
given medium the 'observed planes [surfaces] of any body so
that at a certain distance and in a certain position from the
center they appear in relief, seem to have mass and to be
lifelike'.[61] In Dolce's dialogue, Aretino interestingly adds death-
like to life-like, stating that 'Dante pins down the acme of the
painter's excellence nicely in his lines: "*The dead seemed dead,
and the alive seemed living; / Not he who saw the actuality saw
/ More clearly than I found myself perceiving.*"' Varchi, too,
cites the same quotation.[62]

The narrator of *Venus and Adonis* images a painter seeking
to produce a life-evoking artwork limning out the vitality of
procreative urges. This stands in counterpoise to the other
images in the poem of a 'lifeless picture' and 'cold and senseless'
carving, and of a delusive painting of grapes that abuses the
senses that should sustain life.

Ekphrasis in *The Rape of Lucrece*

A pictorial artist's means and aims, as well as the active role of
an art-viewer, are deeply explored when Shakespeare presents
the most extensive of all his *ekphrases* of artworks, in lines

1366–1568 of *The Rape of Lucrece*. That poem, which was almost as successful in the literary marketplace as the previous year's *Venus and Adonis*, contains a long section describing how Lucrece seeks a 'means to mourn some newer way', and so turns to a 'piece / Of skilful painting, made for Priam's Troy'. Our question is, as always: what does the description of this artwork tell us about its maker? As we shall see, it tells us that this maker did not purvey illusionism that might even fool an animal or a bird, but relied rather on imaginative human perception fed by prior knowledge of culture and the world at large. It also tells us that this maker had the skill to evoke complex and profound responses in viewers willing to play an active role in the communication offered them.

This maker employed great skill in painting what Alberti called an *istoria*. An *istoria*, Alberti's editor John R. Spencer explains, is a painting with 'dramatic content', usually 'derived from ancient literature', in which the 'figures' are 'so ordained that their emotion will be projected to the observer', and which contains 'variety and richness'. Spencer adds that the *istoria* 'is to be built around antique themes with human gestures to portray and project the emotions of the actors',[63] again recalling the painting in *Lucrece*.

Clearly such a painting must be complicated in construction. Accordingly, in a number of distinct vignettes the Troy painting in *Lucrece* depicts a sequence of various scenes that lead up to a notorious terrible outcome (just as does Figure 18 on p. 200, to be discussed in detail in Chapter 6). Thus the painting displays 'a thousand lamentable objects' while simultaneously presenting temporally incompatible events (such as Priam welcoming Sinon and the wounded Priam dying, or Hector alive and the fall of Troy). This deliberate flouting of spatial and chronological possibility actually makes impossible any overwhelmingly illusory impact (such as that of Zeuxis' grapes).

Lucrece shows herself aware of the artificial conventions used in such a painting, and apparently subscribes to them willingly, if sometimes wryly. Mock-naively, she remarks that the painter 'was no god' able to 'lend' words to painted Hecuba, commenting humorously on the painter doing 'wrong' to Hecuba by denying her a 'tongue'. Here Shakespeare alludes to frequent *paragoni* remarks that a visual artist lacks a poet's ability to give their characters speech. But, immediately afterwards, Lucrece shifts her level of attention to refer to the 'wrong' done to Priam by Pyrrhus and to the Trojans by Helen. With deliberate exaggeration, she offers to put out the flames of Troy with her tears and to deface the images of Pyrrhus and Helen with her nails or a knife (1457–72). In pronouncing this hyperbole asserting the identity of the images with the lives depicted, she actually acknowledges their difference.

Another convention that Lucrece accepts is the portrayal of significant characters by means of a visual analogue to the rhetorical figure of *synecdoche pars pro toto*:

> For much imaginary work was there;
> Conceit deceitful, so compact, so kind,
> That for Achilles' image stood his spear
> Gripped in an armèd hand; himself behind
> Was left unseen save to the eye of mind;
> A hand, a foot, a face, a leg, a head,
> Stood for the whole to be imaginèd.

>   (1422–8)

To see these slight indications as persons, the viewer must supply 'the eye of mind' enriched with knowledge of the world.

According to Ernst Gombrich, a tactic employed in visual art with ancient antecedents that abbreviates or withholds information from the viewer 'must have been' the inspiration for this very passage in *Lucrece*.[64] This raises again Gombrich's belief that a visual artwork may be more effective or enjoyable when it is made somewhat indistinct or blurry – as, for instance, when viewed from a distance. This effect, Gombrich says, may be caused by 'the very act of stepping back . . . and watching our imagination coming into play'.[65] We might note that Horace's text proposing *ut pictura poesis* continues with the observation that with some pictures, 'you have to stand a good way from that one . . . that one will go on giving pleasure no matter how often it is looked at'.[66] Shakespeare's contemporary Sir Henry Wotton wrote: 'Picture is best when it standeth off.'[67]

Indefiniteness is implied to play the role of inciting the imagination when we are told in *Lucrece* (1382–6) that the Troy painting allows us to gather the expressions of eyes peering through remote 'loop-holes'. Thus, 'one might see those far-off eyes look sad' refers to how the viewer's imagination, coupled with knowledge and judgement, may access what are actually invisible details. It is clear that the maker of a 'skilful painting' of Troy deliberately demands this exercise of the beholder's share, for otherwise the crucial figure of Achilles would not be represented only by a spear. The beholder agreeing to supply their share enters into a mutually beneficial contract with the artist. This metaphor of a contract is weakened because the viewer may be instinctually inclined to agree to supply the imagination,[68] but to the extent that they are aware of their own agency they will not be overcome as are the poor birds coerced by Zeuxis' painting adumbrated in *Venus and Adonis*.

Possible benefits to beholders who supply their 'share' can be multilayered, as in the case of those spectators of *Henry V* who are willing to accept the Chorus's demand to 'work, work your thoughts' (3.0.25). Their immediate benefit will be the enjoyment of historical storytelling despite practical limitations on the theatrical portrayal of huge armies, armadas or prancing steeds. The Chorus introducing Act 3 describes another kind of benefit, even more enjoyable, by stating that if willing spectators will allow time and space to be condensed, then the dramatic narrative can attain the exceptional dynamism of 'motion of no less celerity / Than that of thought' (3.0.2–3). Indeed, the beholder's 'thought' is the main product of applying the beholder's share.

In the Troy painting in *Lucrece*, as in *Henry V*, the logic of space and time must submit to the willing beholder's share. More importantly, Lucrece's imaginative participation, stimulated when studying the painting, allows her to conceive an intense impression of lives actually lived.[69] It is not in spite of, but actually *because* of its textural, temporal and spatial lacunae that Lucrece's 'deceitful' artwork is able to be 'so compact, so kind', which here most probably means being so integrated with and natural to the lives it vividly portrays.

Another aspect of the visual sleight of hand of the skilful painter of the Troy painting is described in:

> In scorn of nature, art gave lifeless life.
> Many a dry drop seemed a weeping tear
> Shed for the slaughtered husband by the wife.
> The red blood reeked to show the painter's strife.

> (1374–7)

The words 'nature' and 'strife' in the first and last of these lines may recall the narrator in *Venus and Adonis* saying of the imaginary painter of the horse that 'His art with nature's workmanship at strife, / As if the dead the living should exceed' (291–2). As argued above, this means that this imagined painter strives for life-likeness and not just for idealization.

The above-cited ability to make drops of paint seem to be weeping tears connects with the techniques developed in the Renaissance whereby highlighting and shadowing effects enabled dry paint to represent the wetness of tears (or of blood). Renaissance artists also mastered simulating the gleam of gold and jewels but they could not, of course, represent the reek (the vapour or smell) of blood by any other means than by provoking a viewer's imaginative contribution, the beholder's share. In general, the comment that 'much imaginary work was there' in the Troy painting (1422) does not concern a passive recipient, but rather work that has to be shared between the artist and spectator. The Troy artist conveying 'lifeless life' (1374) thus names their aim to employ dry paint or lifeless materials to convey a sense of a living being, impressive, present and vital. Dolce's Aretino describes this kind of a painter's aim:

> What is needed is that the figures [in a painting] should stir the spectators' souls – disturbing them in some cases, cheering

them in others, in others again inciting them to compassion or distain, depending on the character of the subject matter. Failing this, the painter should not claim to have accomplished anything ... Exactly the same thing happens with the poet, the historian and the public speaker [Oratore]; if their products, that is, whether written or recited, lack this power to move, they lack also spirit and life.[70]

To conclude this chapter, let us consider the striking sequence of ways in which Lucrece is 'moved' or 'stirred' by the portrayal of the traitor Sinon in her painting. The impact on Lucrece of viewing this one character is evidently of importance in the poem, for its description occupies a full third of the thirty stanzas concerning the complex Troy painting. A crucial question about that impact is raised by a recently published claim that 'The extent to which Lucrece's state of mind determines the shape of her interpretation of the tapestry is demonstrated in her reaction to Sinon ... The tapestry is merely a tool facilitating her deliberations, and not the real object of her attention at all.'[71] This implies that Lucrece's beholder's share in the perception of the artwork exceeds a 'share' and becomes a fixation that overrides the artist's expression, and so suggests the problem of differentiating an informed imaginative response to an artwork from a solipsistic one.

To pose the question specifically, do we see Lucrece projecting her personal concerns on to the Troy painting, or are we to understand that the Troy artist purposely induces *both* of her two ways of seeing the image of Sinon, first as a victim and then as a dissembling villain? The latter is not impossible: classical and Renaissance authors analysed the subtle hypocrite and some Renaissance artists represented them (Shakespeare has been well described as one such).[72]

The character Sinon was invented by Virgil to be introduced when Aeneas tells of the fall of Troy in *Aeneid* 2.13–267. This Sinon cunningly pretends to have escaped persecution and death at the hands of his fellow Greeks, and finds refuge with the compassionate Trojans.[73] Virgil's Sinon then induces his

kind hosts to bring the Trojan horse into their city, leading to
its destruction. Sinon's name is a byword for deceptive
treachery in each of the several places where he is mentioned
in Shakespeare's plays.[74] Shakespeare, moreover may have
read in Livy or Ovid's *Fasti* about how the Roman Sextus
Tarquinius (the same Tarquin who raped Lucrece) played an
exactly analogous role to Sinon's when he cunningly pretended
to be a refugee in an enemy camp in order to destroy his hosts
(the Gabii) for the benefit his father.[75] The 'Argument' prefacing
the 1594 first edition of *Lucrece*, most likely written by
Shakespeare, informs readers about other ruthless deeds of the
Tarquins.[76] It begins with an account of the rapist Tarquin's
father: 'Lucius Tarquinius (for his excessive pride surnamed
Superbus), after he had caused his own father-in-law Servius
Tullius to be cruelly murdered, and, contrary to the Roman
laws and customs, not requiring or staying for the people's
suffrages had possessed himself of the kingdom.' An additional
point, which has been much disputed, is that the rape of
Lucrece arguably led to the end of the Tarquin dynasty and the
ejection of the kings of Rome.[77] However that may be
interpreted, it is an undisputable fact that the concluding
section of *Lucrece* takes the story to the point of an agreement
struck to achieve the Tarquins' expulsion. Crucially for that
development, the future consul Junius Brutus dissuades
Lucrece's husband, Collatine, from joining his wife in suicide:

> Why, Collatine, is woe the cure for woe?
> Do wounds help wounds, or grief help grievous deeds?
> Is it revenge to give thyself a blow
> For his foul act by whom thy fair wife bleeds?
> Such childish humour from weak minds proceeds;
> Thy wretched wife mistook the matter so
> To slay herself, that should have slain her foe.

(1821–7)

Thus a political and historical background looms over the
poem. For our purposes, what is important about this

background is that a beholder's knowledge of it must inform their share in the making of meaning; the implicit contract between the artist and beholder limits interpretive latitude as well as offering it.

To see this in action, consider Lucrece's reaction of immediate and extreme commiseration to the portrayal of Hecuba in the Troy painting. Hecuba is a classic figure of grief, presented as such in several Shakespeare plays.[78] But Lucrece's response to the portrayal of Sinon in the painting is not so straightforward. Rather, we are shown that over a period of time Lucrece entertains a *series* of reactions to the figure of Sinon, traversing considerable mental distances. Among other things, this contradicts the claim made in one of Leonardo's combative *paragoni* that the 'painter is able to show you in an instant' scenes that would require a very long time to 'describe with words'.[79] Indeed, modern experimental studies confirm that viewing a painting or graphic artwork with careful attention is actually a process that is far from instantaneous.[80]

Temporal and dynamic processes of scanning a painting are clearly indicated when we are told that Lucrece 'throws her eyes about the painting round', searching for 'forlorn' figures. She only 'at last' focuses on the seemingly pitiable figure that, unbeknown to her, is the traitor Sinon (1499–1501). Continuing to process the painting mentally, Lucrece at first pities the 'wretched image' of a bound and weeping figure whose finely painted face shows no evidence of guile or villainy, and rather seems mild, patient, and humourally well balanced:

> In him the painter laboured with his skill
> To hide deceit and give the harmless show
> An humble gait, calm looks, eyes wailing still,
> A brow unbent that seemed to welcome woe;
> Cheeks neither red nor pale, but mingled so
> > That blushing red no guilty instance gave,
> > Nor ashy pale the fear that false hearts have . . .

> (1506–12)

The description concludes:

> The well skilled workman this mild image drew
> For perjured Sinon, whose enchanting story
> The credulous old Priam after slew;
> Whose words like wildfire burnt the shining glory
> Of rich-built Ilion, that the skies were sorry.
>
> (1520–4)

These lines indicate that as Lucrece's perceptions evolve she realizes that the seemingly attractive and sympathetic captive whom she had spotted is actually Virgil's infamous Sinon. Once she realizes that,

> This picture she advisedly persu'd,
> And chid the painter for his wondrous skill,
> Saying some shape in Sinon's was abused,
> So fair a form lodged not a mind so ill.
>
> (1527–30)

The painter's blameworthy 'wondrous skill' is so called ironically, for it seems a skill to mislead. At this stage, Lucrece thinks that Sinon's picture is inaccurate, 'belied', and that the artist is at fault in creating it (1529–33).

However, in the midst of reaffirming her view that the Troy artist failed to represent a credible reality, Lucrece suddenly realizes that in fact he did do so, having realistically represented an instance of concealed hypocrisy, 'inward vice'. So she is compelled to reverse herself. Thus she consciously inverts the expression of her beliefs by replacing, mid-sentence, her word 'cannot' with 'can' (1534–7). Lucrece's corrective insight arrives when she remembers Tarquin's initial 'outward honesty' and thus realizes that fraudulent traitors may present fair outward forms. Consequently, the artist's workmanship is at last seen by Lucrece to be sound (1538–47). Then sorrow and anger overcome her, and she uses her nails to deface the painting in earnest, as she had threatened to do before in half-jest. But when 'She tears the senseless Sinon with her nails' (1564), she only momentarily violates the implicit contract concerning the duties and limits of the beholder's share. For she quickly realizes her mistake, and regaining her former grim humour, 'she smilingly with this gives o'er' and remarks, 'Fool, fool . . . his wounds will not be sore' (1567–8).

Let us return to the question of whether all this complexity derives only from Lucrece's projections of her personal concerns on to the painting. Militating against that are two factors seen in Shakespeare's poem, although of course there cannot be any conclusive way of interpreting the inner workings of either Lucrece or the painter. One factor is that Lucrece is fascinated by the figure of the tearful captive who seems so genuine before she identifies him as Sinon. This suggests that the artist's intention was specifically to draw attention to a dissembler. The other factor is the historical analogy of the betrayal of the Trojans by Sinon and the betrayal of the Gabii by Tarquin that may be a deliberate allusion planted by a republican painter, later picked up by Lucrece. On balance it seems to me reasonable to suppose that Lucrece's sequential interpretation of the figure in the painting as disarming and then as deceptive discovers elements of a subtle artwork placed by the artist in order to be seen.

We will next consider visual artists in Shakespearean plays, and will find again that they and their works interconnect with historical-cultural actualities, the knowledge, willingness, and tact of spectators, and complicated scales of intrinsic and assigned value.

2

Painters and Sculptors in Shakespeare's Plays

Painting as falsification

The noun 'a painting', referring to an artwork that is admired or valued, appears twice in *The Rape of Lucrece* (1367 and 1499), and twice in *Timon of Athens* (1.1.91 and 1.1.159–61). Apart from that, however, and often in Shakespearean contexts, 'paintings' are said to be ridiculous or misleading.[1] More frequently, Shakespeare uses 'painting' to denote the act of painting (as a gerund from 'to paint'). The verb 'to paint' and its derivatives appear over a hundred times in Shakespeare's works, in nearly every play or poem. In the majority of these places the act of 'painting' is associated with falsity, deception, folly or immorality.[2] Counting again, the noun 'a picture' appears in two-thirds of Shakespeare's plays.[3] About half of those uses arise in negative or dubious contexts involving a picture's lack of speech, reason, or motion, or involving elements of misogyny, ill-intent or destructive eroticism.[4] Usages of this sort may correspond with ambivalences in some plays concerning the arts of design that will be considered later in this chapter. But counterpoising this trend, and belying a theory of a universal Elizabethan 'iconophobia',[5] are a number of positive representations in Shakespeare plays of visual art or its makers.[6] We will begin with these positive representations, first considering portraits or statues that are looked upon with admiration or even devotion.

Portraits in Shakespeare plays

Paintings or statues representing admired persons, who are for the most part also admirable persons, feature in many Shakespeare plays.[7] For convenience, we will call these their 'portraits', although the word 'portrait' was hardly used by Shakespeare.[8] Subtle Renaissance portraiture began with the work of northern European masters such as Dürer, Holbein and van Eyck. Its development continued in northern Europe and Italy, where portraiture became increasingly sophisticated down to and including the works of Bronzino, Pontormo and Giulio Romano. Portrait painting in England, begun by Holbein in the sixteenth century, later flourished in the work of foreign-born and native masters including Gower, Hilliard and Oliver.

Those were all well-known names, the most famous among them in Shakespeare's England being Nicholas Hilliard. Hilliard's prolific output, especially of miniature portraits, has stirred disagreement among experts. Their differences may in fact help to set parameters for what will be most significant for us concerning Elizabethan painting (and indeed Elizabethan art generally), which is a contrast between verisimilitude and expressiveness. Roy Strong finds Hilliard's aversion to using chiaroscuro and Albertian linear perspective retrograde.[9] However, Eric Mercer emphasizes that it is 'beyond dispute' that the miniature painting ('limning') of both Hilliard and his pupil Isaac Oliver 'is of great merit, and that they are at least the equals in their field of any foreign artist of the time'.[10] Graham Reynolds goes further, alleging that Hilliard is 'a master of the alienation effect', who 'developed a system of linear stylization which was extreme even for those mannerist days',[11] thus seeing his eschewing of perspective and the like as advanced rather than unsophisticated choices. But whether or not they were in some ways 'moldy' in the sense of old-fashioned (as Jonson said of Shakespeare's *Pericles*),[12] there is general agreement that Hilliard's paintings have extraordinary vivacity. That is not because Hilliard's portrait miniatures are brilliantly painted in watercolours on card-backed vellum using the rich gem-like techniques of goldsmiths and manuscript illuminators.[13] Indeed, despite finding much of Hilliard's work old-fashioned, market-driven and uneven, Roy Strong still describes his portrait miniatures as not only 'astoundingly vibrant' but also 'executed with a brilliant sureness of touch and a mercurial response to the fleeting mood of the human face'.[14]

In his manuscript *Treatise Concerning the Arte of Limning* (*c*. 1600), Hilliard claims that he emulates the great Dürer in several ways: for instance, when creating shadow effects by means of 'little touches' (this phrase should be remembered for later).[15] Roy Strong supports that claim, concluding: 'The lines of the limner are those of the engraver.'[16] However, Strong denies validity to Hilliard's further claim to have followed 'Holbein's manner of limning'.[17] This is no doubt correct in one sense, but perhaps not in another. Strong shows that the technical *methods* of limning used by Holbein and Hilliard were dissimilar, but Hilliard refers to the *manner* of Holbein's limning, by which he might have meant something quite different. Given what Strong says about Hilliard's sensitivity to facial expressions and moods, it is reasonable to claim that Hilliard, like Holbein, possessed a 'gift for expressing profundity of character, the face as a mirror of the human soul' (see Figure 5 on p. 52 for a stunning Holbein example).[18]

Shakespeare repeatedly alludes to painters' or sculptors' abilities (or inabilities) to accomplish a programme that Giovanni Lomazzo set out at the start of his 1584 *Tracte* on Painting, Carving and Building. Described as 'Englished', or translated, by Hilliard's friend Richard Haydocke, Lamazzo's *Tracte* begins by defining painting as 'an arte' that 'doeth so imitate the nature of corporall thinges, that it not only representeth the thicknesse and roundnesse thereof upon a flat, but also their actions and gestures, expressing moreover divers affections and passions of the minde'.[19]

The cost of having the 'passions of the minde' recorded by the brilliant Nicholas Hilliard was very moderate: apart from the price of their sometimes jewelled settings, Hilliard's miniatures were valued at, or sold for, between three and six pounds each.[20] Similar prices of 'up to a few pounds' were charged for Elizabethan easel paintings.[21] Before a new cult of connoisseurship came into play under the Stuarts, paintings were not at all costly.[22] This may be reflected in how the house of Shakespeare's Posthumus Leonatus, 'a poor but worthy gentleman' (*Cymbeline* 1.1.7), contains several paintings (2.2.25, 5.6.204).

Hilliard limned portraits of royalty, aristocrats, fashionable youths (sometimes unidentified), poets, and citizens or their wives. In respect of the last sort, the recent work of Tarnya Cooper and others has shown that there was some basis in fact for an exaggerated claim made in 1598 that 'nowe every citizens wife that weares a taffeta kirtle and a velvet hatt . . . must have her picture in the parlour'.[23] That is to say, members of the Elizabethan middling classes increasingly commissioned portraits (see Figure 2, a portrait of a woman in Shakespeare's milieu, and the extremely lively Figure 3). Many portraits were made of writers or other artists, including (probably or certainly) George Chapman, Samuel Daniel, William Camden, Christopher Marlowe, Reginald Scott, John Donne, Michael Drayton, Ben Jonson, Thomas Middleton, Richard Burbage, Nathaniel Field, Edward Alleyn, John Fletcher and (most disputably) William Shakespeare.[24]

The until recently understudied genre of Elizabethan citizen portraiture finds a reflection in *The Merry Wives of Windsor* when Falstaff is told by Mistress Quickly that Mistress Ford will be at home alone between 'ten and eleven . . . and then you may come and see the picture, she says, that you wot of' (2.2.83–6). This mock-lewd invitation, where 'picture' is a euphemism, is contrived by the middling-class merry wives to entrap Falstaff by making him expect a sexual liaison. It nonetheless shows that it was plausible for a citizen household like the Fords' to possesses a painted 'picture'.

However, Shakespeare was also aware that commissioning art could enhance the status of both upper and middling sorts.

FIGURE 2 *British School, Joan Alleyn, 1596 (née Woodward), wife of Edward Alleyn and step-daughter of Philip Henslowe, oil on panel, 79.1 x 63.2 cm, DPG444. By permission of the Trustees of Dulwich Picture Gallery, London.*

Thus we find the wealthy, but apparently not aristocratic, Capulet and Montague families (who would be glad to marry with a County Paris) intent on 'rais[ing]' two statues 'in pure gold' of Romeo and Juliet.[25] The families put emphasis on

46   SHAKESPEARE'S ARTISTS

FIGURE 3 *Anon., portrait of Mary Wittewronghele (née Everdey), wife of the successful London brewer Jacob Wittewronghele. Reproduced by kind permission of the copyright owners, Lawes Agricultural Trust, Rothamsted.*

ostentation and costliness: 'whiles Verona by that name is known / There shall be no figure at such rate be set' (5.3.298–303). So the tragically misunderstood young lovers provoke displays of competitive affluence, yet at the same time the intended artworks signal sorrow and respect.

Magnificence in display was of the essence in the official English royal portraits that were produced from the time of Richard II, often in full-length and richly embellished. Poorer Elizabethan subjects purchased modest copies of royal likenesses that were mass-produced by a regulated industry, while courtiers would need grander versions. Shakespeare's Hamlet is disgusted that his uncle's new flatterers, who 'would make mows a him while my father lived', now 'give twenty, forty, an hundred ducats apiece for his picture in little' (2.2.364–7). Hamlet's mention of 'picture[s] in little' may allude obliquely to the 'little eyasas' he had just been discussing (Folio only 2.2.340–63), but literally these pictures must be portrait miniatures. Hamlet's claim that his uncle's courtiers pay up to a hundred ducats for them makes them an order of magnitude more costly than Hilliard's miniatures, for which a typical price of several pounds was equivalent to roughly six to twelve ducats.[26] That disproportion would no doubt have struck Elizabethan audiences as an index to the inflation or overvaluation of Claudius' majesty.[27]

Gifting, possessing, commissioning, exchanging or even wearing miniature portraits carried strong significance for Elizabethans. It is possible that their artistic qualities were also so familiar that Shakespeare was able to make a recognizable allusion to limners' specific techniques, for it has been suggested that a description of Olivia's complexion in *Twelfth Night* accords with how Hilliard in particular wielded colouring and modelling techniques when representing faces.[28] If so, Shakespeare would have gathered his knowledge from observing Hilliard's work, for it is very unlikely that he had access to Hilliard's manuscript *Treatise* where his techniques are explained. Yet Hilliard's fame and that of his sophisticated pupil Isaac Oliver were great and allusions to their work could easily be made, as they may well be in *Hamlet*.[29]

Royal portraits of Hamlet Senior and Claudius, most probably miniatures,[30] are crucial to the 'closet scene' of *Hamlet*. In this, hot from murdering Polonius and in an almost unbelievably abusive manner, Hamlet compels his terrified mother to view the two portraits side by side:

Look here upon this picture, and on this,
The counterfeit presentment of two brothers.
See what a grace was seated on this brow –
Hyperion's curls, the front of Jove himself,
An eye like Mars, to threaten or command,
A station like the herald Mercury
New lighted on a heaven-kissing hill;
A combination and a form indeed
Where every god did seem to set his seal
To give the world assurance of a man.
This was your husband. Look you now what follows.
Here is your husband, like a mildewed ear
Blasting his wholesome brother. Have you eyes?
Could you on this fair mountain leave to feed,
And batten on this moor? Ha, have you eyes?

(3.4.52–66)

Queen Gertrude's response, 'O Hamlet, speak no more!', is overridden and Hamlet rants on: 'Nay, but to live / In the rank sweat of an enseamèd bed, / Stewed in corruption, honeying and making love / Over the nasty sty' (3.4.81–4). His excoriating words and gestures continue while his mother repeatedly implores him to stop. No doubt Gertrude cannot focus on the pictures, being overwhelmed by Hamlet's outrageous behaviour, including speaking with an invisible ghost. Nothing Hamlet says about the pictures, except that his father is made to look handsome according to some curly-headed standard, gives any sense of their or their makers' artistic propensities. Those artists' identities are rendered invisible by a psychological violence in the scene that is so intense that it pales the actual murder that takes place in it.

The miniature portrait paintings found in the lead casket in *The Merchant of Venice*, or pressed on Cesario by Olivia in *Twelfth Night*, or compared pair-wise by Emilia in *Two Noble Kinsmen*, are all supplied by lovers and/or contemplated by a beloved. Illustrating with anecdotes concerning the Queen and her courtiers, Graham Reynolds shows that an Elizabethan cultural code endowed the secretive possession or wearing of love-token miniature portraits with intense, and sometimes unrecoverable, significances.[31] Eric Mercer similarly describes the emergence of the Elizabethan miniature as 'private art' invoking 'an intimate personal secret'.[32] In his *Treatise*, Hilliard wrote that limning 'is for the service of noble persons very meet in small voloms in privat manner for theem to have the portraits and pictures of themselves, their peers, or any other forraine'.[33] Such 'privat' use is illustrated in Marlowe's play when King Edward II and his lover Gaveston exchange miniature portraits upon being forced to part (1.4.128–9). Thus the mere appearance of miniature paintings onstage might have conveyed a penumbra of delicate private emotions.

The same was not necessarily the case with larger easel portraits. One such is named in *The Two Gentlemen of Verona* as 'The picture that is hanging in [Silvia's] chamber.' Proteus begs this painting from Silvia so that he can 'speak' to it and 'sigh and weep' over it (4.2.117–19). His idolatrous wish is granted, but why Silvia would donate her portrait to him, knowing him to be the inconstant lover of Julia who is also betraying his friendship with Valentine, is a weirdness that has never been explained.[34] The messenger sent to bring Silvia's portrait to Proteus is Julia, disguised as the pageboy Sebastian. Collecting it, poor Julia is at least gratified to learn that the compassionate Silvia will not accept the counter-gift of the ring that she (Julia) had given to Proteus (4.4.130–4). Although unaware that Julia gave the ring to Proteus in a manner closely resembling the formation of an indissoluble marriage by *spousals*,[35] Silvia still says that she will not do 'his Julia so much harm' (4.4.134). Immediately after this scene in which a woman in disguise sues for the love of another woman on behalf of a man whom she herself loves (anticipating *Twelfth Night*), Julia finds herself alone with Silvia's portrait. Examining it, she comments:

Here is her picture. Let me see, I think
If I had such a tire, this face of mine
Were full as lovely as is this of hers.

And yet the painter flattered her a little,
Unless I flatter with myself too much.
Her hair is auburn, mine is perfect yellow.
If that be all the difference in his love,
I'll get me such a coloured periwig.
Her eyes are grey as glass, and so are mine.
Ay, but her forehead's low, and mine's as high.

(4.4.181–90)

Although Julia next refers to this painting as her 'rival', which will be 'worshipped, kissed, loved and adored', her description of it may still be clear-eyed. After all, she has just seen and conversed with the actual Silvia. Thus Julia is able to confirm the painting's accuracy in depicting Silvia's desirable eye colour and hair colour. Cataloguing feminine charms that conform to arbitrary ideals resembles the depersonalizing Renaissance poetic genre of the *blazon*: high foreheads, blonde hair and grey eyes were the Provençal poets' feminine ideal. That very genre is spoofed in *Two Gentlemen* itself (3.1.294–358), as well as in *Twelfth Night* 1.5.233–7.

Comparing conventions of beauty cannot answer Julia's question when looking at Silvia's portrait: 'What should it be that he respects in her' (4.4.191). For what Julia does not detect in the painting is far more telling than what she does describe: she fails to find in it any sense of a lively presence, anything at all that conveys the 'affections and passions of the minde'. Rather, Julia says that the painter 'flattered her a little'. Sentimentalizing and conventionalizing a sitter's appearance was characteristic of the Renaissance portraits of unmarried children that were commissioned by high-placed families seeking suitable marriages.[36] In a precursor to Internet dating, such portraits were dispatched for approval or even shipped abroad. A famous instance was Holbein's portrait of Anne of Cleves, which so badly misled Henry VIII that he could not bring himself to consummate his marriage with her when they met in the flesh (compare Figure 4, Holbein's Anne of Cleves, with the much more lively Holbein portrait of Mrs Jane Small, Figure 5).

FIGURE 4 *Hans Holbein the Younger, miniature of Anne of Cleves depicting a prospective wife for Henry VIII. An exquisite painting, yet idealizing, and so making the sitter seem some what insipid. Courtesy of the Victoria and Albert Museum.*

It is easily conceivable that the picture Silvia gave Proteus was indeed a flattering one intended to market her for marriage, commissioned by her father, the Duke of Milan. The play certainly shows the Duke ready to marry Silvia off to the unworthy Sir Thurio. If the painting's intended purpose were advertisement of a high-value female, Silvia certainly would not cherish it, for she is the sort to reject a 'good match' with Thurio in favour of her own chosen lover, Valentine. That would make

FIGURE 5 *Hans Holbein the Younger, miniature of Mrs Jane Small, formerly Mrs Pemberton, a London merchant's wife. Courtesy of the Victoria and Albert Museum.*

sense of her willingness to dispose of the painting while angrily and dismissively saying to inconstant Proteus, 'since your falsehood shall become you well / To worship shadows ... / Send to me in the morning and I'll send it' (4.2.126–8).

Conversely, in *The Merchant of Venice* the miniature portrait of Portia confirming her availability for marriage is far from despised. Rather, when Bassanio finds it hidden in the leaden casket, it inspires his wonder:

> What find I here?
> Fair Portia's counterfeit. What demi-god
> Hath come so near creation? Move these eyes?
> Or whether, riding on the balls of mine,
> Seem they in motion? Here are severed lips
> Parted with sugar breath. So sweet a bar
> Should sunder such sweet friends. Here in her hairs
> The painter plays the spider, and hath woven
> A golden mesh t' untrap the hearts of men
> Faster than gnats in cobwebs. But her eyes –
> How could he see to do them? Having made one,
> Methinks it should have power to steal both his
> And leave itself unfurnished. Yet look how far
> The substance of my praise doth wrong this shadow
> In underprizing it, so far this shadow
> Doth limp behind the substance.

(3.2.114–29)

Despite Bassanio's passion, this *ekphrasis* need not be inaccurate. Apart from the conventional trope of her eyes being so bright as to be blinding, Bassanio's account of the painting describes none of the standard attributes of feminine allure, but rather an almost uncanny impression of liveliness. Thus the miniature in the lead casket is the diametrical opposite of a type of Elizabethan portrait in which the 'representation of the individual' has 'all individuality other than the mere facial features . . . processed away'.[37] On the contrary, it bears comparison with the characteristics of the best of Hilliard's productions. This may even help to date the composition of Shakespeare's play, for, according to Roy Strong, 'an abrupt stylistic change occurred' in Hilliard's miniatures 'in the year 1593'. Strong explains that 'foremost among' the 'new characteristics' was Hilliard's 'handling of the hair, which suddenly tightens in a direct imitation of the manner of his pupil Isaac Oliver'. Strong repeats: 'Up until that date [1593] Hilliard always rendered hair and costume in his usual free bravura manner.'[38] So we may suppose that the free treatment of the hair, whereby 'the painter' of Portia's picture 'plays the spider', conformed with a kind of handling employed in Hilliard miniatures before 1593 and not thereafter.

Indeed, Bassanio's description of the miniature seems to describe real painterly tactics – not in the implausible hyperbole that it shows eyes of blinding brightness – but in the report that the portrait endows Portia's painted eyes with life and seeming motion. Hilliard's *Treatise of Limning* describes the importance of achieving such effects: 'chiefly the drawer should observe the eys in his pictures, making them so like to another as nature doeth, giving life to his worke, for the eye is the life of the picture.' Hilliard concludes, 'So shall the worke by weel placing and tru[el]e doing of the eye have great life; for of all the features of the face of a picture the eye showeth most life.'[39] Bassanio's description of Portia's portrait emphasizes the artist's subtle treatment of her seemingly alive mobile eyes and breathing mouth; the portrait thereby conveys the impression of a face not so much conventionally beautiful as vividly alert, and for that reason fascinating.

Thus the portraits of Shakespeare's Silvia and Portia could not be more different. One lifelessly conveys the conventional attributes of feminine 'beauty', and is unwanted by the sitter. The other is described as depicting no such features, but rather an eager liveliness consistent with the sitter's individual character and thirst for life.[40]

Lastly in this section, let us consider another pair of portraits that present a problem to a Shakespearean viewer who struggles to discriminate between them in terms of the portrayal of outward allure versus of a more profound individuality. Following a stage direction in Shakespeare and Fletcher's *The Two Noble Kinsmen*, '*Enter Emilia alone, with 2. Pictures*',[41] Emilia contemplates two undoubtedly miniature portraits of the cousins Arcite and Palamon. Knowing that they will battle in tournament to win her love, her reactions to their images are confused and confusing. First she notes, 'Good heaven, / What a sweet face has Arcite!', and observes that he is depicted as (to paraphrase in brief) a smiling beauty, the darling of fame and honour possessed of sparking sweet eyes and a brow as high as Juno's and as smooth as ivory. She adds that his appearance in the picture would be an irresistible lure both for maids and for the enflamed (male) Jove (4.2.6–25). Emilia next describes the other portrait, of a lean, unsmiling, dark-complexioned, unebullient, even brooding, Palamon:

> Palamon
> Is but his foil; to him a mere dull shadow;
> He's swart and meagre, of an eye as heavy
> As if he had lost his mother; a still temper,
> No stirring in him, no alacrity,
> Of all this sprightly sharpness, not a smile.
>
> (25–30)

But then she immediately corrects herself with:

> Yet these that we count errors may become him:
> . . .
> I have lied so lewdly
> That women ought to beat me. On my knees
> I ask thy pardon, Palamon, thou art alone
> And only beautiful, and these the eyes,
> These the bright lamps of beauty, that command
> And threaten love – and what young maid dare cross 'em?
> What a bold gravity, and yet inviting,
> Has this brown manly face? O, love, this only
> From this hour is complexion. Lie there, Arcite,
> Thou art a changeling to him, a mere gypsy,
> And this the noble body.
>
> (31–45)

Thus she cannot decide between the two, saying:

> I am sotted,
> Utterly lost – my virgin's faith has fled me.
> For if my brother, but even now, had asked me

Whether I loved, I had run mad for Arcite;
Now if my sister, more for Palamon.

(45–9)

Lastly, Emilia places the two pictures side by side and expresses her perplexity in most amusing terms: 'What a mere child is fancy, / That having two fair gauds of equal sweetness, / Cannot distinguish, but must cry for both!' (52–4).

The issue is resolved because when Emilia's own true wishes eventually emerge they are seen to correspond with the particular 'beauty' of Palamon that she perceived in the painter's account of a man of strong character. Before the contest, Emilia prays to Diana that it will be won by the man who 'best loves me' (5.3.22). Which of them that will be is revealed by their respective prayers before the battle: Arcite prays to Mars for victory (5.1.48–59), while Palamon prays to Venus for 'true love's merit' (5.2.9–61). The outcome is that each gets what he or she prays for: Arcite wins the contest (but is killed afterwards by his falling horse); Palamon gets to marry Emilia. Consequently, Emilia marries the lover who prefers winning her to the glory of martial triumph.

A fundamental theme of *The Two Noble Kinsmen* is the contrast between love engendered in the eyes (as is the Jailor's daughter's) and love embedded in the soul (as is Palamon's). That contrast links with the difference between a painting that shows outward glamour and one that represents an inwardly intense personhood. That contrast implies in turn diametrical sorts of painters and portraiture.

Elizabethan painters and self-advertisement

The contrasting paintings of Arcite and Palamon are given to Emilia as love tokens, effectively as advertisements for the rival suitors. They are used in a private context, but other Elizabethan portraits are made specifically for public advertisement. Such paintings include official portraits of sovereigns, which are often laden with didactic iconography of, for instance, victory, empire or a unified nation. Elizabethans other than royalty or nobility also self-advertised through the medium of painted imagery. Among them was George Gower, who was Queen Elizabeth's Sergeant-Painter from 1581 until his death in 1596. That position had formerly involved only decorative painting projects and Gower was apparently the first Sergeant-Painter who also produced portraits. They include his 1579 self-portrait, the only known sixteenth-century English self-portrait in large (that is, not in miniature). Gower depicted himself holding his painter's pencil (brush) and palette, and just above these he placed scales showing his family coat of arms in one pan and in the other the implements of his artistic profession. The implements outweigh the coat of arms, and a verse inscribed above explains why (Figure 6). Gower writes that he has maintained by 'skill' in 'pensils trade' the chivalric honour his forebears had accrued:

> The proof whereof thies balance show, and armes my birth displayes
> What Parents bare by just re[n]owne my skill mayntenes the prays.

This assertion that artistic merit outweighs birth has been judged 'startling' for its time.[42]

In a close parallel, the Elizabethan musician Thomas Whythorne (whom we will meet again later) laid claims in his pioneering manuscript *Autobiography* for the dignity of both his art and his birth. He did this also by means of commissioning at least four portraits of himself that indicated his standing, in 1549, 1550, 1562 and 1569. He also had a woodcut made from the 1569 portrait, which he prefaced to the songbooks he published in 1579 and 1590. The only portrait that survives, the one of 1569 (which is possibly by George Gower), shows Whythorne's family arms quartered.[43] The derived woodcut

FIGURE 6 *George Gower, self-portrait with allegory and inscription, 1579. Public domain.*

repeats the quarters in four crests, and adds the inscription '*Aspra, ma non tropo*'. This motto puns on part of his name ('thorn' or 'horn') in order to assert his sharpness despite his small stature. Whythorne writes that he did this to show himself 'as free a man born, both by fathers and mothers side, as he that may dispend thousands of pounds of yearly inheritance'.[44] Whythorne further explains that he placed his portrait and arms at the 'beginning' of all his books in order to 'show himself . . . a gentleman . . . both in the outward marks as in the inward man'. For evidence 'of the which inward man' Whythorne propounded 'the music, with the ditties and sonnets therewith joined, shall show to the sufficient judge in that respect'.[45] By this he means that his musical and poetic compositions prove his inward nobility as an artist, while his portraits proclaim it.

Assertions of the value of his art are made also by the unnamed 'Painter' in Shakespeare's *Timon of Athens*. These arise in discussions with the equally unnamed 'Poet', but those discussions have often been alleged to reflect no more than a competitive *paragone* between two arts. This idea is not convincing. It was first proposed in 1938 by an art historian who was sceptical of Shakespeare knowing or caring about visual art at all.[46] In common with many who have followed him, that critic based his position mainly on the Painter's response to the Poet's outlining of a moral allegory he is writing:

A thousand moral paintings I can show
That shall demonstrate these quick blows of Fortune's
More pregnantly than words.

(1.1.91–3)

Of course, asserting that 'a thousand' paintings can function 'more pregnantly than words' may be competitive, but it does not present a *paragone* argument of any weight. It does, on the other hand, reflect often repeated Renaissance advice that visual artists ought to 'associate with poets and orators' in order to acquire 'beautiful invention[s]': that is, in order to acquire useful topics and ideas, especially for their history paintings.[47]

I believe that, rather than implying competition, the Painter's remark about 'a thousand' paintings accords with Tom Adair's subtle comments on the relations between the two artistic professionals, in which 'seemingly cordial rapport' overlies 'deeper suggestions of frustration and impatience'.[48] His comments were made with regard to the Poet, but his explanation of tendencies to outbursts of boasting and frustration would apply to both artists. Adair argues that *Timon* follows the pattern in one of Horace's *Epistles*, which semi-comically describes a poet seeking patronage and therefore needing to self-advertise immodestly and to self-deprecate modestly at the same time. Similarly, both the Painter and the Poet in *Timon* repeatedly boast and then retract their boasting, practically in one breath (sometimes in chorus, at 1.1.20, 1.1.28–30, 1.1.36–8). Shakespeare, I believe, astutely links their stumbling over contradictory demands with a wholly believable upwelling of Adair's 'frustration and impatience'.[49]

Other critics, not detecting the subtle naturalism in Shakespeare's creation of serio-comic characters, find only animosity between and hypocrisy in the two artists. These suppose that the Poet's and the Painter's expressions of high regard for one another's productions are only 'a pretty play of egotisms, dressed up as courtesies' or else 'hypocritical and patronising'.[50] One of these critics considers the Painter's 'thousand moral examples' remark a gross misreading of 'the Poet's speech', and labels the poem that the Poet outlines 'confused and hackneyed at the same time . . . His ill-nature is such that he cannot even produce a straightforwardly conventional panegyric.'[51] Similarly derogatory views of the Poet and Painter in *Timon* are widespread.[52] Is this because critics find it unacceptable that these artists reveal commercial motives?

It is certainly true that the Poet says that his book will appear only after he has been paid for the dedication (1.1.26–7), and the Painter says that he will seek a commission for an 'excellent piece' before beginning it (5.1.18–19). But I can attest that our own contemporary artists mention the problems of making a living, at which their friends and colleagues do not blush. The same must have been so when George Gower inscribed the poem on his self-portrait in which he thanks God 'for his good gift' in 'pensils trade' whereby he has won a living 'with gayne and lyfe to leade in rest'.[53] Likewise, in Whythorne's *Autobiography* and Hilliard's *Treatise* questions of making money are discussed with urgency, and sometimes anxiety. In fact, sixteenth-century London was a magnet for visual artists seeking employment, drawing the likes of Hilliard and (probably) Gower from the English regions, absorbing artists of religious refugee stock like Isaac Oliver, and attracting many other artists from Antwerp and other northern European cites.[54] Thus visual artists seeking paid work would have been familiar in Shakespeare's world, and not shockingly rude to behold.

A following chapter about Shakespeare's poets will further discuss how some critics seemingly align themselves with the misanthropic Apemantus' claims that the artists in *Timon* are parasites who give nothing of value to their patrons. One critic even extends such a judgement to Shakespeare's career, proposing that when he moved his quest for gain from aristocratic patronage to the public playhouse this 'released' him from 'telling lies at court . . . at the price of delivering [him] as a hostage to the modern tyranny of consumer demand'.[55] However, in contrast to the gloominess of such points of view (a *paragone* between slobs and snobs, with no winners), we should remember that the Poet and Painter in *Timon* sometimes seem in genuine accord. Early on, they concur in their approval of a portrait made by the Painter, which the Painter himself initially calls 'a good piece'. Although, following the Poet's unfocused 'This comes off well and excellent', the Painter faux-modestly modifies his self-praise to 'indifferent', more is said in its praise in the *ekphrastic* interchange of views that follows:

POET   Admirable. How this grace
        Speaks his own standing! What a mental power
        This eye shoots forth! How big imagination
        Moves in this lip! To th' dumbness of the gesture
        One might interpret.

PAINTER   It is a pretty mocking of the life.
    Here is a touch; is 't good?
POET   I will say of it,
    It tutors nature. Artificial strife
    Lives in these touches livelier than life.

                                              (1.1.30–8)

Thus the Poet praises the painting for conveying a sense of the
sitter's 'mental power', 'imagination' and even incipient
speech. Saying that the painted figure evokes so strong a
pressure towards communication that 'one might interpret'
does not amount to a competitive claim on the Poet's part
that the image is *less* communicative than language would
be. Rather, the Poet's commendation that the painting
'tutors nature' parallels Sir Philip Sidney's claim that the
poet 'dooth growe in effect another nature, in making
things either better than Nature bringeth forth, or, quite a
newe'.[56]

Next, the colloquy mentions a painterly 'touch'. One or
both of two senses of the word *touch* may be in play. The
'touch' or 'touches' might resemble the 'little touches' discussed
in Hilliard's *Treatise*, which, as noted above, are carefully
calibrated and delicately executed painterly manoeuvres which
enable 'artificial' painted surfaces to convey the sense of a
human presence that is so vital-seeming as to be 'livelier than
life'. Or, as discussed earlier, the 'touch' of a painter could
denote their individual, identifying, painterly style. Either way
the word is understood, the Poet's praise of the Painter's
touches is obviously not competitive.

Another arena in which the Poet and Painter in *Timon* are
not competitive is, surprisingly, the commercial one. At the
start of Act Five these two appear as friends travelling together
(and not just as colliding acquaintances, as in Act One).
They agree that Timon's former bankruptcy was 'but a try
for his friends' (5.1.9–11), and each hopes for new
commissions. Neither artist is ashamed to admit to a pecuniary
motivation:

POET   Nay, let's seek him.
Then do we sin against our own estate
When we may profit meet and come too late.
PAINTER   True.
When the day serves, before black-cornered night,
Find what thou want'st by free and offered light.

(5.1.39–44)

Some editors, by the way, reverse the speech prefixes above (seen here as they appear in the only source for the play text, the First Folio). But the speech pattern of the first speaker does seem to me more typical of the Poet than the Painter, being more stretched in metaphor ('sin . . . against estate') and less visually oriented ('by free and offered light').[57] In any case, the frank admission that these creators plan to 'pitch' their work to potential sponsors would not, I think, seem discreditable to hearers less jaded than Timon.

When Timon overhears the two artists saying that they will seek his support, he speaks aside with Apemantus-like anger and disgust.[58] Revealing himself, Timon next baits the artists in a manner that will be described in our chapter on Shakespeare's poets, then viciously berates them, and finally beats or pelts them as they flee. All of that is symptomatic of Timon's mental instability.

A similar mental derangement also motivates the beating and ejection of the painter Bazardo at the conclusion of the 'Painter scene' addition to Thomas Kyd's *The Spanish Tragedy*. The first appearance in print of that added scene was advertised on the title page of the 1602 fourth quarto: 'Newly corrected, amended, and enlarged with new additions of the Painters part, and others.'[59] It now seems likely that Shakespeare wrote this scene (and possibly the three other additions made to the old play in that quarto), most probably in the late 1590s. The qualifiers 'likely', 'possibly' and 'probably' point towards controversies over the Painter scene that began as early as 1808. But recent analyses, further supporting a notable mid-twentieth-century study,[60] have produced a consensus that Shakespeare authored the Painter scene.[61]

This scene, the longest and subtlest of the 1602 additions to
Kyd's play, opens with the 'a Painter' calling on Hieronimo, the
Knight Marshal of Spain. Being shown in, his visitor's salutation
is 'God bless you, sir', which is met with unhinged responses
from Hieronimo, including 'thou scornful villain / . . . by what
means should I be blessed?' (3.12A.73–80). When the Painter
reveals that he has come seeking justice, Hieronimo replies that
there is none, addressing the suppliant as 'O ambitious beggar!'
(82–7). But when the Painter names himself 'Bazardo' and cites
his reputation, Hieronimo offers a new greeting: 'Bazardo,
afore God, an excellent fellow' (110–11). By then, Bazardo has
piqued Hieronimo's interest because he has come to seek justice
for the murder of his only son, while Hieronimo is also
mourning a murdered son. Therefore Hieronimo dismisses his
attendants and sits down with the Painter, intending to 'talk
wisely' (that is, not madly). Their talk begins, however, with a
comparison of the hallucinations experienced by both bereaved
fathers, and swiftly moves on to Hieronimo's mad-seeming
demands, beginning, 'Art a Painter? canst paint me a teare, or a
wound, a groane, or a sigh? Canst paint me such a tree as this?'
Trees, tears and wounds can be painted, but not groans or sighs,
or so we hear in many *paragone* discussions, although a painted
image may *seem* to groan if beholders are willing. Therefore,
when the Painter is asked to paint 'a doleful cry', he replies that
he can do this 'Seemingly, sir' (112–25). That is not enough for
Hieronimo, who demands rather, 'Nay it should cry' (126).
Next, Hieronimo requests that the Painter represent a series of
scenes depicting Hieronimo rising in terror on hearing a noise,
going out to search, finding his murdered son hanged on the
tree in the orchard, cutting him down, cursing and raving, and
in the end being left 'in a trance' (141–58). Hieronimo's
descriptions of these actions are excellent, but it would require
a motion-picture camera to depict them. Thus the Painter
answers this string of requests with an ironic, 'And is this the
end?', meaning, I believe, 'is *that* all?' (133–58). Hieronimo's
reply is, 'Oh no, there is no end: the end is death and madness.
I am never better than when I am mad' (159–60). He then

proves his point by raving and enacting the final stage direction of the scene: '*He beats the Painter in.*'

Hieronimo is initially drawn to Bazardo because he seeks fellow feeling from another bereaved father (99–101). The principle behind his commissioning of a painting is that a painter must be able to feel the emotions they set out to portray, which accords with Alberti's explanation that: 'It happens in nature that nothing more than herself is capable of things like herself; we weep with the weeping, laugh with the laughing and grieve with the grieving.'[62] Dolce's Aretino similarly says, 'Nor is it possible that someone whose hand is cold should warm the person he touches.'[63] However, because of the impossible demands made by the patron Hieronimo, the Painter's empathy is sterile and no artwork can be made. So Hieronimo finds no way to advertise through art (as it were) his unique situation and emotions.

The self-advertisement of unique personal situations and emotions was precisely the designated purpose of the very peculiar Elizabethan artistic genre called the *impresa*. An *impresa* comprises a brief enigmatic text (usually in a foreign language) inscribed on an equally enigmatic allegorical picture. The connections of text and image are made deliberately riddling and no additional sententious verses are supplied to explain them (as in the emblem). In Shakespeare's era *imprese* were painted on pasteboard shields that were presented at ceremonial chivalric jousts by or on behalf of the participants entering the lists. These not only announced the contestants, but also expressed, although with deliberate obfuscation, their 'intentions, aspirations, and state of mind'.[64] They therefore made semi-public the private or internal, and challenged the boundaries between artistic and social activities. Michael Leslie holds that Elizabethan *imprese* could be significant works of art, giving access to 'individual minds at moments of intensity'.[65] He also asserts that interpreting *imprese* demands a particularly strenuous degree of involvement and effort on the part of the reader, which can be repaid with 'peculiar pleasures and excitements'.[66]

In *Pericles*, six such *imprese* are paraded before the princess Thaisa and the court of her father, the wise King Simonides. Each of the six obscure images and mottos is described in turn and read out, and then each is interpreted (6.18–50). Only one of these devices is presented by a knight himself, rather than by his page: this is the 'stranger knight', whose rusty armour and makeshift equipment are the best that the shipwrecked Prince Pericles can muster. The impoverished Pericles is likely to have been both author and painter of his own device.

The compatibility of high rank with making visual art arrived relatively late in England, yet many Elizabethans would have read in Hoby's 1561 translation of Castiglione the Count's opinion that courtiers should not only understand and play music, but also practise drawing and painting.[67] Working artists of the Renaissance of high birth included the Italians Leonardo da Vinci and Sofonisba Anguissola, the Flemish Karel Van Mander and the English Sir Nathaniel Bacon (1585–1627).

All six *imprese* in *Pericles*, by whomever made, satisfy the dual requirements that they be difficult to decipher and yet decipherable. Pericles' *impresa* is described and read out by Thaisa and then interpreted by Simonides to mean: 'From the dejected state wherein he is / He hopes by you his fortunes yet may flourish' (6.44–50), which is indeed a true representation of Pericles' current 'intentions, aspirations, and state of mind'.

Hilliard's *Treatise on Limning* mentions the expressiveness of *imprese* in a startling way:

Now knowe that all painting imitateth nature or the life in everythinge, it resembleth so farre forth as the painters memory or skill can serve him to expresse, in all or any manner of story worke, embleme, empresse, or other device whatsoever; but of all thinges the perfection is to imitate the face of mankind, or the hardest part of it, and which carieth most prayesse and commendations, and indeed one should not attempt until he weare metely good in story work, soe neare and so weel after the life as that not only the party in all liknes and favor and complexion is or may be very well resembled, but even his best graces and countenance notabelly expressed . . .[68]

The main aim of this sentence is to elevate portraiture that 'imitate[s] the face of mankind' over other kinds of painting, but for our current purposes its salience is in its bracketing of a strangely wide range of kinds of painting as all being capable of imitating 'nature or the life in everythinge'. That range includes 'empresse', and one possible implication is that such an abstract genre is seen by Hilliard (as it is by Michael Leslie) as capable of conveying Lomazzo's 'affections and passions of the minde'.[69]

If *imprese* were intended to convey human interiority in an especially powerful way, it is not amazing that a writer of Shakespeare's stature was commissioned to author one. Indeed, he was paid the substantial sum of forty-four shillings to provide the motto for the *impresa* that was presented by Francis Manners, sixth Earl of Rutland, at the King's Accession Day tilt, on 24 March 1613. Richard Burbage, the leading actor of the King's Men and also a painter, was likewise paid forty-four shillings for painting it.[70] Their total reward exceeds payments made to Hilliard for a miniature or to easel painters for larger portraits. Thus, at a late stage in his career Shakespeare produced the verbal half of a combined artwork that was used by a member of the aristocracy to give a riddling impression of – and thus make partly public – private inner intensities. Noting this may launch the final quest in this chapter, which will be to attempt to understand the power of an only apparently artistically fashioned visual object. That is the 'statue' of Hermione in *The Winter's Tale*, which functions as an artwork only because it is said to be one.

These matters will be approached circuitously, beginning with consideration of several painter figures seen in dramas that may or may not be Shakespearean.

Painting, poison, passion, naming and social position in *Arden of Faversham*

Numerous works of visual art crop up in Shakespeare's plays and poems, but their makers are very often nameless.[71] Perhaps the not-naming of the Painter in *Timon of Athens* is a deliberate gesture indicating that his social position is on a par with the unnamed strolling players in *Hamlet* and *The Taming of the Shrew*.[72] The above-mentioned painter Bazardo in *The Spanish Tragedy* does name himself, and lays claim to an artist's reputation, yet (in ways to be discussed presently) he is not treated with respect. Possibly no more than two visual artists are both named and treated with high regard on Shakespearean stages: these are Pericles (who may be the maker of his own *impresa*) and his daughter Marina.

Two additional *possibly* Shakespearean theatrical texts each presents a named painter, but these do not function as artists and rather use the cover of being artists to carry out violent designs involving poisoning. The first of those named but non-functioning visual artists is the painter 'Clarke' in *Arden of Faversham*, a play that was first published anonymously in 1592 and has increasingly often been attributed to Shakespeare.[73] This play is based on the actual 1551 murder of Thomas Arden by his wife and her lover Thomas Mosby. It takes most of its plot from the account of the murder in Holinshed's 1578 *Chronicles*.[74] Holinshed and the play alike portray Arden as a greedy landlord who had greatly profited from seizures of church lands, and Mosby as a no less rapacious former tailor who aims to kill Arden, and then steal his wealth by marrying his powerfully connected attractive wife.

To fulfil his own wish to marry Mosby's sister Susan, Clarke agrees to use his painter's skill to supply chemicals with which Mosby and Alice can poison Arden. The historical prototype for the character Clarke was a painter named William Blackborne,[75] but Holinshed refers only to 'a painter dwelling in Faversham'. For one reason or another, Clarke does not keep his historical name in the play, although most of the other participants in the murder do. It is plausible that 'Clarke' was so-called for a purpose. A parallel might be the naming in the play of a wholly fictional character called 'Franklin' whose name evokes a middling social standing, and also matches that character's frankness and lack of subterfuge. The assignment of the name 'Clarke' to the painter/poisoner in *Arden* might likewise have a double significance. On one hand, Thomas Arden was an unjust recipient of church lands called in Holinshed 'a covetous man and a preferer of his private profit before common gain'.[76] At the same time, *OED* indicates that the usual Elizabethan word for a religious person was a 'clerk' (the term 'cleric' coming into use somewhat later).[77] Therefore, calling an accomplice to Arden's murder 'Clarke' might symbolize retaliation against land grabbing. On another front, from 1512 'a clarke', was used to designate a person 'employed in subordinate position' to do such tasks as 'the mechanical work of correspondence'.[78] The painter Clarke in *Arden* seems to be of middling standing at best, although he is less wretched than the poor Apothecary in *Romeo and Juliet*, who is forced by desperate 'penury' to sell poison (5.1.57–84).

Clarke alleges that his motives to help to kill Arden are not mercenary, and that he is motivated, rather, by his passion for Mosby's sister Susan (who is a fictional figure conflated from two historical ones). Thus he presents himself as an idealistic lover, averring that all painters 'Must have a love. Ay, love is the painter's Muse, / That makes him frame a speaking countenance, / A weeping eye that witnesses heart's grief' (1.255–8).[79] Clarke's claim to double nobility, as lover and artist, echoes Renaissance notions that love is the ultimate of the fine arts and that the perfect visual artist and the lover are one and the same.[80] However, other possibilities emerge when we see that Clarke has a rival in love, the servant Michael, who also agrees to assist in the murder of his master Arden. The resulting erotic triangle highlights social and economic configurations whereby marriage with Susan would also bring very tangible rewards to Clarke.

Even before Michael comes into the story, Alice Arden promises Clarke that when his poison works, the 'next day / Thou and Susan shall be married', whereupon Mosby adds, 'And I'll make her dowry more than I'll talk of, Clarke' (1.286–8). Moreover, if the poisoning were to succeed in elevating Mosby, Clarke would acquire a powerful and influential brother-in-law. Social hierarchies are a constantly recurring theme in the play, seen, for instance, when Arden seizes Mosby's sword, citing a statute against 'artificers' wearing swords. Arden then berates him as 'a velvet drudge, / A cheating steward and a base minded peasant' (1.310–23). During one of their violent fallings-out, Alice calls Mosby 'a mean artificer' with a 'low born name' (8.77). Even the play's cutthroat ruffians, Black Will and Shakebag, are repeatedly at one another's throats over questions of status and precedence. What then can be said about the standing of the painter Clarke? Arden's 'serving-creature' Michael calls him a 'lurdan' and says he is 'too weak to win Susan' (10.44–71). Michael himself considers a plan to murder his own elder brother to gain possession of the family farm in Bolton, which would bring him land and render him able to offer Susan a higher station than 'twenty painters can' (1.169–75).

Let us look back briefly at reflections of the social standing of the Painter in *The Spanish Tragedy*. Although he can say to a grandee, 'Sir, I am sure you have heard of my painting. My name's Bazardo' (110–11), he is forced into a peculiarly deferential position when reporting the death of his son. Hieronimo raves that a single hair of *his* son 'did weigh' (that is, *outweigh*) 'A thousand of thy sons', and the poor Painter replies, 'Alas, sir, I had no more but he' (92–4). Bazardo must finally abandon hope of finding justice for *his* murdered son and submit to the demand that he devote his skill to the remembrance of Hieronimo's son.

In *Arden of Faversham*, as well, a painter's activities are at the command of the powerful. Thus Mosby introduces Clarke into the play:

I happened on a painter yesternight,
The only cunning man of Christendom,
For he can temper poison with his oil
That whoso looks upon the work he draws
Shall, with the beams that issue from his sight,
Suck venom to his breast and slay himself.
Sweet Alice, he shall draw thy counterfeit,
That Arden may be gazing on it perish.

(1.227–34)

This passage alludes to the tension between the rival technical theories of sight known as 'extramission' and 'intromission',[81] but also suggests that the valued 'cunning man' who can produce such a magic portrait is a magician who does not belong in 'Christendom'.[82] Alice rejects the idea of obtaining Clarke's portrait for fear, she says, of harm to herself or Mosby (1.235–41). I believe that it is implied here that Alice's fear does not rest on a naive belief in a painting's basilisk-like properties, but rather on her awareness that a portrait may reveal the true inner nature of its sitter, Lomazzo's 'affections and passions of the minde'. If so, then Alice fears that anyone, including herself, who might see a true representation of the horror of her murderous self would be poisoned spiritually. Thus, in his *Autobiography* Thomas Whythorne claims that portraits have powers to speak uncomfortable truths. As we have seen, Whythorne commissioned several portraits of himself (as well as painting a peculiarly candid one in prose). In the longest of the explanations he gives for doing this, he writes: 'divers do cause their counterfeits to be made, to see how time doth alter them from time to time; so thereby they may consider with themselves how they ought to alter their conditions, and to pray to God that, as they do draw towards their long home and end in this world, so they may be the more ready to die in such sort as becommeth true Christians.'[83] The prospect of viewing an image of herself unfit for her 'end in this world', I suggest, terrifies Alice Arden. Her fear of confronting her own conscience is consistent with the most notable structural feature of the play, the blundering and hesitation that repeatedly delay the killing of Arden. In parallel with this, Mosby and Alice repeatedly waver in their commitment to their plan, and also to one another. Mosby even considers murdering Alice after he has taken over Arden's estate (8.43).

There is some black humour in the play's portrayal of many missed or bungled attempts at murder, but also a reflection of a miserably dark world of distrust and despair. At the end, Bradshaw, a wholly innocent bystander to the murder, and the maid Susan, who knew nothing about it before it was done, are condemned along with the guilty parties and sent to savage executions (most of the women are burnt for petty treason). These terrible miscarriages of justice are adapted from Holinshed's account of the affair. The play's epilogue states that of all the murderers and accomplices to murder, only the painter escaped punishment.

The painter in *Arden of Faversham* offers three poisoning schemes. The first, a poisonous portrait of Alice, having been rejected, Clarke supplies a simpler poison intended for Arden's broth (1.278–85). That is the only poison mentioned by Holinshed. Arden is coerced by Alice into taking some broth, but survives (1.364–95). Then Mosby asks Clarke to make 'a crucifix empoisoned / That whoso look upon it should wax blind, / And with the scent be stifled, that ere long / He should die poisoned that did view it well' (1.611–14). Inconsistent with his prior willingness to provide poison, Clarke is reluctant to make this object, saying 'I am loth, because it toucheth life' (1.617). This may be inserted to explain a textual incompleteness, for although agreed upon the crucifix never appears in the play. But also, to depict a painter willing to make a crucifix that will poison by mere proximity or on sight may have suggested a position too strongly sectarian for safety on the Elizabethan stage.[84]

The compounding of bizarre poisons by the painter in *Arden of Faversham* accords with a motif in Elizabethan drama in which poisoning is seen as the worst kind of murder.[85] This poisoning motif is often linked to female cosmetic practices,[86] and also to painting, because on one hand Elizabethan makeup artists were known as 'paynters',[87] and on another artistic painters handled the same toxic colouring materials as those often employed in cosmetic practices. The dangers of poisonous cosmetics are discussed at length in Lomazzo's above-mentioned 1584 *Tracte* on artistic painting,[88] and moralistic objections to cosmetic adornment, often misogynistic, were frequently expressed.[89] A powerful example appears in Edward Guilpin's 1592 anti-woman, anti-Catholic and anti-cosmetic 'Satyre II':

> Then how is man turnd all Pygmalion
> That know these pictures, yet we doate upon
> The painted statues, or what fooles are we
> So grosly to commit idolatry? . . .
> A painted wench is like a whore-house signe . . .
> Or generall pardons, which speake gloriously,
> Yet keepe not touch: or a Popish Jubily.[90]

Let us turn next to a play, just possibly Shakespearean, in which Pygmalion-like idolatry and poisonous face painting combine in a shockingly direct manner.

Poison, passion, blasphemy and painting in *The Second Maiden's Tragedy*

Before turning to *The Winter's Tale*, we will consider an anonymous play surviving only in a manuscript dated 1611, which has only occasionally been attributed to Shakespeare but that may offer a deep insight into relevant issues. It was assigned the name *The Second Maiden's Tragedy* by the Master of the Revels, George Buc. As it was a King's Men play, it would have been known to Shakespeare, whether or not he had a hand in writing it.[91]

In this play a so-called 'Lady', beloved of the deposed King Govianus, kills herself in order to escape the sexual advances of the usurping 'Tyrant'. The Lady is buried, but the Tyrant, undeterred, calls for 'the keyes of the *Cathedrall*' and 'close lanthornes and a pickax' and declares that 'neither death nor the marble prison my love sleepes in / shall keep her bodie lockt up from myne armes / I must not be so coozned' (1702–10). In the next scene (4.3), '*The Toombe here discovered ritchly set forthe*' is forced open by the Tyrant and his comically blaspheming soldiers, despite the weeping eyes of a painted funeral effigy. The Tyrant exclaims to the statue, 'thow grey-eyed Monument shall not keep her from us' (1750). The fearful soldiers refuse to use their pickaxes, so the Tyrant violates the tomb himself. The soldiers then carry the Lady's corpse to the Tyrant's 'pallace'. In the next scene the Lady's true lover Govianus weeps at the tomb and then the Lady's ghost tells him that her body is in the Tyrant's 'owne privat chamber', where he

> foldes me within his armes and often sets
> a sinful kiss upon my senseles lip,
> weepes when he sees the palenes of my cheeke,
> and will send privatlie for a hand of Arte
> that may dissemble life upon my face
> to please his lustful eye.

> (1963–8)

By 'a hand of Arte' the Lady's ghost means the Tyrant's hired painter, who will not produce a symbolic representation of the Lady, but only an outward 'dissembl[ing of] life'. Govianus, conversely, responds to the Lady's monument as a symbolization of inwardness, and addresses it so:

I bring to be acquainted with thy silence
sorrows that love no noyze, they dwell all inward,
where Truthe and love in everie man should dwell.

(1885–7)

The Tyrant, who could not weep upon seeing the Lady's effigy on her monument (1736–41), fails to supply the beholder's share that allows an artwork to convey meaning. Rather, with obsessive literalism, he makes the Lady's corpse into a fetish to worship in private, where he verges on necrophilia.[92]

The Tyrant 'circumspectlie' sends for an artist, a 'Picture drawer', to repair the Lady's rotting face (2254, 2281). Govianus enters, disguised as this painter. Malign face painting is done onstage, as in a number of other dramas of the period,[93] and this evokes the Tyrant's deluded response: 'o she lives agen . . . does she not feel warm to thee?' (2341, 2345).[94] The Tyrant then embraces and kisses the painted corpse. Govianus reveals that the 'colour' he used was 'the best poison I could get for monie' and the Tyrant dies. Govianus is reinstalled as king and the honoured Lady is carried off for reburial, accompanied by her ghost.

The viewing of a 'richly' painted funeral effigy offering an inward vision only to those imaginatively able to receive it, the work of an only pretending visual artist, the danger of wet paint that has been applied to the image of a dead woman, and a finally a painted icon that seems to become warm flesh, are all elements in common between this play and *The Winter's Tale*, to which we turn next and finally in this chapter.

'Julio Romano' in *The Winter's Tale*

A short description of an artist by the Third Gentleman in *The Winter's Tale* opens many questions:

The Princess, hearing of her mother's statue, which is in the keeping of Paulina, a piece many years in doing, and now

newly performed by that rare Italian master Julio Romano,
who, had he himself eternity and could put breath into his
work, would beguile nature of her custom, so perfectly he is
her ape. He so near to Hermione hath done Hermione that
they say one would speak to her and stand in hope of
answer. Thither with all greediness of affection are they
gone, and there they intend to sup.

(5.2.93–102)

This courtier, in discussion with two others, is mainly concerned
about the royal party (including where they will eat), but he is
also careful to show off his connoisseur's knowledge of 'that
rare Italian master Julio Romano'. Although some have
proposed that Shakespeare's Third Gentleman refers to
someone other than the famous painter and architect Giulio
Romano, their suggestions all seem far-fetched or fanciful.[95]
Why then did Shakespeare name 'Julio Romano', an actual
sixteenth-century visual artist, in a unique gesture in all his
works? I have no single answer to that, but many topics that
we have explored, or now will explore, converge toward a
satisfactory understanding.

Marie-Madeleine Martinet's erudite article 'The Winter's
Tale et "Julio Romano"' demonstrates that mythological and
other motifs deployed by Julio in his great designs for the
Palazzo Te in Mantua resonate with the play. To oft-heard
objections that the historical Giulio was not a sculptor, but
rather a painter and architect, Martinet replies that this
anomaly is deliberate, and enhances rather than vitiates the
significance of naming Julio in the play. Her arguments for this
connect with several topics we have met before, including the
prevalence of non-contentious 'celebration[s] of the affinity of
the arts ... in the Renaissance', the value of standing at a
distance when viewing pictures, and Shakespearean uses of a
'deliberate change of register which produces an effect in
accord with the whole' (such as we have seen in The Rape of
Lucrece).[96]

An issue not addressed by Martinet arises from the peculiarity that Julio Romano's statue in *The Winter's Tale* is said to have been very long sequestered. The fantastic plot in which Hermione has been hidden requires that this 'piece many years in doing' (5.2.95) must have been kept 'Lonely, apart' (5.3.18), but its secrecy is over-determined, serving thematic ends as well. Outwardly, it excuses the peculiarity that the play's in-the-know courtiers apparently chatter about Julio's reputation without having seen him. It indicates, more deeply, a kind of artist demanding extreme privacy when working, and a kind of artwork that is isolated from viewers until completion. Vasari describes several of his beloved eccentrics, especially the mannerists Michelangelo and Pontormo, taking extraordinary steps to ensure their privacy when working; that connects with a new conception of the visual artist as spiritual master.[97] More practically, Hilliard advises that limners should find places to work 'wher neither dust, smoak, noisse nor steanche may offend'.[98]

However, a demand for privacy, which was significantly on the rise among the higher classes in the seventeenth century,[99] could be associated with reprehensible, or even damnable, behaviour.[100] Giulio Romano seems to have accepted a more public role than Pontormo or Michelangelo, but he did decorate Pope Clement VII's private tiny bathroom, or *stufetta*, in the Castel Sant'Angelo in Rome. One of his frescos there shows a naked Venus gazing into a mirror in *her* private chamber spied upon by her husband, Vulcan, just as her lover, Mars, strides in (Figure 7). This images secrecy, surveillance and marital infidelity. A striking example of the destructive power of such a complex is seen in a fresco designed by Giulio for the eloquent *Room of Cupid and Psyche* in the Palazzo Te (Figure 8). This shows Jove as a great serpent committing adultery with the mortal Olympias, wife of Philip of Macedon. Olympias steadies herself to receive Jove's penis by holding on to the painted frame of the image while the serpent defies gravity in a phallic manner. Above this, Olympias' husband looks on, but one of his eyes is struck with a bolt of Jove's

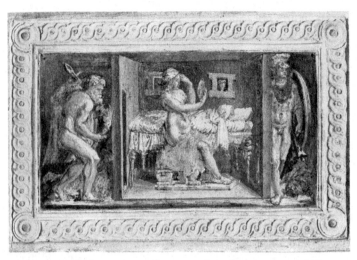

FIGURE 7 *Giulio Romano, fresco in the private* stufetta *of Clement VII. Castel Sant'Angelo, Rome. Museo Civico di Castel Sant' Angelo, Fototect neg. no. 19390.*

lightning and he is blinded by what he sees.[101] Similarly, in Leontes' spider-in-the-cup metaphor for discovering adultery in *The Winter's Tale* 2.1.45, the eye is the channel of taking poison.

Leontes' mistaken belief in Hermione's sexual infidelity, a monolithic obsession devastating to himself and all his family, dominates the first half of *The Winter's Tale*. In contrast, in the play's country festival scene, its hinge from a tragic to a tragic-comic mode, many other responses to sexuality are seen. In one, Perdita is alarmed at the possibility that festive costuming, or, worse still, cosmetic painting, might produce an untoward allure. Abandoned as an infant, she thinks herself a shepherd's daughter and is somewhat anxiously in love with a young gentleman calling himself 'Doricles'. Dressed as the queen of the festival, she exclaims upon 'me, poor lowly maid, / Most goddess-like pranked up' (4.4.9–10). She then enters into

FIGURE 8 *Giulio Romano, fresco of Jove and Olympias. Room of Cupid and Psyche, Palazzo Te, Mantua. Azienda di Promozione Turistica, Mantova.*

dialogue with King Polixenes, who is present in disguise in order to spy upon his son Florizel, who is in fact the supposed Doricles. In the course of this encounter Perdita refuses to supply artificially bred 'carnations and streaked gillyvours' that 'some call nature's bastards' to King Polixenes and his attendant. This elicits the king's famous response that when human artifice (such as grafting) mends nature, 'The art itself is nature' (4.4.81–97). Also using sexual/horticultural metaphors, Perdita's repeats that she will not set 'one slip' of such flowers, 'No more than, were I painted, I would wish / This youth should say 'twere well, and only therefore / Desire to breed by me' (4.4.99–103).

Perdita's frank hope that Doricles will experience procreative desire without the need for her to wear cosmetics evokes linked themes of painting, or art generally, being threatening, and of the complications of sexuality. Those complications are elaborately developed during the festival, where Perdita describes her own sensual (in addition to procreative) desire for Doricles, saying that she would like to 'strew' him with spring flowers. Asked, 'What, like a corps?', she replies, 'No, like a bank, for love to lie and play on, / Not like a corpse – or if, not to be buried, / But quick and in mine arms' (4.4.129–32). 'Corpse' here has its early modern meaning of a living, or 'quick', body.

A diametrically opposed understanding of sexual relations finally disrupts the festival when the unmasked King Polixenes alleges that Perdita has lured his son with sexual favours, and so threatens her:

> if ever henceforth thou
> These rural latches to his entrance open,
> Or hoop his body more with thy embraces,
> I will devise a death as cruel for thee is as
> As thou are tender to 't.

(4.4.437–41)

Before that, however, the festival scene exhibits more than ten different aspects of the erotic, or ways of viewing sexuality. They include the above-mentioned procreative and sensual aspects of which Perdita speaks, and the hateful sexual suspicions of Polixenes. It is possible to argue that the dire threats against innocence that Polixenes makes when he realizes that his son's interest in Perdita is not just to sow wild oats mirror the fury of Leontes' insane misogynistic jealousy. Surely, suspicions of bastardy and fears of concubinage are complexly embedded in the scene.[102] The scene displays many other diverse aspects of sexuality as well, including the innocent (Florizel as an 'unstained shepherd'), the passionate ('How prettily the young swain seems to wash / The hand was fair before!'), the besotted (Florizel's 'all your acts are queens'), the licentious (Autolycus 'tumbling in the hay' with his 'aunts'), the ribald (ballads' 'delicate burdens of dildoes and fadings, "Jump her and thump her"'), the rivalrous (Mopsa and Dorcas), the courtly-complimentary (Camillo on Perdita) and the cynical (Polixenes on 'rural latches'). This terrific variety, exceeding even the widely varied takes on love, sex and marriage embedded in *Romeo and Juliet*, is a key factor for understanding the most discussed aspect of the naming of Julio Romano in *The Winter's Tale*. To approach that, let us begin with some history.

Giulio Pippi, known as Romano (*c.* 1499–1566), began his career in Rome where he was Raphael's favourite assistant and his heir. Giulio later served Federico Gonzaga in Mantua where his many remarkable works in architecture, drawing, painting and the erection of monuments won him fame throughout Europe. In England, Ben Jonson placed his name first among the greatest contemporaries working 'in picture or in stone', listing 'Romano, Tintaret, / Titian, or Raphael, Michel Angelo'.[103] Giulio Romano, however, may have been most famous, or infamous, because he made sixteen drawings of heterosexual couples engaged in sexual intercourse in various positions, which were subsequently engraved in the prolific workshop of Marcantonio Raimondi and then published together with sixteen sonnets written by Pietro Aretino. This, the most notorious book of the sixteenth century, was called *I Modi*, a title translated *The Postures*. Elizabethan satirists mentioned this work frequently; they may or may not have actually seen Marcantonio's plates, because the original edition was severely suppressed, although counterfeits and copies may well have been widely distributed throughout Europe.

One peculiarity is that in England the *I Modi* images engraved from Giulio's designs were often called 'Aretine's pictures': for instance, in Jonson's plays (multiply), and by Donne, Marston, and others.[104] Vasari's comments on this book also seem confused, because he says that there were twenty (not sixteen) pictures, probably because he did not see

the original images. Nevertheless, Vasari condemns the entire
book, images and poems:

> Giulio Romano caused Marc' Antonio to engrave twenty
> plates showing all the various ways, attitudes, and positions
> in which licentious men have intercourse with women, and
> what was worse, for each plate Messer Pietro Aretino wrote
> a most indecent sonnet, insomuch that I knew not which
> was the greater, the offence to the eye from the drawings of
> Giulio, or the outrage to the ear from the words of Aretino
> . . . And since some of these sheets were found in places
> where they were least expected, not only were they
> prohibited, but Marc' Antonio was taken away and thrown
> into prison . . . Of a truth, the gifts of God should not be
> employed as they very often are, in things wholly abominable,
> which are an outrage to the world.[105]

Aretino, who habitually advertised himself as wildly sexually
transgressive,[106] told the same story from his own perspective,
in a letter where he stated that having once seen the
Marcantonio engravings he was 'filled with the same spirit that
had moved Giulio Romano to draw them', and so wrote his
sixteen sonnets to accompany them.[107]

Aretino's poems are indeed *Sonetti lussuriosi*, as they were
known, and they are also wildly funny in Bette Talvacchia's
translations.[108] But these poems do not, as Aretino claimed,
convey the spirit of Giulio's much more serious drawings.
Instead, they record outrageously libertine pillow talk between
the lovers, much of it urging anal eroticism. The poems do not
correspond in style or content with the surviving traces of the
Marcantonio engravings, which can be seen through woodcut
copies and a number of fragments that have survived
destruction.[109] Rather, as can be seen from the illustration here
(Figure 9), the images show couples striving in pursuit of
mutual ecstasy with such intense concentration that the notion
that they are conversing is absurd. None of the traces of
Marcantonio's engravings from Giulio's designs are libertine,

FIGURE 9 *Marcantonio Raimondi, after Giulio Romano, from* I Modi. © *Albertina Museum, Vienna.*

and they do not invite a voyeuristic perversion as defined by Freud.[110] Neither do they accord with Steven Marcus's observations about pornography evoking a 'pornotopia', an easy and strife-free realm that is 'nothing more than a representation of the fantasies of infantile sexual life'.[111] For, as I see it, there is more heroic striving than infantile ease in Giulio's Michelangelo-like images.

Opinions of these images have varied widely, however. Some assessments have been sharply censorious, including that of Pope Clement VII (who may have succeeded in having all complete copies of *I Modi* destroyed), of Vasari (as we have seen), and of many others up until recently.[112] A reaction from 1977 that is of special interest because by a noted Renaissance scholar, is that 'Perhaps Giulio Romano was best known, alas, as the originator of the obscene drawings of "postures".'[113] Andrew Gurr took more detailed notice of the *I Modi* images in relation to *The Winter's Tale* in a 1982 article which concludes that most of Shakespeare's public would not have heard about the scandal of that book, but for those who had – those very few sophisticated 'Jonsons' in his audience – Shakespeare's allusion would have seemed 'simply an embellishment to his ending, not an ironic undermining of it'.[114] Gurr's article spells out what he understands to be two deliberately inserted off-colour Shakespearean locutions. I use the phrase 'off-colour', but Gurr actually describes one of these locutions as a 'dirty word'.[115] Gurr claims in particular that Aretino's play *Il Marescalo* uses '*occupato*' (taken to mean to occupy the vagina in sexual intercourse) as a 'dirty word', and that, analogously, Shakespeare's 'Othello's occupation's gone' (3.3.362) can be heard as a lament for loss of (dirty?) sexual pleasure. Gurr cites in parallel Leontes' exclamation 'her natural posture' in *The Winter's Tale* (5.3.23) as alluding to *The Postures*, the title of *I Modi* in translation.[116] But, although Shakespeare's Cleopatra fears lest 'Some squeaking Cleopatra boy my greatness / I' th' posture of a whore' (5.2.216–17), his Coriolanus is described as appearing as if some god 'Were slily crept into his human powers / And gave him graceful posture' (2.1.216–18). That is to say, the word 'posture' once does, but certainly does not always, imply smutty indignity when used by the late Shakespeare.[117]

We will return to a more promising aspect of Gurr's argument presently, but first let us consider two other Renaissance scholars' responses to *I Modi*. Keir Elam finds Aretino's *I Modi* sonnets 'projections of male pornographic fantasy' and 'phallocentric', and also maintains that the 'book's reader-spectator [is uncomfortably] invited to indulge the scopophiliac pleasure offered by image and text'.[118] The *I Modi* images and text are not considered as distinct here, and neither are they distinguished in Elam's first comment on the Lord's lasciviously treasured 'wanton pictures' in *The Taming of the Shrew*: 'There can be little doubt that the model for the promised wanton pictures in the Lord's chamber is the art of Giulio Romano and Marcantonio Raimondi, transmitted throughout Europe thanks to Aretino's literary sponsorship.'[119] However, after discussing classical and Renaissance uses of pornographic imagery and performances to inspire lust, Elam does significantly distinguish *I Modi* from the 'wanton' pictures described in *The Shrew*, noting rightly that the description of pictures infused with subtle Ovidian eroticism in *The Shrew* (1.2.49–59) 'seems to have little to do with Arenentian sexual acrobatics'.[120]

Further distinctions of great importance are made in Bette Talvacchia's discussion of 'The Posture of Hermione in *The Winter's Tale*'. One is that 'if Giulio's couples were composed of elegant lines, those in Aretino's couplets lacked any touch of delicacy'.[121] In addition to making this necessary distinction between the wholly dissimilar aesthetic of those words and images, Talvacchia proposes the further discrimination that, although in the statue scene 'The appearance of Hermione is such that it rekindles Leontes' erotic impulses', yet 'This reading is in keeping with the import of the drama, for the erotic nature of the scene, though highly charged, is not smutty.' I certainly agree with that, but think that a different assessment should be made of the impact of the statue's supposed maker being Julio Romano than in Talvacchia's next remark: 'the "natural posture" of the sculpture arouses Leontes' lust; the figure must therefore be understood as disturbingly erotic in its simulation of real flesh'.[122]

I find two problems here. One is that 'lust', even the 'kindly lust' described in Thomas Morley's wonderful madrigal 'The Fields Abroad',[123] may not be the aspect of the eroticism implicit in Leontes' re-encounter with his wife. We have noted a huge range of other aspects of the erotic in *The Winter's Tale*, and here, I propose, we meet yet another aspect again. This is an aspect portrayed in Giulio's *I Modi* images that involves intense efforts to interlink with another (efforts that are quite distinct from 'lust'). Also, remembering how unpleasant it can be to encounter waxwork-like verisimilitude, we may be wary of accepting that a 'disturbingly erotic . . . simulation of *real* flesh' (emphasis added) properly describes either Giulio's images or the qualities of Hermione's 'statue'.

To consider these points, let us first return to Gurr's article which proposes that only very few sophisticated 'Jonsons' in

The Winter's Tale's original audience would have caught Shakespeare's allusion to *I Modi*. In a later article, Gurr enlarges on this proposition, claiming that this particular Shakespearean 'in-joke' was 'designed for even smaller elements in the audience' than the regular habitués of the Globe theatre.[124] If indeed only very few in Shakespeare's audiences were aware of Giulio's reputation, either for good or ill, then the erotic implications of 'Julio's' involvement with Hermione's statue would have had small significance in the play. Gurr's premise, however, seems unlikely because researchers have produced long lists of contemporaries of Shakespeare (some in his own milieu) who were well aware of Giulio's *I Modi* images.[125] Thus, let us take it that when the courtiers mention 'Julio' many in Shakespeare's audiences, although perhaps not the courtiers themselves, would have picked up an allusion to the famous images in *I Modi*.

It is interesting to consider whether the courtiers in *The Winter's Tale* are presented as not so knowing as they pretend. Indeed, Shakespeare's work from early on satirizes the fashionable attitudes of aspiring aesthetes who fancy themselves to be far more artistically knowing than they actually are. The presence of such satire, some of it involving coteries or academies central to whole plays, indicates that Shakespeare's audiences at large were aware of the comical possibilities of conventional-minded pretentiousness of a sort that may attach to Leontes' courtiers.

In fact, in an elaborate joke which would not have been lost on all but the few in the audiences of *The Winter's Tale*, the play's would-be sophisticated courtiers prove to be quadruply mistaken or deluded about Julio's statue. The first of the courtiers' errors surfaces when one of them remarks that 'had [Julio] himself eternity and could put breath into his work, would beguile nature of her custom, so perfectly he is her ape'. The first part of this, about beguiling nature, simply echoes an encomiastic commonplace that a great artist outdoes nature – as seen, for example, in Bembo's epitaph for Raphael: 'This is that Raphael, by whom in life / Our mighty mother Nature fear'd defeat; / And in whose death did fear herself to die.'[126] But the second part, the claim that Julio is 'perfectly' nature's 'ape', shows the ignorance of would-be connoisseurs who hold that excellence in visual art equals mere verisimilitude.

The next part of the joke at the expense of Leontes' courtiers is that Paulina's statue, which they extol unseen, does not fulfil up-to-date criteria for excellent sculpture. Discussions of such criteria, as derived from Italy, were highly *au courant* in England just at the time of the appearance of Shakespeare's play. By then the more knowing understood that fine sculptures should be left unpainted, both to allow subtle details of carving to show, and to accord with the Renaissance belief that classical sculpture was not coloured. Of course, the statue in *The Winter's Tale* could not have been monochrome because the boy actor who posed as Hermione's statue could not be drained of natural colour. But beyond that, Shakespeare insists on the paint on the statue, even calling it 'wet'.

I have argued in detail elsewhere that by 1608 or 1609 a range of English cognoscenti, including Ben Jonson, Inigo Jones, Sir Henry Wotton, the Earls of Salisbury and Arundel, and Prince Henry himself, had begun to praise unpainted, Italianate statues and to show contempt for brightly coloured, English ones, and that soon after some put the new taste into practice (compare Figures 10 and 11).[127]

To mention just one facet of that argument, near the start of Jonson's 1609 play *Epicoene*, Truewit sarcastically praises the long secretive painting of the statues that had just been unveiled on the new Aldgate in the City of London. He does this to parallel the equally secretive face painting of a group of very unpleasant, and indeed pederastic, 'collegiate ladies'. Additionally, by the time of *Epicoene*, letters and documents indicate that English aesthetes had already formulated among themselves the rejection of coloured statues that was to be expressed explicitly some years later in a sarcastic interchange in Jonson's 1632 *The Magnetic Lady*:

FIGURE 10 *Batholomew Atye and Issac James, detail of the monument to Sir Edward Denney and his wife Margaret in Waltham Abbey Church, 1600.* © *David Tyrrell.*

DR RUT
    I'd have her statue cut now in white marble.
    And have it painted in most orient colours.
SIR MOTH INTEREST
    That's right! all City statues must be painted;
    Else they be worth nought i'their subtle judgments.

                                (5.7.90–3)

Even more damning is Sir Henry Wotton's comment on 'the *Fashion* of *colouring*, even *Regall Statues*, which I must take leave to call an *English Bararisme*'.[128]

The Winter's Tale presents Julio's painted statue as not only coloured, but also newly 'performed' (meaning, on the first level, 'completed'). So Leontes is warned that 'The ruddiness upon her lip is wet. / You'll mar it if you kiss it, stain your own / With oily painting' (5.3.81–3). Here the joke at the expense of would-be sophisticates darkens, because it evokes correlated

FIGURE 11 *Maximilian Colt, detail of the tomb of Robert Cecil, Church of St Etheldreda, Hatfield, 1612. © John Midgely.*

images of painting, cosmetic painting, unpleasant textures ('oily'), soiling and Pygmalion-like perversity.

We will return to those dark matters presently, but first let us note the third of Shakespeare's jokes at the expense of

Leontes' courtiers. This involves the revelation that their understanding of what makes a statue excellent is completely wrong not only in terms of aesthetic theory, but also in terms of actual impact. This joke aligns with Shakespeare's several other expositions of self-assured ignorance in judgements of art that come up against the demonstration of genuine artistic excellence (for example, when Holofernes' ignorant judgements confront the wonderful poetry heard at the end of *Love's Labour's Lost*). Thus, rather than encountering a work of art that perfectly apes nature and being overwhelmed by it (as if by Zeuxis' grapes), Leontes quickly overcomes his perception of only the verisimilous surface of the statue (that it is 'wrinkled') and is then brought with Paulina's help to 'seeing-in' the work of art, as Richard Wollheim puts it,[129] achieving an imaginative connection with 'Julio's' representation of Hermione. This allows him better to comprehend – in fact, actually to relive – his own internal life and his perception of her internal life at a crucial time in their mutual past. That was the time when, during his first wooing, Leontes had been bitterly frustrated by Hermione's hesitancy. He'd recalled that time just before the birth of their second child, shockingly describing it in a courtly setting:

> Three crabbèd months had soured themselves to death
> Ere I could make thee open thy white hand
> And clap thyself my love.

> (1.2.104–6)

In the presence of the 'statue', Leontes is able to revise, and to invert, that old anger. He recognizes at last, with gratitude and respect, the dignified inner life of the statue's model:

> O, thus she stood,
> Even with such life of majesty – warm life,
> As now it coldly stands – when first I wooed her.

> (5.3.34–6)

This is only made possible by Leontes' contribution of the beholder's share, whereby his encounter with the image releases new meanings.

The fourth and final joke about the courtiers' misunderstanding of Julio's statue is that its art does not ape or vie with nature, but actually *is* nature. This, however, is not a cheat, for the pretend statue functions exactly as an artist-made one would have done if the viewer had given it their full imaginative attention. The converse is also true: Leontes' belief that he views an artwork mediates the process, but the internal transformation seen in his reconciliation with the image of his 'good' wife would be the same in either 'real life' or in artistic perception.[130]

Let us turn, finally, to the issue of the alleged wet paint on Hermione's statue which is potentially soiling, and to the linked question of how viewing a seeming statue of his wife can redeem Leontes' shattered marriage. As mentioned above, cosmetic paint on women was often decried by satirists and moralists, among them Ben Jonson. It has also been mentioned that Jonson's 1609 *Epicoene* contains satiric commentary on the time-consuming painting of its collegiate ladies. In fact, at the very start of the play their face painting is noted by their pageboy, as follows: 'The gentlewomen play with me, and throw me o' the bed; and carry me in to my lady; and she kisses me with her oil'd face . . . and then she hits me a blow o' the eare, and calls me innocent, and lets me goe' (1.1.13–18). Clerimont comments on the cosmetic painting *cum* sexual abuse of 'the lady Haughty': 'there's no man can be admitted till she be ready, now-a-days, till she has painted, and perfumed, and wash'd, and scour'd, but the boy here; and him she wipes her oil'd lips upon, like a sponge' (1.1.86–9). So it was certainly possible in Elizabethan contexts for 'oily painting' on a woman's face to be seen as sexually transgressive.[131] No such dangerous possibility is implied when Perdita makes to kiss the statue's hand and is warned by Paulina, 'O, patience! / The statue is but newly fixed; the colour's / Not dry' (5.3.46–8). But when she issues a similar warning to Leontes, the terms 'mar', 'stain' and 'oily', ensure that he does not approach the statue until it has descended and is 'stone no more'.

There is, then, a psychic danger in the statue scene of short-circuiting the process of recognizing the symbolization in art. This would have been readily identified in a culture that produced, for instance, John Marston's truly pornographic *The Metamorphosis of Pigmalions Image* in 1598. The dangers of Leontes overstepping the bounds of married life into a condition of obsession, or of evading the seriousness demanded by sexual relations (as depicted by Giulio), are at last mediated because artworks can speak to dangerous parts of the unconscious and enlist even there, in defence of life, allies to a true linkage between the self and others. *The Winter's Tale* presents a perfect model for that process when Hermione's firstborn son Mamillius whispers in his heavily pregnant mother's ear a 'sad tale ... for winter ... / Of sprites and goblins' (2.1.27–8). By creating a scary story he sublimates, as we would say, his monstrous feelings of jealousy and his terror about being displaced in his mother's affections by a 'fine new prince' about whom he has been teased (2.1.18–20). I have argued that Mamillius' father Leontes undergoes similar anxieties about his wife's pregnancy, but without sublimation his reaction becomes violent and he becomes a vicious tyrant.[132]

In this same scene Mamillius banters with a waiting-gentlewoman about facial cosmetics, noting that her fashionable 'eyebrows' may have been 'made with a pen', and when questioned says, 'I learned it out of women's faces' (2.1.8–12). However, Mamillus' experience of cosmetics is nothing like that of the poor pageboy in *Epicoene*. And although he has been a difficult child, and perhaps even a tyrannical one (his mother was driven to say 'He so troubles me / 'Tis past enduring' (2.1.1–2)), and although the waiting-women have teased him, he is able to use art to help reform his passionate perversity and regain his vital connections. This is just what his father will do sixteen years later.

3

Poets in Shakespeare's Plays

Boundaries

T.S. Eliot's two essays 'Poetry and Drama' (1951) and 'The Three Voices of Poetry' (1953) address a question he first posed three decades before: can one write verse drama for a modern audience?[1] In the first of these essays Eliot harshly criticizes his own verse drama to date as either excessively limited or actually inept, conveying no *ex cathedra* sense of infallibility. The 1951 essay also includes a strong admonition that authors should ensure that audiences perceive only unconsciously that a play is written in verse. Thus Eliot pronounces it 'unfortunate' when modern playgoers 'are repelled by verse', but supposes it *a fortiori* 'deplorable when they are attracted by [verse] – when that means that they are prepared to enjoy the play and the language of the play as two separate things'.[2]

Eliot's 1950s essays addressed contemporary sensibilities, so it might seem unfair to compare his views on writing plays in the mid-twentieth century with Shakespeare's practice long before. However, Eliot does cite Shakespeare as an ideal user of dramatic verse, so it might be fair to point out that he seems to have entirely overlooked one significant aspect of Shakespeare's use of verse in drama. This is the point at which we hear the work of a Shakespearean poet-character recited and we are intended to hear this *as* poetry, indeed it becomes of specific interest because it *is* poetry. Here it would be 'deplorable', to invert Eliot's phrase, if it is *not* recognized as poetry. The verse in question must be *consciously* recognized as the verse of a particular character, quite distinct from any verse that the author may use as a medium of expression (perhaps to be noted only unconsciously).

Another way of putting this is to assert that there is a fourth 'voice of poetry' beyond the three that Eliot went on to propose in his 1953 essay. Eliot's three voices are those of (lyric) poets meditatively speaking for themselves to themselves, of poets speaking for themselves to an audience from behind the mask of one single other imaginary person, and of (dramatic) poets speaking for a range of sympathetically portrayed interacting characters. Eliot illustrates the second, masked, voice by citing Browning's dramatic monologues.[3] To these we may add a fourth voice of poetry: the voice of a poem heard (or heard about) within a work of fiction where the author of that poem is a character in that fiction. In Shakespeare's case, the fiction will take the form of a poetic drama or of a poem.

Shakespeare's work contains quite a lot of that fourth voice and therefore many figures who are poets or who exhibit actual poems by means of recitation or description. However, for our purposes we cannot accept that Shakespeare's poets are as ubiquitous as some critics have suggested. For instance, Gary Schmidgall claims, 'The poet-as-courtier is ubiquitous in Shakespeare's plays', and then identifies all the many Shakespeare characters he perceives as being involved in 'the courtly rat race' as poets in the Renaissance poet-suitor tradition.[4] Going even further, Patrick Cheney claims that 'so many [of Shakespeare's dramatic] characters qualify as poet-figures that it would be hard to count them'.[5] Probably in line with that notion, Cheney indicates, for instance, that when Duke Vincentio soliloquizes in rhymed couplets in *Measure for Measure*, 'Shakespeare concludes Act 3, scene 2, with a poem'.[6] However, from our perspective we must insist that Vincentio's rhymed soliloquy is not a poem *inserted* into the play *as* a poem, but rather that its verse appears only as a medium for formalized dramatic utterance.[7]

So a certain kind of slippage appears in criticism that does not distinguish verse as a medium of expression in Shakespeare's work from the verses actually made by dramatized poets. Such slippage was not in play in T.S. Eliot's analyses because Eliot did not even imagine that voices speaking verse *as* verse could be presented to modern theatre audiences, and therefore did not consider the possibility of a fourth voice of poetry. By contrast, Elizabethan theatre audiences would not have found the dramatized presence and voice of a poet-character far-fetched or exotic. Indeed, writing or attempting to write poetry was a common and fashionable Elizabethan activity, and not only among the best educated or highest-placed in society. Renaissance courtiers were advised by conduct literature to turn a hand to poetry, and some did so excellently.[8] At least as portrayed by Shakespeare, wooers from a wide range of social levels (down to Romeo's, and even Abraham Slender's) were conventionally expected to emulate the great sonneteers. Elizabethan writers in other media also wrote poems. Poetry books and manuscripts were eagerly circulated and consumed. Even the London citizen Henry Petowe (b. 1576), who was a scrivener made free of the Clothworkers' Company, wrote and published quantities of poetry.[9]

Since for many Elizabethans writing, reading or hearing verse was not unusual, they would have discriminated with ease between characters who speak merely *in verse* in a drama, and characters in drama who are deliberately exhibiting poetry. We make analogous discriminations when a character in an opera bursts into song; we do not assume that that character is consciously singing and thus is an amateur or professional musician. Accordingly, with some exceptions to be explained presently, we will exclude from our consideration Shakespearean speakers who show no conscious intention to produce poetry, despite the fact that they speak in blank or rhymed verse, or even present elaborately patterned lyrics.[10] Often a transition to the use of rhymed verse in a Shakespeare play does not indicate any present artistic intention, but rather accords with conventions for choruses, soliloquies, masques, prophecies and epilogues, or for the use of couplets to cap blank-verse scenes.

The rule, then, will be that we will distinguish poetry that is *embedded* in Shakespeare texts as a medium from poems that are deliberately *inserted* into texts in order to indicate that poetry *per se* is being heard or written, and give our attention only to the latter. Exceptions to the rule will occur only when particular *inserted* poems are deliberately juxtaposed with particular instances of *embedded* poetry in order to induce comparison or to express specific ironies. In such places, the *embedded* poetry in question will be seen to have a direct bearing on the activities or qualities of identified poet-characters.

We might ask if we should assign the title of 'poet' to the several Shakespearean characters who attempt to make 'all the world' into *their* 'stage' in the sense that they are given to creating and acting out false roles to impress or deceive others, seeking their own benefit. The shameless coney-catching mountebank Autolycus in *The Winter's Tale*, who says he has produced puppet plays (4.3.95), shams many roles, changing accents and costumes to suit. Iago deliberately sets up misleading situations, and then extemporizes gestures and appropriate lines when the opportunity emerges to advance his aims.[11] There are also a few Shakespeare characters that create theatrical parts for others to enact. These include Hamlet, who supplies the actors visiting Elsinore with 'a speech of some dozen or sixteen lines which I would set down' to 'insert' into their play (2.2.543–4). Another is Camillo, who counsels the lovers Florizel and Perdita to escape in *The Winter's Tale* (4.4.543–64). Here he instructs them to enact a plausible fiction capable of inducing an affective reaction ('Methinks I see / Leontes opening his free arms and weeping') and proposes how Perdita must be costumed ('habited'), and also actually scripts what Florizel must say ('What you . . . shall deliver . . . I'll write you down'). The lines Camillo writes down are no more known than are Hamlet's play-patching lines, but in both cases the motives of the playwrights are revealed. Hamlet's personal and political aim is to 'catch the conscience of the king' (2.2.607), and Camillo admits in soliloquy that his real intention is not to help the lovers, but rather to betray them to the angry King Polixenes in order to serve his own selfish ends (4.4.663–8).[12] So both these playwrights fall foul of Freud's noble stricture that 'the aesthetic attitude toward an object is characterised by the condition that we do not ask anything of the object, especially no satisfaction of our serious needs'.[13]

Several well-founded recent studies show that even when writing his plays Shakespeare deliberately acted as a 'literary' author as well as a man of the theatre.[14] Shakespeare himself as a poet is not our topic, but we will adopt from those studies, and from Shakespeare's own usages, the suggestion that for Shakespeare the creation of poetry was not fully equivalent to spontaneous or inspired extemporizing.[15] Therefore, poets for Shakespeare are responsible for their own crafted productions. Shakespeare also apparently holds that an element of a poet's responsibility is aesthetic answerability, as we shall next see.

'Literary criticism by example' and the poets in Shakespeare's plays

At the height of the Elizabethan sonneteering craze of the mid-1590s some poets satirized the excesses of would-be love poets who indulged in absurdly inflated emotionalism, or who were apparently self-delighted when grotesquely parroting stupefying poetic conventions. These include Shakespeare who describes such poetry in his *Venus and Adonis* (1593), and Sir John Davies who parodies it in his 'Gullinge Sonnets' (1594). The next chapter will consider this phenomenon more closely, but for now we should note that in addition to a satirical intent Shakespeare sometimes also showed a corrective one when parodying poetasters. This he did by deliberately dramatizing the creation of lame verses in several plays, and presenting alongside these verses examples of far greater poetic skill and quality. I will call such configurations '*literary criticism by example*'.

When Shakespeare dramatizes a weak poet, the critique is often as much of that character's behaviour as it is of their poetry. However, Shakespeare is typically droll when doing so, rather than severe, usually linking the poor artistry of a would-be poet to a mild degree of vanity and self-deception, or with overconfidence and conventionality pardonable by immaturity. In contrast, Ben Jonson was censorious about makers of bad poetry, especially in his *Poetaster* (1601–2). Jonson even expressed the position, especially in his extraordinary Carey-Morrison Ode,[16] that poetic language and the poet are indistinguishable, so that literary criticism *is* moral criticism. Although exaggerated, Jonson's position derived from a widespread concept of artistic virtue which paralleled a concept of civic virtue that had far more impact in Shakespeare's age than in ours.

Ben Jonson's fascination with the topic of literary excellence leads to his nearly explicit description of the above-mentioned practice of *literary criticism by example*. This appears in Jonson's only gesture at a Renaissance sequence of 'love poems', a ten-poem sequence which he titled *A Celebration of Charis*. This is a kind of spoof overall, yet contains one very serious turn. In the third poem of the sequence Jonson's narrator amusingly details 'What He Suffered' at the hands of a tyrannous Cupid, using mock-conventional Anacreontic imagery. But then the narrator concludes this third poem with a promise

> To revenge me with my tongue,
> Which how dexterously I do
> Hear and make example too.

Thus Jonson's narrator promises to provide an *example* of contrasting poetic excellence. He makes good on this promise, for the immediately following (fourth) poem in the sequence is the extremely lovely lyric beginning 'See the chariot at hand here of Love'.[17] This was a risky thing for Jonson to have attempted, and it illustrates how delivering *literary criticism by example* requires that an author supply both a convincing parody of weak conventional poetry, and also serve up on order, for contrast, excellent poetry. In another art form, some musical composers have *inserted* inferior musical passages into their works alongside superior ones, also for the sake of parody or contrast (Hadyn and Shostakovich come to mind).

Love's Labour's Lost was the earliest play in which Shakespeare undertook such a challenge. This play is filled with poets and would-be poets whose lyrics are repeatedly recited or sung in poetry's fourth voice, so distinctions are clear between verse *embedded* in the play as its medium of expression and verses *inserted* into it to be recognized as deliberately made poetry.[18] All of the play's *inserted* poems are encountered, moreover, as written-down verses that are read out loud onstage, giving emphasis to their deliberately made aspect. In addition, a stage character reading a text from a paper will use a different tone of voice from their normal speaking voice, and the piece of paper they read from is a visible prop, all making evident the presence of literary poetry.

The literary quality of one of the poems *inserted* into *Love's Labours Lost* is further underscored when the pedantic Holofernes, hearing that an intercepted letter contains 'verses', asks to hear 'a staff, a stanza, a verse' (4.2.104). The materiality of this same poetry-bearing letter is emphasized when its author, Birone, later 'tears' it up for shame (4.3.198–217). Moreover, the onstage reading out loud of a text from a written paper had a special standing in Elizabethan stage practice: at issue was whether or not it was necessary for a member of the repertory company to memorize the text.[19] The First Folio text of *Love's Labour's Lost* probably indicates this point by using italics when printing the majority of the poems that are read out loud in the play.[20]

In addition to being deliberately identified *as* poems, most of the poems *inserted* into *Love's Labour's Lost* are more or less gently satirical both of their genres and of their authors. Thus, when first declaring himself 'in love' the absurdly bombastic Don Armado proclaims, 'I am sure I shall turn sonnet. Devise wit, write pen, for I am for whole volumes, in folio' (1.2.173–6). He then pens a letter to his illiterate lady love, which when later read out loud is heard to contain absurdly preening overblown prose followed by a love poem that images the male lover as a lion and his beloved as a helpless lamb (4.1.60–92).[21] Although their poems do not similarly celebrate predatory male violence, the four male protagonists of *Love's Labour's Lost* are all love-struck, and each writes a love poem. These comprise three sonnets (the King's at 4.3.24–39 has an extra couplet) and Dumaine's song-like lyric in ten tetrameter couplets (4.3.99–118), which is called in the Folio stage direction '*his Sonnet*' (tln 1438). Rather than being absurd, like Armado's poem, all of these qualify as competent, if not outstanding, Elizabethan poetry.[22]

Literary pretensions, together with stereotyped wooing behaviour, are at last repudiated in Birone's famous recantation speech. Although Birone's language in this speech is *embedded* poetry and he is not reciting a deliberately composed poem, it remains notable that this recantation speech exhibits excellently fluent blank verse that stands in stark contrast to the stiff and frigid phasing of Birone's formerly *inserted* love poetry. Explicitly commenting on that difference, Birone promises to desist from 'speeches penned', a 'schoolboy's tongue', and wooing in 'rhyme':

O, never will I trust to speeches penned,
Nor to the motion of a schoolboy's tongue,
Nor never come in visor to my friend,
Nor woo in rhyme, like a blind harper's song.
Taffeta phrases, silken terms precise,
Three-piled hyperboles, spruce affectation,
Figures pedantical – these summer flies
Have blown me full of maggot ostentation.
I do forswear them, and I here protest,

By this white glove – how white the hand, God knows! –
Henceforth my wooing mind shall be expressed
In russet yeas, and honest kersey noes.
And to begin, wench, so God help me, law!
My love to thee is sound, sans crack or flaw.

(5.2.402–15)

In the penultimate line, Birone imitates a rough country
wooer's dialect, but then in the last line he comically slips into
French, drawing Rosaline's reply of 'Sans "sans", I pray you'.
Yet Birone's recantation speech also incorporates the lovely
monosyllabic cadence and vowel harmonies of 'By this white
glove – how white the hand, God knows!' Even more chastened
is the simple but stirring quality of Birone's slightly later
monosyllabic poetic line, 'Honest plain words best pierce the
ear of grief' (5.2.745). So, Birone's repudiation of verbal
excesses is expressed in *embedded* 'Honest plain words' that
possess great poetic value. Here we find our first example of
literary criticism by example. In this instance it might also be
called 'literary education by example', because our sensibilities
are instructed when we observe the difference between the
excellent verse in which Birone regrets his 'affectation' and
'ostentation', and his former schoolboy poeticizing with which
he attempted to 'woo in rhyme'. Thus his far superior *embedded*
verse contrasts with his inferior *inserted* verses – that is to say,
third-voiced poetry is contrasted with fourth-voiced poetry.

Love's Labour's Lost contains yet another contrast of
inferior with superior verses where both are *inserted*, both
fourth-voiced. The inferior *inserted* verses in question are
those heard in the absurd Pageant of the Nine Worthies,
consisting of clumsy and stale poetic jingling, reeking of
pedantry.[23] The superior verses are heard in the superb ditties
of the two sparkling songs *inserted* at the play's very end,
'When dasies pied and violets blue' and 'When icicles hang by
the wall'. So, after the ridiculously stilted Pageant has been
aborted and its musical postlude alone called for (5.2.871–5),

we hear these two lyric poems that far surpass it in quality (and surpass the courtiers' poetry as well).

Connecting them with the Pageant, Don Armado identifies these lyrics as a 'dialogue . . . in praise of the owl and the cuckoo', which 'should have followed in the end of our show' (5.2.872–4). This inverts the tradition in which sung postludes to Elizabethan plays were much coarser in style than the staged works they followed.[24] The excellence of the Pageant's postlude in *Love's Labour's Lost* thus alerts us to another instance of *literary criticism by example*. Recognition of this may help to untangle a famous crux. Both the quarto and Folio texts of the play include, after the splendid final songs, an additional line, 'The words of Mercury are harsh after the songs of Apollo', but neither text indicates a speaker for the line. Who, if anyone, speaks it has been much debated, as well as what the line means. A solution to these mysteries (but not to an allied, less-noted mystery)[25] may lie in the following hypothesis. I believe that the line is intended to be delivered by one of the Nine Worthies on behalf of all of them in order to say that the their silly and pedantic Pageant is as charming as the songs of Apollo, while the wonderful lyrics that follow are merely workmanlike efforts inspired by the lesser deity Mercury. If this reading is correct, then the play concludes with its pedants continuing to flaunt their ignorance of and insensitivity to great poetry. This final reiteration of the folly of Navarre's self-satisfied arbiters of literary taste would emphasize the centrality of *literary criticism by example* in *Love's Labour's Lost*.

Literary criticism by example is also significant in *Romeo and Juliet*, another play of the sonneteering 1590s. Here the poor poetry on display is actually bad poetry, slackly and incompletely made by the immature Romeo in love with Rosaline. We do not hear much of this bad verse because Romeo has to be capable of evolving first into a genuine lover, and then into a tragic one,[26] and so cannot be as much a figure of fun in his play as the ridiculous Spaniard Don Armado, or the pedants of Navarre, are in theirs.

Romeo's immature, if fashionable, poeticizing attracts Mercutio's adverse commentary. Offering one of the diverse voices in the play that present a wide range of differing views of sex, love and wooing, Mercutio scoffs at Romeo 'beryhm[ing]' his beloved with exaggerated praise, and says 'Now is he for the numbers that Petrarch flowed in' (2.3.36–8). Earlier Mercutio mock-'conjure[s]' Romeo with

> Romeo! Humours! Madman! Passion! Lover!
> Appear thou in the likeness of a sigh.
> Speak but one rhyme and I am satisfied.
> Cry but 'Ay me!' Pronounce but 'love' and 'dove'.
>
> (2.1.7–10)

This indicates that Romeo has actually attempted poetry – or at least rhyme.

Before turning to that rhyme, we may note that a very high proportion of the language of *Romeo and Juliet* consists of *embedded* poetry,[27] most in the form of varied but always vigorous blank verse. There are also many traces of the sonnet tradition:[28] the play opens with a Chorus reciting a sonnet; a joint sonnet is spoken during the first encounter between the play's lovers; and Act Two also begins with a sonnet-reciting Chorus. Less obviously, several sonnet sestets are *embedded* in the speeches of Benvolio and Romeo, as has been detected by both Brian Gibbons and René Weis.[29]

Justly famous *embedded* poetry also appears in the dialogues spoken by Romeo and Juliet as their love evolves. Those dialogues share the blank verse format heard throughout much of the play, but surpass in poetic quality all the other verse in the play. They are notably superior as verse to the stiff mutual sonnet spoken by the two lovers at their first meeting (1.5.92–105). This suggests that the love between them progresses far beyond the conventional love-religion motifs playfully echoed in their initial sonnet.

Even more in contrast with the superb blank verse spoken by the rapidly maturing Romeo and Juliet is a dire sole

poetic *insert* in the play pronounced by Romeo in the fourth
voice of poetry. This poem or poetic fragment, crafted when
Romeo thinks himself in love with Rosaline, is produced
seemingly in response to a unrhymed two-line poetic lead-in
pronounced by Benvolio. That was realistic – an actual instance
of an Elizabethan poet following his poet-friend's poetic lead
will be discussed in the next chapter.[30] Benvolio's lead-in verses
are unoriginal in content, yet are actually admirable in terms
of their alliteration, cadence and vowel harmonies: 'Alas that
love, so gentle in his view, / Should be so tyrannous and rough
in proof' (1.1.166–7). The would-be poet Romeo picks up on
Benvolio's 'Alas that love', but his continuation, which is
distinctly in the fourth voice of poetry, does not match the
quality of Benvolio's lines. Romeo begins, 'Alas that love,
whose view is muffled still, / Should without eyes see pathways
to his will' (168–9), the 'invention' here borrowed from the
super-trite Anacreontic topos of a blind and wilful Cupid.
Apparently this opening couplet is so tedious to even the poet
himself that he immediately self-interrupts with a practical
question: 'Where shall we dine?' (170).

Romeo next receives a new impetus for poetic invention
when he notices evidence of a recent street fight. In response to
this, however, his resumed poem only enunciates hackneyed
paradoxes in baggy lines overladen with oxymoron, his lame
verses failing to dignify his mooning over Rosaline. Phrased in
the language of what G. Blakemore Evans wittily labels 'mere
sonnetese',[31] these lines run:

> Alas that love, whose view is muffled still,
> Should without eyes see pathways to his will
> Where shall we dine? O me! What fray was here?
> Yet tell me not, for I have heard it all.
> Here's much to do with hate, but more with love.
> Why then, O brawling love, O loving hate,
> O anything of nothing first create;
> O heavy lightness, serious vanity,
> Misshapen chaos of well-seeming forms,

Feather of lead, bright smoke, cold fire, sick health,
Still-waking sleep, that is not what it is!
This love feel I, that feel no love in this.

(1.1.168–79)

These verses show none of the *cantible* that Shakespeare's own poetry possesses even at its weakest,[32] and are also beset by uneven rhyming, including the clunking concluding half rhyme 'it is' / 'in this'.

In the third of these dozen lines Romeo asks two questions: 'Where shall we dine?' and 'What fray was here?' Being besotted with Rosaline has not reduced his healthy teenage appetite for food, so he notices his stomach even before his attention strays to his environment. Returning to his poem, Romeo next alleges with hollow hyperbole that his woes as a thwarted lover exceed the miseries of any other conflict. Although contrasts between feuding and loving permeate the play, Romeo's facile remarks on that contrast are here not only shallow, but also heartless. The bloody evidence of a fight suggests to Romeo only a way to emphasize his own love sufferings by way of a series of timeworn, hackneyed, oxymoronic paradoxes.[33]

Literary criticism by example becomes pertinent to this feeble poeticizing if we notice that later in the play Juliet is driven to use oxymoron passionately in a blank-verse soliloquy. As in the case of Birone's blank-verse recantation of his former wooing in rhyme in *Love's Labour's Lost*, the contrast here is between weak *inserted* and strong *embedded* verse, but here the link is the shared use of a notable rhetorical figure. Juliet's paradoxes, in contrast to Romeo's, express painfully real enigmas. The contradiction in her oxymoron matches her genuine internal conflict upon hearing that her new husband has killed her cousin. Not knowing that Tybalt's death followed his underhanded killing of Mercutio, or that Mercutio's death resulted from Romeo's efforts to abate the violence of the feud, she is driven to describe Romeo as a

> Beautiful tyrant, fiend angelical!
> Dove-feathered raven, wolvish-ravening lamb!
> Despised substance of divinest show!
> Just opposite to what thou justly seem'st –
> A damned saint, an honourable villain.

Adding, 'O nature, what hadst thou to do in hell / When thou didst bower the spirit of a fiend / In mortal paradise of such sweet flesh?' (3.2.75–85), she clothes her emotions about losing both kinsman and husband in wholly appropriate oxymoronic language.

Just before learning of Romeo's exile, Juliet expresses her longing for 'love-performing night' in an ecstatic soliloquy beginning 'Gallop apace, you fiery-footed steeds' (3.2.1–31). Because of Romeo's banishment, her ardent anticipation of the consummation of her marriage is thwarted, while she is at the same time confronted with the horror of her kinsman's death. Thus her paradoxes are not flat-footed like Romeo's, but rather, searingly, 'fiery-footed'. Poetry-aware Elizabethan audiences would have been alert to the *embedded* oxymoron in Juliet's agonized reflections on real paradoxes, and would have noted the wholly conventional *inserted* oxymoron bandied in Romeo's immature poetic maundering. If comparison of these two occurred to them, as it may well have done, both literary-critical and literary-educational functions would have been served.

However, purposes other than the literary-critical may also be served when Shakespeare inserts deficient poetry into his plays. As Inga-Stina Ewbank puts it, 'deliberately "bad" Shakespearean poetry is sometimes functional *rather than* parodic'. In these cases, it is 'part of and subordinated to a dramatic exploration of the false as against the genuine, fiction as against reality'. The italics are Ewbank's own, and she adds several examples of where 'literary satire' is not 'the main point'.[34] To her examples of mainly *embedded* bad poetry may be added, relevant to our purposes, Orlando's paltry poetry which is *inserted* into *As You Like It*.[35]

Orlando's wholly inexpert poetry is heard against a background of the play's brilliant prose passages and beautiful songs, but it is presented entirely humorously and not in a comparative framework, as in *criticism by example*. Thus, emulating the shepherd-poet conventions of pastoralism, Orlando hangs silly verses on the trees of the Forest of Arden. When Rosalind reads some of these lines out – a farrago of couplets whose jogging rhythms and jingling rhymes extol her excellence – Touchstone accurately describes them as a 'very false gallop of verses'. Then Touchstone (who otherwise speaks only in prose) reels off extempore a stream of very funny off-colour parodies (3.2.86–112). At this point Celia enters, reading out more of Orlando's love lyrics (3.2.122–51). Their poor scansion and forced rhyming make these cross-rhymed tetrameters even more ludicrous than the earlier couplets. In them, Orlando first professes dedication to writing poetry about mortality, mutability and the perfections of a 'Rosalinda' made up of the parts of famous historical women. Such smatterings borrowed from conventional models are followed by a feeble run of religious-erotic metaphors. Upon hearing these, Rosalind comments, 'What tedious homily of love have you wearied your parishioners withal' (3.2.152–3). Rosalind disguised as Ganymede therefore needs to educate and reform Orlando's immature emotions, for she is in love with him. When he eventually graduates from her schooling, he will abandon his poetic pretensions.

As You Like It was the last play in which Shakespeare mocked an author of lame non-dramatic verse.[36] From such mockery, let us turn our attention to sorrowful Shakespearean poet-figures who are not presented as ridiculous, but rather as tragic.

Tragic and neglected poets in Shakespeare's plays

It is arguable that the deposed king in *The Tragedy of King Richard II*, who deliberately 'stud[ies]' how to express himself in his prison scene, is one of Shakespeare's sorrowful poet-figures, soon to become a tragic one.[37] In that scene, Richard is entirely alone on stage (uniquely in the play), and also does not seem desirous of auditors. And yet there was a Renaissance view that poets become particularly unhappy when unheard. This is illustrated in Samuel Daniel's Sonnet 54, beginning 'Unhappy pen, and ill-accepted lines', and is half-spoofed in Ben Jonson's 'My Picture Left in Scotland', which begins 'I now think Love is rather deaf than blind'.[38] The desperate plight of a poet lacking an appreciative audience is exaggeratedly described in *As You Like It* when Touchstone (speaking, as Rosalind says at another point, 'wiser than thou are ware of') says, 'When a man's verses cannot be understood . . . it strikes a man more dead than a great reckoning in a little room.'[39]

Death, literally, comes to the unheard poet Cinna in Shakespeare's *Julius Caesar*. Because he is not 'understood' by an unheeding mob, despite his insistence that 'I am Cinna the poet, I am Cinna the poet', his profession is simply discounted when he is mistaken for the political conspirator Cinna. The bloodlust of the mob overwrites his language, so that one plebeian jests, 'Tear him for his bad verses, tear him for his bad verses' (3.3.1–35). The parody of antiphonal cadences in Cinna's doubled-up plea to be heard and in this unhearing response is chilling.

Also in *Julius Caesar*, a character called only 'a Poet' is unheard, dismissed, ejected, and humiliated when he attempts to become a truce-maker between the squabbling Cassius and Brutus (4.2.178–90). When Cassius berates this intruding poet with 'Ha! ha! How vilely doth this cynic rhyme', the ghost of his origin is glimpsed. Shakespeare's unnamed poet-peacemaker derived from Plutarch's account of one Marcus Phaonius, a headstrong, would-be cynic philosopher, who in exactly parallel circumstances frantically quoted Homer.[40] In Shakespeare's play, the Poet's quotation from the *Iliad* is unrecognized by Brutus, who remarks, 'What should the wars do with these jigging fools?' (4.3.185–9). The point made here is not that Brutus is uncultured, but rather that there is no space for a poet in the midst of civic upheaval and contention.

A parallel notion is expressed by Nicholas Hilliard, who wrote that should a particularly talented painter 'live in time of trouble, and under savage government wherein arts be not esteemed . . . woe be unto him as unto an untimely death'.[41]

As mentioned in the last chapter, the 'Poet' in *Timon of Athens* is also rejected and driven away by his former patron Timon. The once over-generous and then bankrupted Timon becomes monumentally bitter because his false friends abandon him. He regains his wealth (accidentally), but not his trust in humanity, including artists. He therefore rejects the Poet and his friend the Painter, first warning each about 'trust[ing] a knave / That mightily deceives you' (5.1.92–3). Timon then avers that those knaves, the traitors that they 'Know . . . love . . . feed . . . / Keep in your bosom' (5.1.95–6), are the two artists themselves. Here Timon focuses his anger and hatred on artists who had formerly provided him with aesthetic and intellectual pleasure. It is true that his association with their productions promoted Timon's heedless self-esteem, on which he looks back with disgust, but he forgets that the Poet and Painter (unlike his mere sycophants) gave him things of value in return for his support. He finally pelts the two fleeing artists with missiles, holding them less worthy than the whores, renegades and thieves who had visited him before. Artists regarded in such a manner must suffer. An open question is whether Shakespeare's poets, many of whom are treated satirically, deserve better esteem and treatment.

Shakespeare's 'feigning' poets and honest poets

A lexeme encompassing the words 'deceit', 'deceiving', 'deceive' and 'deceiver' is represented in nearly every Shakespeare play and poem, with 140 instances in the Oxford Shakespeare and 138 in the First Folio.[42] The lexeme embracing 'feign' and 'feigning' is also frequent, making about thirty-five appearances in Shakespeare texts. Words referring to poets or poetry are also highly frequent in Shakespeare's works,[43] and this dilutes the potential significance of the dozen collocations in Shakespeare texts between the word 'poet' and terms such as 'feign', 'lie', 'trick', 'flatter' or [falsely] 'devise'. Nevertheless, many critics remark that Shakespeare often associates the making of poetry with various kinds of fraud or dishonesty.

Sometimes when poets are said by Shakespeare to 'feign', that only means that they write or compose their poetry, in accord with the old meaning of to 'feign', which is to 'fashion, form, shape'.[44] Moreover, many remarks made by Shakespearean characters about dishonest poets are closer to jests or sallies than to moral opprobrium. So, when in *Twelfth Night* Olivia replies with 'It is the more likely to be feigned' to Viola's claim that her conned speech is 'poetical' (1.5.187–8), she only light-heartedly gestures towards the sense of 'feign' meaning to 'contrive (a deception)'.[45] Other similar remarks are merely pompous or stilted. Thus the Poet in *Timon of Athens*, who is given to overblown diction, replaces 'wrote about personified Fortune' with 'Feigned Fortune' (1.1.65), and Lorenzo in his 'purple passage' on music in *The Merchant of Venice* asserts that 'the poet / Did feign that Orpheus drew trees' (5.1.79–80).

Shakespeare's unscrupulous Richard, Duke of York, describes his limitless ambition for 'all that poets feign' (3 *Henry VI* 1.2.31), and Touchstone famously proclaims that 'the truest poetry is the most feigning, and lovers are given to poetry; and what they swear in poetry it may be said, as lovers, they do feign',[46] here showing little positive regard for artists. While attempting to seduce 'foul' Audrey, whom he hopes will not prove 'honest', Touchstone parodies the subtle position taken in Sidney's *Defence of Poetry* about poets never being able to lie. A poet's 'feigning' is treated with distaste when Egeus in *A Midsummer Night's Dream* angrily claims that his daughter has been seduced by Lysander, who has 'by moonlight at her window sung / With feigning voice verses of feigning love' (1.1.30–1).[47] In all these cases the speakers alleging poets' 'feigning' are more discredited than the poetry they accuse.

Nonetheless, many critics have proposed that all of Shakespeare's poet-figures are dishonest, immoral or inauthentic. Phillip Edwards extends this to a broader view that 'in Shakespeare's plays, most of the remarks about the nature of poetry are uncomplimentary', attributing this to Shakespeare's own continuing scepticism about 'the value of art'.[48] Kenneth Muir alleges that there was an earlier critical consensus that Shakespeare always regarded 'the art [of poetry] and its practitioners with irony, satire, or contempt', and himself finds reasons to praise only three of Shakespeare's poet-figures: Lodowick in the possibly Shakespearean *Edward III*, and the unnamed Poets in *Julius Caesar* and *Timon of Athens*.[49] More recently, Patrick Cheney has inverted the thrust of Muir's tepid view that 'if Lodowick was Shakespeare's creation he is the only one of his poets who emerges with much credit',[50] instead finding Lodowick in *Edward III* a 'poet working harmoniously with his sovereign' and yet brave enough to be 'a critic of a king trying to commit adultery'.[51] Thus Cheney's Lodowick is no flatterer, and is opposed to immorality.

A similar figure, this time certainly Shakespearean, is the unnamed court poet who arrives in *The Winter's Tale* just after Leontes promises never to remarry without Paulina's permission, and Paulina replies that that will be 'when your first queen's again in breath' (5.1.81–4). This poet brings news of the arrival of Florizel and Perdita, and he extols the beauty of Perdita, 'the most peerless piece of earth, I think, / That e'er the sun shone bright on' (5.1.94–5). Paulina objects to this remark, naming of the former queen: 'O, Hermione.' She then makes it clear that the courtier formerly wrote verses asserting that Hermione's beauty was unsurpassable: 'Sir, you yourself / Have said and writ so . . . / your verse flowed with her beauty once' (5.1.98–102). Paulina is the dominating force in Leontes' court, so the courtier-poet is under great pressure to agree. He apologizes to Paulina, 'Pardon, madam . . . your pardon!' but he then insists on repeating that Perdita is so lovely that women and men, and Paulina herself, must 'love her' (5.1.103–12). Patrick Cheney comments that in doing this, 'this gentle poet, intimate with king and counselor, appears precisely to announce the play's momentous event: the return of Perdita to her home and parents, a stunning prophesy of the apocalyptic resurrection of Hermione through visionary perception of the lost one'.[52] Cheney thus makes this poet into a seer, or *vates*. Whether that is accepted or not, this poet is at least honest and brave, a court poet who will not disguise the truth even when pressured by the most powerful.

This poet will not withhold Perdita's deserved praise, but more usually court poets were accused of being all to ready to flatter with undeserved praise. Thus a poet abandoning court life in Sir Thomas Wyatt's stunning satire 'Myne owne John Poyntz' complains, 'I cannot frame my tune to feign, / To cloak the truth for praise without desert'. The poet-speaker in Samuel Daniel's Sonnet 53 likewise avows, 'For God forbid I should my papers blot / With mercynarie lines, with servile pen; / Praysing vertues in them that have them not'.[53] The stereotypical view that poets seeking patronage must be timeservers underlies scurrilous Apemantus' accusations that the Poet in *Timon of Athens* purveys flattery for reward (1.1.219–30). Apemantus alleges that merely *being* a poet means being a liar, and offers as proof, 'Look in thy last work, where thou hast feigned [Timon] a worthy fellow.' The Poet replies, 'That's not feigned, he is so'. Here the Poet's word 'feigned' takes on its modern negative meaning; moreover, abandoning his usual inclination towards over-elaborate diction, he shows his sincerity by using what the narrator in Shakespeare's Sonnet 82 calls 'true plain words'.[54] Misanthropic Apemantus is not convinced, and so insists that the Poet's praises are offered not because Timon is 'worthy' in himself, but because he is 'worthy of thee, and to pay thee for thy labour. He that loves to be flattered is worthy o' th' flatterer.' It is interesting to observe how Apemantus indulges in word play here (conflating 'worthy' with financial 'worth'),[55] while the Poet veers away from it.

Apemantus' view of poetic patronage is not the only one possible. Patricia Thomson has argued that in Shakespeare's time 'the system of patronage could be either a spur or a check to genius. Within it the poet could lose or maintain his integrity, raise or lower his standards.'[56] And indeed, there are reasons to allow Timon's Poet his integrity, despite him seeking patronage. For one, he expresses dismay at the debasing of the language of praise when it is misapplied to the unworthy: 'When we for recompense have praised the vile, / It stains the glory in that happy verse / Which aptly sings the good' (1.1.15–17). Writing 'In Defense of Timon's Poet', Kenneth Muir saw these lines as 'poetry which wells up, unbidden, from the depths of his being, the "gum which oozes from whence 'tis nourish'd"'.[57] An even stronger indication that Timon's Poet is no flatterer rests on his description of the allegorical poem that he is currently composing to present to Timon (1.1.85–95). This poem, far from flattering Timon, rebukes his behaviour and warns him against continuing it.[58]

Self-analytical poets in Shakespeare's plays

The self-awareness of Shakespeare's poets takes two forms, one objective and one subjective. The first involves their observations of the aesthetic qualities in their art, or of the mental phenomena involved in making it. The other involves the personal psychologies of the individual artist.

Some poets in Shakespeare's plays question or reform their work based on reality-oriented aesthetic judgements, while others are entirely divorced from realistic criticism. Holofernes in *Love's Labour's Lost* judges Birone's reasonably graceful sonnet to be 'very unlearned, neither savouring of poetry, wit, nor invention' (4.2.155–7) just after he has fully approved of his own absurd poetical attempt (4.2.57–62). By contrast, Birone's valid self-criticism when he deplores the 'maggot ostentation' of his former overblown style of 'woo[ing] in rhyme' leads to his vastly improved diction and self-expression (if not to further poetry).

In more complicated contexts, the Poet in *Timon of Athens* twice attempts to describe the experiences of poets when creating poetry, thus addressing the phenomenology of creation rather than the psychology of a particular creator. His first attempt at this reads, with emendations that have been adopted for centuries:

> Our poesy is as a gum which oozes
> From whence 'tis nourished. The fire i' th' flint
> Shows not till it be struck; our gentle flame
> Provokes itself, and like the current flies
> Each bound it chafes.

> (1.1.21–5)

Whatever position one takes about the traditional emendation in which 'a gum which oozes' replaces the Folio's 'a Gowne, which uses',[59] the general import of the first part of this passage (up to 'like the current') is clearly that the poetic impulse is experienced by poets as self-generating and self-propelling. This phenomenological observation has been repeated innumerable times by working poets.[60]

The remainder of the above passage about flying (over?) bounds is best considered alongside the Poet's second observation on the phenomenology of poetic creation. This is expressed in a manner that is, in common with many of the Poet's utterances, high-flown to a fault:

>   My free drift
> Halts not particularly, but moves itself
> In a wide sea of wax. No levelled malice
> Infects one comma in the course I hold,
> But flies an eagle flight, bold and forth on,
> Leaving no tract behind.

> (1.1.45–50)

This passage is extremely obscure, probably because of printing-house errors.[61] Nonetheless, it does cohere with the Poet's earlier comment about the 'current' of poetic creativity in so far as both passages describe a self-propelled 'flight' over bounds. Here the bounds are identified with the 'malice' of suggesting a particular external reference.[62]

The question of how Shakespeare speaks to the individual emotional experiences of particular poets (as opposed to the phenomenological experiences of poets generally) is best considered when we will next examine the poets represented in some of Shakespeare's poems. This will be in our next chapter.

4

Poets in Shakespeare's Poems

A goddess and a ditty in
Venus and Adonis

Shakespeare's Venus partly resembles a male lover with a 'cruel' mistress, and the parody is undoubtedly deliberate. The failure of her ingeniously verbal and vigorously physical attempts at the seduction of a young man leave her frustrated and disappointed, and so she turns to grief-stricken poetry-making. The narrator presents her 'extemporally' made verses (line 836) as overblown and ridiculous, but at the same time, Venus must retain enough dignity to figure eventually in a tragic outcome. This may be one reason why her actual 'ditty', although described at length, is not transcribed in *Venus and Adonis*. Another might have been an awareness of classical strictures against poets ridiculing the gods, as enunciated in Plato's *Republic* II, 377e–378e. Alternatively, Shakespeare chose not to burden his elegant poem with more than fleeting glimpses of Venus' literary monomania and conventionalism.

We have already seen how Shakespeare treats the poor poetic performances of the young male lovers Romeo and Orlando with derision. On the other hand (as will be seen in the next chapter), Shakespeare presents passionate love laments of several women in *Hamlet*, *Othello* and *The Two Noble Kinsmen* as not in the least ludicrous. Yet he does ridicule Venus' overblown poetic expression of her entanglement in erotic suffering. This is because a comedy of disproportion attaches to Shakespeare's Venus. As we have seen, she is described as so large and powerful that she is 'Courageously' able to sweep her beloved from his saddle with one arm (29–32). Physical power and great beauty notwithstanding, Venus fails to elicit a response from Adonis, giving rise to another disproportion, between her hot passion and his cold disinterest. She achieves her best result when she pretends to be half-killed in order to draw Adonis' pity and attention, but even then she reaps only comic pinches and nose-wringing, followed by, for her, all too pallid erotic rewards (463–612).

Venus and Adonis mocked male lust by inversion, but this did not impede its great success in the marketplace, attested to by many reissues. The poem is grotesque but not cruel, sophisticated in its explicit eroticism and it manages to elicit sympathy for both its pawed-over Adonis and tantalized, sweaty, and thwarted Venus.

Our main concern now will be with Venus' poetic productions following her frustrating encounters with her totally unwilling beloved:

> And now she beats her heart, whereat it groans,
> That all the neighbour caves, as seeming troubled,
> Make verbal repetition of her moans;
> Passion on passion deeply is redoubled.
> 'Ay me,' she cries, and twenty times 'Woe, woe!'
> And twenty echoes twenty times cry so.
> She, marking them, begins a wailing note,
> And sings extemporally a woeful ditty,
> How love makes young men thrall, and old men dote,
> How love is wise in folly, foolish-witty.
> Her heavy anthem still concludes in woe,
> And still the choir of echoes answer so.

Her song was tedious, and outwore the night;
For lovers' hours are long, though seeming short.
If pleased themselves, others, they think, delight
In such-like circumstance, with such-like sport.
  Their copious stories oftentimes begun
  End without audience, and are never done.

(829–46)

In 'How love makes young men thrall, and old men dote' we get our only glimpse of the contents of Venus' 'ditty'. Strikingly, Venus herself is neither male, nor of any particular age, being immortal. Thus the conventional unoriginality of her 'extemporally' created poetry is revealed. This poetry is responded to only by echoing pastoral 'caves', so a Shakespearean poet again suffers neglect. But this time neglect is deserved because the poetry lacks all merit and focus. We are told that audiences hearing poetry like Venus' extended maundering will slip away before it is done. The thrust of the passage above is therefore literary-critical, although it bypasses explicit parody. It is also literary-psychological, for Shakespeare's Venus exemplifies poets who 'If pleased themselves, others, they think, delight', but are quite wrong to think so.

    The narrator says that Venus' 'woful ditt[ies]' are 'copious' and 'tedious'. The Latinate term 'copious' would have reminded late Elizabethans of the still widely used schoolbook, Erasmus's *Copia*. Written in England, this was first published in 1512 and several times enlarged.[1] Its full title translates as *On Abundance of Words and Ideas*, and it covers two areas. Its 'Words' division was often used to teach facility with rhetorical figures but, according to Thomas Sloane, its second section, on 'Ideas', was far less often used in schools.[2] Thus calling Venus' poetry 'copious' may have underlined that it is voluminous in words alone and lacks freshness in engagement with ideas. Labelling Venus' poetry 'tedious' suggests the word's first meaning, 'long and tiresome',[3] but also carries a penumbra of the ridiculous. So Peter Quince in *A Midsummer Night's Dream* advertises 'A tedious brief scene' (5.1.256). In fact, 'tedious' appears in two-thirds of Shakespeare's plays and poems, where it frequently embellishes the malaprop vocabularies of uneducated or prolix speakers such as Dogberry, Pistol, Polonius and an inkhorn Schoolmaster in *Two Noble Kinsmen* who exclaims against 'tediosity and disinsanity' (3.5.2). Therefore the appearance of the adjective 'tedious' in a Shakespearean context suggests comic faults in the use of language.

Shakespeare's Venus is at first verbose in her love-lamenting poetry, but becomes 'Dumbly' unhappy following Adonis' death (1059–61). In this way, the register of Shakespeare's poem evolves from the satirical comic to the Ovidian tragic. One pole of that progress, the element of satirical ridicule, was just becoming particularly *au courant* when *Venus and Adonis* appeared in 1593. By 1594, Sir John Davies's *Gullinge Sonnets*, which brilliantly caricatures Petrarchanism, began to circulate in manuscript.[4] As we have seen, some of Shakespeare's plays of just the same period also ridicule would-be Petrarchs. Similar mockery, and also serious self-critique, appear in Shakespeare's own Sonnets. Those will be the final topic of this chapter, but first let us consider a poem closely linked to the Sonnets.

'Deep-brained sonnets' in *A Lover's Complaint*

The long poem *A Lover's Complaint* was printed just following the Sonnets in the volume *Shakespeare's Sonnets* of 1609. Several scholars hold that it was placed there as a deliberate 'coda'.[5] Perhaps accordingly, this poem, and this one only among all of Shakespeare's poetry, actually contains the word, '*sonnets*'.[6] The exact contents of the 'deep-brained sonnets' to which *A Lover's Complaint* refers (209) are not revealed. *A Lover's Complaint* does, however, describe their fictional makers' intentions in writing and presenting these

poems, and also describes their recipients' very odd uses of
them as a kind of transferable love tokens. Thereby the sole
significances of the 'deep-brained' poems, as far as we are
allowed to know them, are in the transactions between the
persons who first make and give them and the others who then
receive and re-gift them. Such matters require some untangling.

A Lover's Complaint comprises forty-seven rhyme royal
stanzas. All but the first ten of these seven line stanzas comprise
a heartfelt confession to a 'reverend man' made by a 'fickle
maid full pale'. The first eight stanzas describe the maid
lamenting solo, and the next two describe the sympathetic
auditor who having overheard her complaints sits down
enquiring 'the grounds and motives of her woe' (63). The
poem's first eight stanzas depict the maid tearing 'papers' and
breaking 'rings' (6), throwing 'a thousand favours' into a river
(36), and then reading, kissing, tearing, and discarding 'folded
schedules', 'posied rings' and sealed 'letters sadly penned in
blood', all the while weeping and exclaiming against her
inconstant lover (43–56). It is notable that although most of
those discarded love tokens are written upon, none of that
writing is identified as poetic (if we except the trivial 'posy of a
ring', as Hamlet scathingly calls a jingling rhyme).[7]

Serious written poetry enters the maid's discourse in a very
peculiar manner. She gives a detailed account of how irresistibly
attractive her false lover has been to herself and many other
women, explaining that he is a beautiful youth who is
outstandingly gifted in speech, charm and even horsemanship
(manège is again used to imply sexual competence, as it is in
Venus and Adonis). In consequence, 'Many . . . did his picture
get' to dote upon (134), and others did more. Unlike them, while
nonetheless smitten, the maid has not 'yielded', saying, 'I mine
honour shielded' (149–51). But she has been sorely tempted,
even while knowing 'this man's untrue' and having 'Heard
where his plants in others' orchards grew' (169–71). What,
then, reduced her to becoming eventually one of his conquests?

Having been besieged with the usual flattery, tears and
protestations of a Petrarchan lover, she resisted the charming

young man until he gave her, as 'oblations' and proof of his love, the locks of hair, jewels and 'deep-brained sonnets' that numerous other love-smitten women had sent to him (197–238). Then, she says, 'my white stole of chastity I daffed' (297). What overthrew her resistance was precisely the kind of 'mimetic desire' that the critic René Girard repeatedly alleges governs all human desire, his theory being that we desire things or persons solely because others desire them.[8]

Why would the proof that 'several fair' had sent 'deep-brained sonnets' and other gifts to beseech the love of the inconstant man have had such an impact? We do not have to accept the universality of Girard's thesis to see that love triangles appear repeatedly in Shakespearean contexts and that love poetry often plays a part in such configurations.[9] Thus, Proteus in *Two Gentlemen of Verona* attempts to win over, and eventually attempts to rape, Silvia, the beloved of his friend Valentine. But first Proteus advises the foolish Thurio (against the interests of Valentine) to use 'wailful sonnets' in his pursuit of Silvia (3.2.69), and then he attempts to use a song to attract her to himself (4.2.38–52). Similarly, the bestial Cloten in *Cymbeline* first bespeaks a serenade to impress Imogen, a married woman, and later attempts to rape her (2.3.11–29, 4.1.1–25). Both of these corrupt lovers will be further considered in relation to uses of music, but we should note that, despite their evil motives, the ditties of the songs sung by or on behalf of both of them are very beautiful. Yet neither Proteus nor Cloten succeeds in his design, whereas the young man in *A Lover's Complaint* does.

In contrast with the lyrics of Proteus and Cloten, the texts of the deep-brained sonnets sent second-hand to the maid in *A Lover's Complaint* are unheard by audiences (the 'fourth voice' of poetry is silent). However, Shakespeare's poem offers clear contextual indications of the focus and nature of the poems sent by the youth's female admirers; these implore him to relieve their suffering for love. Although rare, analogues to this can be found in contemporary women's poetry. There are few records in Shakespeare's culture of female love sonneteers, but one who was very famous was Mary, Queen of Scots, who was accused of having sent a dozen sensationally passionate love sonnets (written in French) to a married man. Those alleged 'casket sonnets', and associated 'casket letters', were translated and published by George Buchanan in 1571, leading to Mary's execution.[10]

The first English love sonnet *sequence* written by a woman was Lady Mary Wroth's *Pamphilia to Amphilanthus*. This was published together with the first portion of Wroth's prose romance *Urania* in 1621, but circulated earlier in manuscript.[11] *Pamphilia to Amphilanthus* could not have inspired Shakespeare's depiction of Venus writing love poetry because *Venus and Adonis* first appeared in 1593, when Wroth was six years old. However, dates make it just possible that Shakespeare's knowledge of (or about) the *Pamphilia to Amphilanthus* sonnets did help to inspire *A Lover's Complaint*. For by 1611 or earlier, several well-known writers were praising Wroth's poetry,[12] indicating that some of it was circulating privately tantalizingly close to the 1609 date of *A Lover's Complaint*. In addition, Jane Kingsley-Smith argues with strong evidence that Shakespeare not only knew Wroth and her husband very well, but also actually found the context for his Sonnet 116 in their 1604 marriage.[13]

If Shakespeare did hear about or see Wroth's work before 1609,[14] he might have garnered from it more than one notion for *A Lover's Complaint*. One would have been of the very existence of women's passionate love sonnets. Another, requiring somewhat more detailed knowledge, would have been of such love sonnets being directed to an inconstant man. For Wroth's sonnets are addressed to *Amphilanthus*, whose name means 'philanderer', and the likely model for her Amphilanthus was not very different from the young man in Shakespeare's poem who receives 'deep-brained' love sonnets from various women and plants his seeds 'in others' orchards'.

That apparent model was Wroth's cousin William Herbert, the third earl of Pembroke. There is evidence that after her husband died in 1614, Wroth 'gave birth to two children, apparently through a romantic involvement with [Pembroke]'. Moreover, William Herbert was 'Described by Clarendon as "immoderately given up to women"', and 'Herbert's name was linked with various women before and after his marriage on 4 November 1604'.[15] Because Wroth's sonnets, as well as her *Urania*, overly explicitly referred to well-known scandalous events, in the year of their publication (1621), 'apparently in response to public outrage, Mary Wroth requested the duke of Buckingham to procure a warrant from the king to enable her to gather in any books that had already been sold'.[16]

Wroth's sonnets may or may not have provided ideas for *A Lover's Complaint*, but one thing is certain: her literary work became notorious for too thinly disguising its reflections of real life goings-on. Unlike her uncle Sir Philip Sidney, whose writings provided models for both her sonnet sequence and her prose romance, Wroth was not as indirect as she should have been when alluding to 'real world' events in her work.

Considering such literary misadventures may help us to read Shakespeare's own Sonnets. Moreover, the uses of 'deep-brained sonnets' in *A Lover's Complaint* in the service of dishonest erotic aims may prepare us for the frankness of self-condemnation seen in some of Shakespeare's Sonnets: for instance with regard to impulses called in Sonnet 129, 'cruell, not to trust'. Let us, therefore, now proceed to a major concern of this chapter, the artists in Shakespeare's Sonnets.

Artists and conventions in Shakespeare's Sonnets

Shakespeare's most extensive and complex treatment of poet-figures occurs in those of his Sonnets in which the poem's speaker self-identifies as a poet. Such poet-speakers appear in at least forty-two of the Sonnets. Thus a poet appears in 50 per cent more of Shakespeare's Sonnets than does any alleged 'Dark Lady'. Such poets feature in about 28 per cent of the

Shakespeare Sonnets in total, and we may note the coincidence that poet-speakers also appear in 28 per cent of the 366 poems in Petrarch's foundational *Rime sparse*.

The most frequent gesture of the Shakespearean poet speakers in the Sonnets is self-denigration: in the majority of the Sonnets narrated by poets the narrators harshly censure their own work. Thus they repeatedly apply to their own 'invention', 'books', 'written embassage', 'wit', 'verse', 'lays', 'lines', 'ink', 'rhyme', 'song', 'papers', 'discourse' or 'Muse' (more than forty times in total), epithets including 'barren', 'pore', 'rude', 'slight', 'decayed', 'inferior', 'worthless', 'enfeebled', 'truant' and many more like these.[17]

However, in common with almost all positions expressed in the Sonnets, this one is not consistent. Thus in Sonnet 80 the self-abasement of Shakespeare's poet-speaker is not sincere but conforms rather to what Colin Burrow described as the 'scarcely suppressed irony masquerading as masochism in which the Sonnets abound'.[18] In this sonnet the narrator likens his own writing to a nimble 'sawsie barke', and contrasts it mock-unfavourably with a rival writer's poetry 'of tall building, and of goodly pride'. The image almost certainly recalls nimble English shipping defeating the tall galleons of the Spanish Armada,[19] rendering the poet-speaker's reference to his own poetry's 'humble . . . saile' being 'inferior farre' to a rival's 'prowdest saile' indeed ironic.

However, Sonnet 80 also appears in the midst of a cluster of poems among which some are self-critical, without irony, of the poet-speaker's verse. This clustering illustrates how certain widespread tendencies in the construction of sonnet sequences are adopted in Shakespeare's 1609 collection. One of those is to cluster together poems that treat similar materials from varied vantage points or in varied moods; this results in contrary directions or thrusts in poems on similar topics even when they are immediately adjacent. Another is in the disposition of entire sequences along the lines of theme and variation, as opposed to linear narration based on chronology, argument or consistent logic. The typical use of such confounding structures is among the reasons why seeking straightforward dramatic or autobiographical contents in a sonnet sequence is likely to be misleading.

Moreover, sonneteering traditions or conventions were often deliberately varied or played upon by sonneteers rather than followed, and by Shakespeare not least. Even the range of ways in which convention confronted originality is also hard to determine given that an estimated 300,000 sonnets were written in sixteenth-century Europe.[20] I intend here to look at the ways in which some famous and influential sonneteers play upon the long-established sonneteering modes of 'eternizing', Platonizing, and 'naughting', and to consider the ways in which Shakespeare treats similar modes in his sonnets. As numerous ambiguities and ironies characterize his treatments, we may extend by analogy Inga-Stina Ewbank's remark that Shakespeare's language in his sonnets 'is not merely equal to [his] vocabulary',[21] and say the same for his use of the traditional 'language' of sonneteering modes.

Despite conventions of modesty, often the speakers in Renaissance sonnets who present themselves as artists are boastful, even aggressively so. For instance, Michelangelo's Sonnet 92, addressed to Vittoria Colonna, claims 'A thousand years, and more, after we leave, / They will see how most beautiful you were / And in loving you I was most right'.[22] More brutally, Ronsard's 'Quand vous serez bien vieille' envisions a future when, remorsefully murmuring the name of her rejected lover, the beloved will sing the songs of the famous 'Ronsard [who] praised me in the days when I was beautiful'.[23] This poem is relatively tender when compared with Sonnet 8 in Michael Drayton's *Idea*, in which a poet-narrator imagines a fantasy future in which his rejecting beloved, grown ugly with age, will painfully read his lines describing her former beauty.[24]

The survival of a poem across time, treated cruelly in Drayton's sonnet, takes on an entirely different complexion when poets address the stock 'eternizing' theme,[25] as Michelangelo does when he claims he will confer a thousand years of fame, and as Shakespeare does in his great Sonnet 55:

Not marble, nor the guilded monument,
Of Princes shall out-live this powrefull rime,
But you shall shine more bright in these contents
Then unswept stone, besmeer'd with sluttish time.
When wastefull warre shall *Statues* over-turne,
And broiles roote out the worke of masonry,
Nor *Mars* his sword, nor warres quick fire shall burne
The living record of your memory.

Despite this stirring claim, however, contexts in a number of Shakespeare plays and poems indicate that art and artists are vulnerable to social turmoil or query the validity of eternizing.[26] For instance, when the poet-speaker in Sonnet 18 claims, 'So long as men can breath or eyes can see, / So long lives this, and this gives life to thee' (13–14), this only ambiguously lays claim to the eternity of poetry. For the pronoun 'this' in 'this lives' may not refer to the present poem,[27] but rather to the image of the beloved's beauty, and likewise in 'When in eternall lines to time thou grow'st' at the culmination of this poem the word 'lines' may not refer to lines of verse, but rather to the lineaments of ideal beauty.

Such a Platonizing strain, although implied in many of Shakespeare's Sonnets, is undercut in others. Thus, in Sonnet 11 the very matrix used by 'nature' to print off future beauty and virtue is seen as vulnerable to mortality: 'She carv'd thee for her seale, and ment thereby, / Thou shouldst print more, not let that coppy die' (13–14). The more assured poet-speaker of Sonnet 19 demands that the beloved be left 'untainted' by time so as to 'allow, / For beauties patterne to succeding men', but if not, 'Yet doe thy worst oulde Time dispight thy wrong. / My love shall in my verse ever live young' (12–14).

Many of Shakespeare's Sonnets maintain that 'Both truth and beauty on my love depends' (Sonnet 101), and many mention a poet or 'Muse' who, by contagion, is enabled to produce beauty-preserving and long-lasting verse.[28] But doubt assails other poems. The highly ambiguous Sonnet 53, for instance, initially asserts that 'millions of strange shadows on you tend', suggesting that the beloved's perfections are Platonic models or Forms.[29] Indeed, that sonnet claims that the beloved sets the pattern for both Adonis and Helen, and for the 'beautie' and 'bountie' of 'the spring and foyzon of the yeare', and further asserts that 'in every blessed shape we know / In all externall grace you have some part'. But the qualification '*externall* grace' may be a warning. The poem concludes with 'But you like none, none you for constant heart'. This might be read either as 'none are like you in that you have a constant heart', or as stating conversely (with 'like' as a verb) that when constant hearts are at issue, no one will like you, and you will like no one. Reading back from this doubleness, all the earlier parts of this sonnet can also be seen to convey possible double meanings.[30]

In yet other Sonnets, the beloved is praised not as the Ideal, but for down-to-earth reasons. So the 'Mistres' in Sonnet 130 is 'as rare / As any she beli'd with false compare'; and the beloved in Sonnet 21 is only 'as faire / As any mother's childe, though not so bright / As those gould candells fixt in heavens ayer'.[31] Sonnets 115 and 116 also remove the love in question from the eternal or celestial realm, the first seeing it as subject to growth and maturation, and the second seeing it as subject to chosen rather than automatic constancy. In both of these poems the narrator is a writer: the first says his earlier poems were mistaken in claiming his love had already grown to its fullest extent; and the second speaker swears by his own writing that love may remain constant despite changes wrought by time. Here the act of writing is valued in itself, not absorbed into notions of eternal verities.

We conclude that the variety of stances seen here in Shakespeare's Sonnets implies their tendencies towards ambiguity and enigma. We will next see that such tendencies are deployed deliberately with regard to a most mysterious aspect of the Sonnets, the aspect of identification or naming.

What's in a name?

The relationship between Renaissance sonnet sequences and what we might call a 'confessional' mode was complex and unstable. As we have seen, Mary Wroth's sonnets were all too revealingly confessional for her contemporaries. On the other hand, no one is certain who Dante's Beatrice or Petrarch's Laura were, or even *if* they were. Yet there is no doubt about the autobiographical *stance* of many of the sonnets in *La Vita Nuova* or *Rime sparse*. And yet, in Dante's *La Vita Nuova* the Thirteenth Sonnet is narrated by voices other than Dante's own, making a fictional element evident despite this work's self-confessional posture.[32] Some have claimed that 'Renaissance writers . . . did not have a hard and fast understanding of the difference between the poet and persona'.[33] There is evidence, however, that what we might call a semi-sharp distinction was often consciously observed.

From the startling first line of its first sonnet onwards, a poet-speaker proclaims his presence in Sir Philip Sidney's *Astrophil and Stella*. This poet-speaker asserts his 'truth' using rule-breaking iambic hexameters: 'Loving in truth, and fain in verse my love to show.'

Sidney's was the first English sonnet sequence of note. When it was first published, posthumously, its editors titled it *Syr P. S. His Astrophel and Stella*. They apparently took their cues from the repeated naming of the beloved as 'Stella' in Sidney's poems, and also from the naming of Stella's lover as 'Astrophil' in the Eighth and Ninth tetrameter 'Songs' that are embedded within the sequence. The name 'Astrophel', or 'Astrophil' (meaning star-lover, or Stella-lover), punned of course on Sidney's forename 'Philip'. Some of the poems in *Astrophil and Stella* also portray details of the narrator's life that match Sidney's own life experiences.[34] Moreover, following the precedent of Petrarch who often punned on the name 'Laura',[35] many poems in *Astrophil and Stella* play on the surname 'Rich', pointing to Penelope Rich as the model for Stella.[36] The 108 sonnets in

Sidney's sequence allude, moreover, to what was known as the 'Penelope number', which was the number of suitors to Penelope in Homer's *Odyssey*.[37] Not surprisingly, the identification of Sidney's Stella with the (unhappily) married Penelope Devereux Rich swiftly became an open secret.[38]

All that does not make Astrophil identical to Sidney, however, nor Lady Rich identical to Stella. Rather, the details partly reflecting 'external reality' in *Astrophil and Stella* were also shaped, altered and re-imagined for artistic purposes. As W.A. Ringler puts it, 'When we compare the known facts ... with the sonnets and songs of *Astrophil and Stella*, we are immediately struck with how much of his biography [Sidney] left out of the poems'.[39]

Elizabethans encountered another *persona* partly aligned with the author in Edmund Spenser's sonnet sequence *Amoretti*. Although a famous poet, Spenser was not so prominent a public figure as Sidney, and therefore there was nothing as mouth-watering (as Sidney himself put it in his Sonnet 37) in his private affairs as there was in Sidney's. Nevertheless, Spenser's sonnet sequence did probably match in some ways events in his own life by describing a long courtship that resulted (after some frustration) in a marriage. Such a pattern is mould-breaking in a sonnet sequence, as is the celebration in *Amoretti* of the narrator's erotic success and satisfaction (Sonnets 63–77). A connection with Spenser's life is emphasized by the fact that at the end of the same 1595 volume containing the *Amoretti* sonnets (followed by a set of four 'Anacreontic' or Cupid-invoking poems) Spenser printed a marriage hymn called *Epithalamion* which 'glorifies' the author's own marriage in 1594 to Elizabeth Boyle.[40] However, although prosperous wooing was a theme in both the *Amoretti* and the author's 'real life', Spenser's publication does not constitute what we would call 'confessional verse'. For instance, it alters chronology for artistic purposes,[41] and gives no hint that Spenser was widowed with two children when he courted an initially reluctant young woman who was finally 'with her owne will beguyled' (Sonnet 47).

Shakespeare's Sonnets are not less sophisticated than Sidney's and Spenser's, and speculations about 'real world' persons corresponding with a purported cast of a 'Lovely Boy', 'Dark Lady' and 'Rival Poet' have repeatedly been shown to be erroneous.[42] Nevertheless, observing traditions in which sonnet sequence narrators may at one and the same time both be and not be mirrors of their authors may help in our pursuit of the poet figures in Shakespeare's Sonnets. The Sonnets are definitely more elusive about naming protagonists than *Astrophil and Stella*. Shakespeare's Sonnet 81 actually seems to tease about naming the beloved, for its poet-speaker first boasts that 'Your name from hence immortall life shall have . . . your monument shall be my gentle verse', but the 'monument' mentioned has no visible inscription. Indeed, the beloved's name is always suppressed in Shakespeare's sonnets, with only one possible exception: in 1971 Andrew Gurr suggested that Sonnet 145, written in anomalous octosyllabics, was a wooing poem written by the teenaged Shakespeare in which the phrase 'hate away' punned on the surname of Anne Hathaway, whom Shakespeare married in late 1582.[43]

The aim here is to pursue the poet-figure correlating with the 'my' in the phrase 'my verse'; this phrase appears just short of a dozen times in Shakespeare's Sonnets and an implied poet-speaker appears far more often. We might think it straightforward to connect that poet-figure with the name 'Will' which is often punned upon when the Sonnets make play with Shakespeare's own forename.[44] But that is not so, for none of the sonnets in which we find phrases like 'my name is Will', or arch references to 'your Will', number among those in which the narrator self-identifies as a poet.

On the contrary, the poet-narrators in Sonnets 71 and 72 request respectively, 'Do not so much as my poore name rehearse', and 'My name be buried where my body is'. These refusals to be named arise because these two adjacent poems are among the many sonnets in which Shakespeare's poet-speakers are highly self-deprecating.[45] Is it a general rule that the greater the self-deprecation the less naming there is in a

Shakespeare sonnet? That, too, turns out to be not quite the case, as we shall see next.

Naming, and the poet-speaker in Shakespeare's central Sonnet 76

I will maintain presently that Sonnet 76 presents a crucial instance of a Shakespearean poet-narrator who sincerely, not ironically, self-deprecates. To explore an intriguing aspect of this poem, I will adopt for the remainder of this discussion an hypothesis, promoted by John Kerrigan and by Katherine Duncan-Jones, that the ordering of *Shakespeare's Sonnets* 1609 was authorial.[46] On that basis, I will argue that the positioning and content of Sonnet 76 follows a model whereby the *placement* of sonnets within Elizabethan sequences implies important meanings.

It will be necessary first to examine similar patterns elsewhere, and then to return to Shakespeare's Sonnets. We have already mentioned Sidney's use of the 'Penelope number' in *Astrophil and Stella*. Fulke Greville's sequence *Caelica* uses the same number of 'sonnets', 108, in a more complex manner. *Caelica* was published posthumously in 1633, in a volume that proclaims on its title page that all of Greville's poetry was 'Written in his Youth, and familiar Exercise with SIR. PHILLIP SIDNEY'. Typically, that publisher's blurb is only partly true.[47] From their school days until Sidney's early death, Greville and Sidney were indeed close companions, and several poems in *Caelica* and in *Astrophil and Stella* posit an identical background experience (throwing doubts on any tight autobiography in either sequence). Moreover, throughout his long life Greville repeatedly memorialized Sidney, even climaxing an impressive list of political achievements in his epitaph with the phrase 'friend to Sir Philip Sidney'.

In an Introduction intended for an unrealized edition of his writings,[48] Greville reveals his late intention to 'examine, and reforme' his early work so as to 'cover the dandled deformities of these creatures with a coat of many seames'.[49] Such a process is indeed seen in the handwritten alterations that Greville made to *Caelica* in a unique surviving scribal manuscript.[50] Those alterations reposition or query the inclusion of several poems, but always keep intact the prominent numbering of the 'sonnets' at the top of each MS page. They thereby adjust the sequence while retaining its fixed number of 108 poems, identical to the number of true sonnets in *Astrophil and Stella*.[51] This practice did not involve occult numerology, but only paid tribute to Sidney (as did Greville's naming his mistress 'Caelica' in parallel with Sidney's 'Stella').

Greville's interventions produced a fascinating numerical ploy. The mid-most poem in *Caelica*, numbered 54 in the manuscript, contains (in its latest version, found in the 1633 edition) just fifty-four lines.[52] This poem, moreover, takes a critical turn at its own central line, line 27. To understand this, we must note that in the latter half of *Caelica* the topic of love is given less and less prominence as the sequence progresses towards a final group of dark and powerful devotional poems. Lying literally at the centre of that transition, Greville's mid-positioned 'sonnet' 54 repudiates romantic ideals, condemning these as merely fanciful. To do so, it parodies and inverts the topic treated in the 'Second Song' of *Astrophil and Stella*, a topic of erotic disappointment due to over-idealization.[53] Greville's 'sonnet' 54, adopting an identical narrative framework or set-up, takes the same notion much further, and its middle line (line 27) reads '*Phancies scales are false of weight*'. This *sententia*, positioned at the mid-point of the central poem in a precisely numbered sequence, indicates a turning point of the sequence by deploying images of pivoting, and also of false assessments due to fanciful self-deception.[54]

Could Shakespeare's arrangement of his sonnets be similarly indicative? Let us recall the tripartite arrangement of Spenser's 1595 volume containing the *Amoretti* sonnets followed by a few pastoral or Anacreontic verses and finally a longer poem. John Kerrigan connects Spenser's arrangement with an Elizabethan pattern begun in Samuel Daniel's *Delia* in 1592 and often repeated, and then associates Shakespeare's 1609 volume with the same tripartite model.[55] Applying this model, Kerrigan and other important critics assert that *Shakespeare's Sonnets* of 1609 consists of 152 love sonnets, capped by two Anacreontic fables in Sonnets 153 and 154, and then the long poem 'A Lovers Complaint'.[56]

The mid-point of the section of 152 love sonnets would then lie in Shakespeare's Sonnet 76:[57]

Why is my verse so barren of new pride?
So far from variation or quicke change?
Why, with the time, do I not glance aside
To new found methods and to compounds strange?
Why write I still all one, ever the same,
And keep invention in a noted weed,
That every word doth almost fel my name,
Shewing their birth, and where they did proceed?
O know, sweet love, I alwaies write of you,
And you and love are still my argument:
So all my best is dressing old words new,
Spending againe what is already spent;
 For as the Sun is daily new and old,
 So is my love still telling what is told.

The central line (line 7) of this central sonnet almost certainly should read, 'That every word doth almost tel my name', because editors take 'fel' to be a typo for 'tell'. So at the centre point of a central poem Shakespeare's poet-speaker refers to words telling 'my name' – and this time, for once, the speaker may reveal that name. For the first and the last words of the very next line begin respectively with 'Sh' and 'pr'. Being statistically unusual,[58] this suggests a concatenation reading 'Sh . . . pr', which does call to mind a familiar name.

Apart from that, the theme of Shakespeare's central Sonnet 76 is a poet taking a dubious view of their work. Stephen Booth thinks that pointless or awkward features were inserted into

this poem in order to indicate an inept poet,[59] and Helen
Vendler thinks the poem dramatizes a poet's scornful reply to a
speech-act in the form of another person's denigrating 'anterior
utterance'.[60] However, I see no call for supposing that the
poet-speaker in this poem is incoherent,[61] or for positing an
offstage 'antagonist' in the form of Vendler's fashionable and
bored 'young man'.[62] I would hold, rather, that the speaker's
tone here corresponds with explicit and genuine self-
questioning. Thus G. Blakemore Evans suggests that in this
sonnet and others the speaker's 'concern . . . may arise in part
from a genuine feeling of uncertainty about the comparative
merit of his verses, despite the conventional modesty expected
of a sonneteer'.[63]

The sorrowful cadence produced by the 'why-why-why'
structure of the octave of Sonnet 76 better accords with almost
despairing self-questioning than with the mocking repetition
of an unkind critique (such a reply would be as petulant as the
critique is carping). If petulance is not in play, personal sorrow,
not sarcasm, permeates the use of the monosyllable 'so' in line
one. To demonstrate this, consider an alternative iambic
pentameter line lacking 'so': 'Why are my verses barren of new
pride?' This presents a sorry variation. For one thing, the
change spoils the original's rising sequence of (second formant)
vowel pitches, moving up from 'o' to 'a' to 'i'. It spoils also a
sibilant progression in 'is . . . verse . . . so', and muddies an
alliterative interplay between 'verse' and 'barren'. The poem's
mournfulness is intensified also because the monosyllabic
modifier 'so' in 'so barren' suggests a sighing, half-involuntary
realization. Such a usage follows a model seen in notable
poems of the period in which monosyllabic words are often
very potent.[64]

The catch-in-the-breath-like word 'so' in line one impacts as
well on the closely following words 'new pride'. On one level,
'pride' may relate to clothing (as it does when Sonnet 52 images
a 'wardrobe . . . unfolding his imprisoned pride'). So, as Stephen
Booth suggests, 'barren of new pride' in Sonnet 76 might suggest
being bare or publicly naked.[65] Further clothing imagery in

Sonnet 76, in 'weed' and 'dressing', may help to reinforce a reading of 'so barren' in terms of shameful nakedness. Yet the sorrowing tone emphasized by 'so' in line one suggests another sense of being barren of *pride*. 'Pride' can indicate 'the best, highest, most excellent or flourishing state or condition', but alternately, more personally, 'The feeling of satisfaction, pleasure, or elation derived from some action, ability, possession, etc., which one believes does one credit'.[66]

If 'pride' is a complex word in Sonnet 76.1, 'new' is even more so. The phrase 'garments . . . new-fangled ill' in Sonnet 91 uses 'new' to mean 'vulgar', so there are grounds for a proposal that 'new pride' in 76.1 may refer to some flashily fashionable new artistic practice.[67] But alternatively, a self-doubting Renaissance poet lacking 'new pride' could refer to a lack of the fresh new 'invention' that was widely understood to be essential for a successful poem.[68] So the poet in Shakespeare's Sonnet 59, seeking the 'new', fears being 'beguiled' by illusory achievements when 'laboring for invention'. Shakespeare's Sonnets 103 and 105 express a similar poet's anxieties about lacking or weak invention.[69]

However, the next appearance in Sonnet 76 of the word 'new', in the phrase 'new found methods, and . . . compounds strange', definitely alludes to a particular poetic tactic or method, not just 'invention' generally. For, despite far-fetched alternatives suggested by some critics (involving medical 'compounds'), the evident first meaning for an Elizabethan poet of 'compounds strange' would be compound words or epithets.[70] The use of compound words in poetry is recommended in Sidney's *Apologie for Poetry*, which praises the English tongue for being 'happy in compositions of two or three words together'.[71] Sidney followed his own advice, for instance, when deploying the five-word compound epithet 'long-with-love-acquainted eyes' in *Astrophil and Stella* Sonnet 31 (I have added hyphens, but the compounding is evident).

When Shakespeare's poet-speaker in Sonnet 76 says he avoids using 'compounds strange', a double irony ensues. For one, his own immediately preceding phrase, 'new found methods', contains the compound epithet 'new-found'.[72] Moreover, compound words are frequently used in Shakespeare's sonnets; editors who modernize by hyphenating these identify as many as seventy,[73] such as 'love's long-since-cancelled woe' (Sonnet 30).

This witty double contradiction (wherein compound words appear not only in Sonnet 76 itself, but also in the poems to which Sonnet 76 refers) does not signal dramatized inept muddling inserted into the poem, or dramatized angry sarcasm, but exemplifies rather how this poem aims to disrupt the logic of either/or. On a larger scale, Sonnet 76 presents overall a poet-narrator who is truly downcast about his artistic barrenness and yet exalts when thinking that he is writing about an ideal beloved. It is not clear which of these two opposed positions prevails, and perhaps neither does.[74] Ambivalence of this sort suggests a mindset in which opposites are asserted at the same time, very similar to that we have seen when discussing Sonnet 53, above.

If examined closely, the self-questioning poet-speaker in Sonnet 76, mock-admitting his lack of 'compounds' on the heels of using one, fails to prove that he has succeeded in more than the mechanics of the poet's trade. Likewise, he may fall short of his claim to a verse style so individual and distinctive that 'every word doth almost [tell] my name' even if he signals a name by making the very next line gesture towards the formula 'Sh . . . pr'. For what would be demonstrated if those consonant digraphs did *steganographically* encode Shakespeare's name? It would not be that '*every* word doth almost [tell, or spell] my name', but only that a few selected (and mechanically manipulated) words do so. The preceding line's boast is fulfilled only in a way that is hollowly reductive. This suggests that the greater boast that dogged repetitiveness, keeping 'invention in a noted weed', can produce a distinctive poetic voice may also fail.

Dire, if witty, aspects of Sonnet 76 reflect the outlook of an artist who suffers from shaken confidence. This, I believe, is analogous with the appearances in many Shakespearean sonnets of lovers who become critics of their own desires and objects of desire (e.g. 33–7, 82, 120, 129, 138). *Odi et amo,*[75] love and loathing, are often entwined in Shakespeare's poems, whether the longed-for object is artistic beauty or human beauty. Love objects, as represented by Shakespeare, are often under threat and must be redeemed from contrary impulses.

Such topics are explored in Shakespeare's Sonnets with a degree of intensity and subtlety that is truly remarkable.

5

Shakespeare's Musicians:

Mimetic

Shakespeare and the Elizabethan musical setting

This chapter will consider those of Shakespeare's musicians who closely resemble the music-makers familiar to Elizabethans, or who parody, satirize or exaggerate their familiar characteristics. I will therefore rely on historical studies of musicians, and consider materials that have bearing on still-open questions about them.[1] In contrast, rather than actual musicians the following chapter will look at Shakespeare's allusions to mythological musicians. So both this and the next chapter consider *musicians* represented by Shakespeare, rather than, more generally, *Shakespeare and music*. That broader topic has been the subject of many valuable studies, but their concerns often fall outside the range of our interest. For example, we will not question exactly what music was heard on Elizabethan stages.[2] Our interests extend instead to the *kinds* of music indicated by Shakespearean play texts, for from those we see what kinds of musicians Shakespeare presented.

Elizabethans were surrounded by music. Fanfares, church bells, popular ballads, work songs, hymns and more elaborate religious music, playhouse music, alehouse music, festival music, all abounded. Public or private occasions, including processions or weddings, were celebrated with music. In Shakespeare's time, several highly cultivated sorts of secular music newly appeared in England. Madrigals, suites for broken consorts and the unique English Ayre were increasingly performed and heard,[3] helping to make the Elizabethan era a highpoint in musical history.

The ubiquity of Elizabethan music was matched by music's near-ubiquity in Shakespeare's plays, all of which contain at least some music-making.[4] There are, moreover, 'over five hundred passages of Shakespeare dealing with musical matters',[5] and over 300 musical stage directions in his plays.[6] Such abundance might seem daunting to the project of tracing Shakespeare's musicians, especially because all the music heard in Shakespeare's plays is seen to be – or is implied to be – produced by musicians who are part of the world of the drama. To avoid confusion,[7] I will avoid calling such music 'diegetic' and instead propose using the term 'practicable music' – borrowing a theatrical technical term where a 'practicable' element of a stage set is both functional and mimetically actual (for instance, a stage set door that can be opened and is walked through, or stairs onstage that can be climbed and are mounted by the dramatized characters). In these terms, the music indicated in Shakespeare plays is almost always theatrically practicable, and is not 'incidental music' that serves only as a 'background soundtrack' intended to evoke or enhance audience responses.[8]

Despite this, our study will not be challenged by an overwhelming number of musicians. This is because a great many of those who purvey music in Shakespeare's plays are relatively featureless exemplars of broad categories of typical Elizabethan musicians. For instance, many pageboy servants are called upon to provide songs redolent of important themes. These themes in the contexts of the plays are of foremost importance, but such performances also reflect the high value placed on musically adept servants (often boys who can sing) in Elizabethan aristocratic and gentry establishments.[9] Shakespeare's plays also reflect the music of Elizabethan tradespersons and manual labourers – urban as well as rural, and male as well as female – who often sang at their work or at leisure.[10] Another broad tendency reflected by Shakespeare is the adoption of folk-like music by the gentry and above, putting 'different levels of taste and education in contact'. Reasons for this may be adduced: there were aristocratic and courtly 'vogues' in Shakespeare's time for enjoying country-style entertainments[11] while, as Bruce Pattison notes, 'The quality of genuine popular music that has come down from the period is amazingly high.'[12]

Some Shakespearean representations of musical interfaces between individuals of higher and lower social status go beyond illustrating good taste or social fashions, and serve thematic aims. Those, however, may bear on matters other than musicianship. For instance, when Shakespeare's love-besotted Count Orsino calls for a rendition of a 'silly' old song about love that 'The spinsters, and the knitters in the sun' are wont to 'chant' (2.4.41–5), his purpose is to further his self-conscious, leisured, emotional self-indulgence. Here he reprises his demand for music to induce 'surfeiting' on love (1.1.1–3); his aristocratic appropriation of folk-like music links with the central themes of over- and under-indulgence in *Twelfth Night*.

In an inverse way, the rough-handed gravediggers in *Hamlet* 5.1.61–94 sing a slightly mangled version of a lyric by a Henrician courtier poet that is printed in Richard Tottel's well-known *Miscellany* (printed in many editions from 1557), advancing a Shakespearean theme of the very wide impact of early Tudor court poetry.[13] Thematic issues also pertain when Stefano in *The Tempest* sings, 'I shall no more to sea, to sea', for he is a lesser court functionary ranking above the 'swabber' and the other mariners in his drunken song (2.2.41–54). When Stefano adopts the stance of a rascally negligent sailor he reinforces a major irony in *The Tempest* 1.1 wherein hard-working mariners strive to save their foundering ship and are cursed and impeded by frivolous indolent courtiers, their supposed betters.[14]

Again thematically, but closer to issues centring on musicians, Stefano wonders at 'a brave kingdom . . . where I shall have my music for nothing' (3.2.147–8). Thus he reflects a popular appetite for secular music provided free of charge. That appetite was fed by 'perhaps the first public concerts in England', in which, from 1571, London's town waits played for all comers gratis at the Royal Exchange.[15] In an age of fewer celebrity artists than ours (although these were increasingly emerging), the invisibility of the musician in *The Tempest* who delights Stefano, after first terrifying him, may refer to the way in which artistic productions could be enjoyed without notice taken of their makers. So in Shakespeare's *Richard II* (quarto only) the aristocratic John of Gaunt proposes to his exiled son, 'Suppose the singing birds musicians', thereby equating the efforts of court musicians with the delightful singing of nameless wild creatures.[16]

Thus *particular* musicians are not necessarily highlighted by Shakespeare, despite the fact that musicians mimetically present in their plays are responsible for what Erin Minear calls the 'pervasiveness of music' in Shakespeare's work. Minear adds that 'Shakespeare's moments of literal music often seem designed to suggest that the music was always there . . . Songs are never sung for the first time.'[17] The Elizabethan theatre could be very literal about the pervasiveness of music in society. Thus Ben Jonson's 1601 *Every Man in his Humour* images barbers supplying musical instruments in their shops for the use of their clients.[18] Shakespeare likewise indicates quotidian musicianship when peaceable times are signalled by 'Our tradesmen singing in their shops' in *Coriolanus* 4.6.8–9.

Shakespeare's plays provide numerous reflections of Elizabethan musicianship at large, but they also present lively and revealing portrayals of particular musical artists. Let us begin with the musician Feste in *Twelfth Night*.

Feste's anxieties and a musician's ambiguous social position

Shakespeare's title '*Twelfth Night*' denotes the end of the twelve-day Christmas festival, thus referring to the temporal limits of seasonally licensed excess and self-indulgence. At the same time, the play's subtitle '*What You Will*' evokes a fantasy of timeless and unlimited hedonistic enjoyment in an imaginary unendingly festive realm. That realm, from a certain point of view in the play, is usurped by the ascendancy of the killjoy household steward Malvolio. But the same play also satirizes the initial limitlessness of Orsino's love-drunkenness, Olivia's love-denial and Sir Toby Belch's bibulation.

Thus the play anatomizes pleasure-oriented modes of being beyond the range of Malvolio and his initially bleakly mourning mistress, Olivia. At the end, inhibiting forces are defeated and Eros prevails (journeys do end in lovers meeting). Yet the aftermath of the liminal festival also sees anarchic Sir Toby married to capable Maria, Sir Andrew and Malvolio shriven of their false erotic hopes, and both Olivia and Orsino moderating wilful passions. Balance is not fully established, however, for the half-humorous subplot of the gulling of Malvolio itself staggers into excess. Malvolio ominously exits promising to be 'revenged'. No less complex than that, equally contributing to an open-ended final texture, is Shakespeare's presentation of the significantly named Feste. Feste, moreover, was first played by Robert Armin, who is identified by Martin Butler as Shakespeare's earliest 'psychologically layered' comedian.[19]

On the socio-historical level Feste closely resembles a roving minstrel of the sort who performs songs, quips, poems, acted-out skits and juggling tricks for varied audiences. Medieval minstrels proudly exhibited versatility and independence while being given licence to be familiar with even the highest-placed clientele. However, the reputation of the 'noble minstrel' declined sadly over the course of the sixteenth century and by the century's end minstrels occupied a position of despised marginality.[20] In accordance with that, the complex character of Feste displays anxieties about his status, evasively anticipates denigration, and suffers from unwarranted attacks, as we shall see.

Shakespeare's special interest in Feste's decayed profession may have arisen because the same interval of time that saw the fall of the 'noble minstrel' also saw the rise of the English playhouse professions.[21] Like minstrels, players looked to paying audiences for their livelihood, selling entertainment for a fee. Some wryness about the players' economic dependence on small individual box-office takings may be echoed in the small handouts Feste repeatedly receives for his fooling or singing (2.3.23–4, 2.3.30, 2.3.32, 2.4.66, 3.1.42, 3.1.52, 4.1.18, 5.1.25, 5.1.32). Although not serving a broad public and court audiences as Shakespeare's company did, Feste does move between two different establishments, Orsino's and Olivia's, which do not at first otherwise communicate. Asked about his itinerant way of life by Viola/Cesario, Feste says of his profession, 'Foolery, sir, does walk about the orb like the sun, it shines everywhere' (3.1.37–8).

So Feste is an economic pieceworker and itinerant. He also resembles a traditional minstrel by engaging in teasing familiarly with his aristocratic employers. When he uses chop logic to prove the Countess Olivia a 'fool' (1.5.35–68), she retaliates with 'Now you see, sir, how your fooling grows old, and people dislike it' (1.5.106–7). Here she probably alludes to the fall of the minstrels' profession out of fashion and into disrepute, rather than to Feste's chronological age. Likewise Malvolio's unkind attacks on Feste's 'barren' fooling may mirror a typically scornful late Elizabethan view of minstrels.

Such a scornful view may be illustrated from the pioneering 1576 autobiography of the musician and composer Thomas Whythorne. Whythorne vehemently despises those who 'will sell the sounds of their voices and instruments' wherever they can find 'such that will hear them', performing in 'cities, towns, and villages . . . also . . . private houses . . . publicly or privately' and at 'markets, fairs, marriages, assemblies, taverns, alehouses', and also playing for 'banqueters, revellers, mummers, maskers, dancers, tumblers, players and suchlike'. 'These,' says the verbose Whythorne, 'in ancient times were named minstrels.'[22] Whythorne placed himself far above 'the rascal and off-scum of [the musical] profession who be, or ought to be, called minstrels', and, as was his wont, superadded for good measure what he called a 'pretty jest'. This is a tedious anecdote in which a 'minstrel', visiting the household of a 'man of worship' where Whythorne himself lived as a music tutor was shown up to be no better than a passing 'stout rogue' of a beggar.[23]

Elizabethan lawmakers concurred with this opinion of minstrels. Whythorne himself alludes with approval to the 1572 statute (14 Eliz. c.5) which classed 'Minstrels' as rogues and vagabonds, and subjected them to harsh punishments.[24] When that statute lapsed in 1597 the Elizabethan Vagrancy Act (39 Eliz. c.4a) used nearly the same wording to define 'Rogues Vagabondes and Sturdy Beggares', and specified even harsher punishments. That latter statute criminalized 'all Fencers Bearewardes common Players of Enterludes and Minstrelles wandering abroad (other than players of Enterludes belonging to any Baron of this Realme, or any other honorable Personage of greater Degree)'.

The very term 'minstrel' has deprecating or ludicrous connotations when King Ferdinand in *Love's Labour's Lost* says of the absurd Don Armado, 'I will use him for my minstrelry' (1.1.174). Despising of minstrels is even stronger in *Romeo and Juliet* when Mercutio gestures to his sword and threatens, 'An thou make minstrels of us, look to hear nothing but discords. Here's my fiddlestick; here's that shall make you dance' (3.1.46–7). In the same play the servant Peter, equally fractious, offers hired musicians 'No money, on my faith, but the gleek. I will give you the minstrel' (4.4.140–1). Shakespeare's Lucrece, having been raped, hates the thought of 'Feast-finding minstrels tuning my defame' (817), while the honest steward Flavius in *Timon of Athens* laments that 'our vaults have wept / With drunken spilth of wine, when every room / Hath blazed with lights and brayed with minstrelsy' (2.2.156–8).

The minstrel Feste is repeatedly shown begging for a second handout on the top of each small gratuity offered to him. For this or other reasons, he is not at all keen to be identified with his profession and replies evasively when the young stranger Viola/Cesario greets him, 'Save thee friend, and thy music, Dost thou live by thy tabor?' (3.1.1–2). Feste replies, 'No, sir, I live by [= near] the church.' Thus, by means of quibbling, Feste dodges acknowledging that he does not receive wages or enjoy noble patronage, but rather sings and jests for meagre payments. There is more in Feste's quibbling. For one thing, because Viola questions his status on first seeing him, it is clear that he does not wear a false livery in order to pretend to belong to one of the establishments he haunts (as some roaming musicians actually did, in order to avoid the vagrancy statutes).[25]

Another implication of Feste's quibbling is more complex. First we must note that, after the English Reformation, church and church-related employment opportunities for musicians were much reduced, although not wholly abolished. Whythorne describes the situation thus: 'In time past music was chiefly maintained by cathedrals, churches, abbeys, colleges, chauntries, guilds, fraternities, & c. But when the abbeys and colleges without the universities, with guilds and fraternities, & c., were suppressed, then went music to decay.' Next he complains of a concurrent decay of 'music in [the] houses' of 'divers noblemen and women' who 'in time past, imitating the Prince' employed both 'organists and singing men to serve God . . . in their private chapels' and also musicians to 'serve for private recreation in [the] houses' of 'the nobility and worshipful' who were 'no less esteemed than the others'.[26] Those claims, however, are partly contradicted by the documentary researches of David Price that indicate a late Elizabethan increase in musical patronage in both Protestant and Catholic 'educated society'.[27] Indeed, Whythorne's autobiography describes his being employed to providing musical 'recreation' and tuition in several private houses, followed by his appointment as chapel master to Archbishop Matthew Parker. Whythorne's complaints, even if exaggerated, do indicate that times were hard for many

Elizabethan musicians.[28] Although psalm singing was universal, and more elaborate religious music was heard in such places as City churches, the Chapel Royal and the cathedrals,[29] arguably the Reformation lay behind the silencing of 'Bare ruined choirs where late the sweet birds sang' (Sonnet 73). Yet generous religious employment was still available to the more fortunate Elizabethan musicians, like those of the Chapel Royal, or Archbishop Parker's employee Whythorne himself. So, when Feste claims that he lives 'by the church' (paralleling 'by thy tabor') he may be insinuating (falsely) that he is among the elite of his profession.

Whythorne's *Autobiography* can further help us to trace Feste's social standing. Following his account of one of his several wrong turnings with a desired woman (this one a music pupil), Whythorne assesses his path in life in a spirit of self-consolation:

seeing that my profession is to teach one of the seven sciences liberal, the which is also one of the mathematical sciences; and in respect of the wonderful effects that hath been wrought by the sweet harmony thereof, it passeth all the other sciences; I do think that the teacher's thereof (if they will) may esteem so much of themselves as to be free and not bound, much less to be made slave-like. And even so did I at this time.[30]

Still attempting self-definition, Whythorne theorizes later in his autobiography:

Ye shall understand that in this our realm [music] was one of the trades and exercises appointed and allowed for such gentlemen to live by who were younger brothers, and neither lands nor fees and goods to maintain them. Ye shall find in the book named *The Accidence of Armoury* that a King of Heralds may give arms to any that is excellently skilled in any of the seven liberal sciences (whereof music is one), although he nor his ancestors might never give any before.[31]

Indeed, more specifically than in *The Accidence of Armoury*, Whythorne's claim is supported in John Ferne's 1586 *The Blazon of Gentrie*. Although condemning 'a certaine sort of bastard and mechanicall' musicians who are mere 'minstrels, wanderers, and vagrants', Ferne cites Pythagoras, Plato, Aristotle, Socrates and others as champions of the 'heavenly science' of music which can alter men's affections, tame wild beasts, cure diseases, inspire warriors and serve divine worship. So Ferne allows that the musician 'meriteth well a coate of Armes' and 'that thereby he is made a Gentleman'.[32]

Discoursing further on what he calls the 'degrees and sorts' of musicians, Whythorne first mentions that at the top of the profession are 'doctors and bachelors'. Whythorne himself, not a university graduate, immediately adds, however, that there are 'musicians uncommenced also ... that have set forth as great mysteries in music as ever did any doctor or bachelor of music'. In accord with convention, he praises scholarly 'musicians that be named speculators ... that become musicians by study, without any practice thereof', and places alongside them amateur musicians in the ranks of the 'nobility and the worshipful' who follow the counsel of conduct books and learn to play music. But, interestingly, he next condemns all who 'do live by music' who 'play or sound on musical instruments' but who cannot compose music of their own as 'no musicians at all' and mere 'pettifogers of music'.[33]

Shakespeare's musical professional Feste is neither a scholar nor a gentleman, and it is not implied that he has written any of the songs that he sings. But, in a further twist, he is a co-producer of music (and of jests), with men of much higher standing than his own. Thus after he has sung the very beautiful lyric 'O mistress mine' (possibly set to the music of Thomas Morley),[34] he joins Sir Toby Belch and Toby's gull, Sir Andrew Aguecheek (who can play a 'viol-de-gamboys', 1.3.23–4), to sing a rousing 'catch' (a catch is a kind of round), disturbing the tranquillity of the household in mourning.[35] The scandalized reaction of Countess Olivia's steward Malvolio to the loud nocturnal singing of this trio has been made famous by

Sir Toby's rejoinder, 'Dost thou think because thou art virtuous there shall be no more cakes and ale?' (2.3.110–11). Equally interesting are several other aspects of this unruly affair. For one, Sir Toby proposes, 'shall we make the welkin dance indeed? Shall we rouse the night-owl in a catch that will draw three souls out of one weaver?' (2.3.56–8). He speaks of the dance of the heavens – a neo-Platonic concept – in relation to his drunken revels, and also to weaving the parts of the song, which probably alludes to the reputation of weavers as noisy and fractious (which is reflected in a half-dozen Shakespeare plays).[36] There might also be an allusion here to a famous jurisdictional dispute, concerning apprentices, between the City guilds of Weavers and Musicians.[37]

More importantly, singing the catch in *Twelfth Night* joins together Feste, apparently an unlicensed minstrel, and Sir Toby and Sir Andrew, who have a much higher social standing (one is a kinsman of Countess Olivia, the other her guest). It is thus ironic when the middling class Malvolio brackets the three singers as equivalent ruffians: 'Have you no wit, manners, nor honesty, but to gabble like tinkers at this time of night? Do ye make an alehouse of my lady's house, that ye squeak out your coziers' catches without any mitigation or remorse of voice?' (2.3.84–8). Two of the three alleged 'tinkers' or 'coziers' (cobblers) rank far above the rebuking steward.

Malvolio's language points up Shakespeare's image of three men from widely diverse social levels performing music together convivially. The spectacle of high-status amateur musicians comfortably joining in recreational performance with lower-status ones would not have seemed bizarre in the Elizabethan world where such conjunctions were not at all uncommon (even when the higher-status participants were not, like Sir Andrew or Sir Toby, foolish or debauched). Thus Christopher Marsh cites a memoir of an Elizabethan establishment 'in which the members of an eminent aristocratic family played and sang in the company of their musical servants, thereby making a "society of musick"'.[38] Marsh also analyses a manuscript collection of catches made in 1580 by Thomas Lant, which contains 'introductory remarks' in which the author seems to have 'imagined himself . . . coordinating the efforts of assorted family members and servants to sing his catches'. Marsh remarks that 'Many of the songs [in Lant's manuscript] aimed clearly at fostering an intense sense of community and an atmosphere of equality, however transient, among individuals of higher and lower social rank.'[39] Marsh's massive study includes many other instances in early modern England of a power of 'musical mediation' that 'bridged the gap that existed between artisan and aristocrat, helping to release some of the tensions that were inevitable consequences of extreme inequality'.[40]

Servants and apprentices, who were integral parts of Elizabethan households, could be highly valued for their musical abilities. Thus Christ's Hospital, a charitable school founded in London in 1552 with a mission to 'place its children as apprentices and servants', is described in 1587 as teaching the children 'to singe, to play uppon all sorts of instruments, as to sounde the trumpet, the cornett, the recorder or flute, to play uppon shagbotts, shalmes, and all other instruments that are to be plaid upon, either with winde or finger'.[41] We may remember, for later, that wind instruments as well as stringed ones were in the curriculum. Several scholars have noted 'great competition' among high-ranking Elizabethans for musically adept servants.[42] Christopher Marsh notes in addition that 'musical servants of aristocrats and monarchs generally had their roots in the middle and lower orders of society, yet within the mansions of the mighty they could find themselves in situations of some intimacy with their employers. This was yet another form of social mediation, and it distinguished musicians from other servants.' Marsh also suggests that professional musicians 'mediated between "high" and "low" society more extensively and continuously than any other group', and that the 'roving recreation' of musicians carrying instruments between venues broke down distinctions between the instruments supposedly suited to upper, middling, and lower classes.[43] To this we may add a particularly poignant anecdote recounted by Walter Woodfill: 'the night before he died, in 1576, the Earl of Essex "willed William Hayes his musician to play on the virginals, and to sing. 'Play' said he, 'my song, and I will sing it myself.' And so he did most joyfully."[44] All of this may be pertinent to how Shakespeare's musician Feste becomes a co-performer, and also a co-conspirator, with men of higher station.

Feste's familiarity with his 'betters' suggests that among the civilizing functions of musical art was the provision of opportunities for contact between diverse social groups.[45] Although status provided a legal framework for Elizabethan society, some, especially those in the arts, moved freely outside of that framework. Despite the severe strictures of moralists, and restrictive laws, boundaries were crossed. When thinking about Elizabethan society, and especially its foundational households, we should be wary of being misled by latter-day ideas that emphasize impermeable class divisions or cultural ghettos. Just so, Christopher Marsh gives many examples of what he calls the 'unstoppable two-way traffic' between 'the cultural pursuits of the gentry and those of the people'.[46] We may also note how the very high-born Sir Philip Sidney averred with mock apology that 'I must confesse my own barbarousnes, I neuer heard the olde song of *Percy* and *Duglas* that I found not my heart moove more then with a Trumpet; and yet it is sung but by some blinde Crouder, with no rougher voyce then rude stile.'[47]

Musical snobbery, musicians' poverty and a musician's amorality

Shakespeare's complex depiction of Feste demonstrates both despised and admired aspects of being an artist. Perhaps accordingly, Feste can 'sing both high and low', and pronounce, in comic rapid alternation, the voices of the Fool and of the grave curate Sir Topas. In this section we note first the 'low' voices of some of Shakespeare's musical artists, then how musicians are regarded both positively and negatively in Shakespeare's works.

In *The Tempest* the 'howling monster' Caliban sings, "Ban, 'ban, Cacalaban', his cacophony the result of roguish Europeans making him 'drunken' (2.2.178–83). However, this is not the limit of Shakespeare's ethnomusicology. Rather, at 3.2.138–45 a sober Caliban shows himself highly sensitive to music, as are his anagrammatical namesakes and models, the New World 'Caniballes' whose 'songs' Montaigne so much admired.[48] More simply, old Silence in *2 Henry IV* 5.3.17–104 progressively falters in stuttering attempts at song as he becomes drunker and more self-deceivingly vainglorious. Other examples of absurd Shakespearean singers include Bottom in *A Midsummer Night's Dream*, who when fitted with ass's ears croaks out a song to the delight of deluded Titania (3.1.118–29). There is also Parson Evans in *Merry Wives*, who is terrified at the prospect of duelling and in his funk falteringly conflates Marlowe's famous lyric 'Come go with me and be my love' with Psalm 137 (3.1.16–29).[49] But such unrefined Shakespearean singers are exceptional, and few now would agree with the snobbish remark (perhaps wickedly) attributed in 1908 to George Bernard Shaw: '[I] should not like to sit down to dinner with [any of] the singers in Shakespeare.'[50]

Wealthy Hortensio in *The Taming of the Shrew* displays a parallel snobbish disapprobation of practical musicians. Having stooped to gain access to a young woman by disguising himself as a music tutor,[51] once he is unmasked he declares:

> Mistake no more, I am not Licio,
> Nor a musician as I seem to be,
> But one that scorn to live in this disguise
> For such a one as leaves a gentleman
> And makes a god of such a cullion.
> Know, sir, that I am called Hortensio.

(4.2.16–21)

This comes after Hortensio, who has been too physically familiar in his tuition for the liking of his spirited female pupil

Katerina, has suffered the indignity of having his own lute broken over his head (2.1.148–59). Amazed Hortensio complains, 'I did but tell her she mistook her frets, / And bowed her hand to teach her fingering' (2.1.149–50).

Hortensio's labelling of a domestic music tutor a 'cullion' denies the dignity of the profession that was so strongly promoted by Thomas Whythorne.[52] For his just deserts, Hortensio is first pilloried in Katerina's lute, and then married to a manipulative widow whom he soon finds he 'fears' (5.2.16). Incidentally, outside of fiction, Whythorne himself reports narrowly escaping marriage to more than one strong-willed householder widow, demonstrating that domestic music tutors 'occupied a nebulous space somewhere between the gentleman and the lowly "minstrel"'.[53]

In *Romeo and Juliet*, the Capulets' liveried servants denigrate a band of professional musicians who have been hired to play at the wedding of Juliet and County Paris. Wedding musicians typically played 'loud' wind instruments suited to public festivities,[54] so we should probably take the Capulets' musicians' decision to 'put up our pipes and be gone' (4.4.123) to be meant literally, despite discrepancies that have led some commentators to other conclusions.[55] Indeed, in Shakespeare's period the town waits, who usually played wind instruments, often performed at weddings to gain extra income. Town waits were also reputed to suffer from poverty,[56] while the musicians in *Romeo and Juliet* are taunted especially in relation to their poverty. Evidently considering his liveried status higher than that of the hireling artists, the Capulet servant Peter sneeringly interprets to them the well-known verse 'Then music with her silver sound' to mean that the musicians will play cheaply, for silver rather than for gold (4.4.155–66).[57] The insults of Peter and his fellows, accompanied by bawdy banter,[58] come immediately after the news has arrived that Juliet has killed herself rather than marry in accord with her father's demands. This continues a theme of thuggish vituperation in the play, reiterating the quarrel in the streets between rival servants (imitating their fractious young masters) that begins it (1.1.1–60).

The Capulets' servants' gratuitous denigration of the wedding players reflects the status of Elizabethan occupational musicians, and especially that they were often impoverished.[59] Peter's claims about musicians' small wages are grotesquely shown to be accurate. The musicians first intend to 'put up our pipes and be gone' when the wedding 'festival' is converted to 'funeral', but actual hunger prompts them to 'tarry for the mourners and stay dinner' (4.4.111–71). Thus the play suggests, very darkly, that the poor musicians exploit a young girl's tragic death so that they can fill their empty bellies for free.

In a wholly contrasting register, without similar pathos, the musician-rogue Autolycus enters halfway through *The Winter's Tale*. When he is asked to 'bear [his] part' in a three-part song he replies, ''tis my occupation' (4.4.293–4). His occupations include itinerant peddler of worthless baubles and absurd broadsheet ballads, and (as he says) musician. He also uses the delights of song to distract his gulls while cutting their purses. But Autolycus also takes personal delight in music, for he enters the play singing with gusto along his solitary way, although the burden of his song is the joy of petty thieving and seducing doxies (4.3.1–12). Confidence trickster, opportunist, pretender at rank, coward and petty thief that he is,[60] he still cheerfully occupies an important niche in the ecology first of an idealized countryside flush with harvest and entirely lacking in material (or sexual) scarcity,[61] and then of a court where country folk are ennobled and therefore require appropriate tutors and followers.

Autolycus is not at all a struggling artist like the jobbing musicians in *Romeo and Juliet*. He at first figures as a thriving rogue in a dream-like, harm-free pastoral world to whom illicit 'booties' come unbidden in profusion (4.4.833). Yet his exploits also suggest more realistic Elizabethan 'coney-catchers' (confidence tricksters), mountebank peddlers and pickpockets. A proud thief and trickster, Shakespeare's Autolycus identifies his lineage: 'My father named me Autolycus, who being, as I am, littered under Mercury, was likewise a snapper-up of unconsidered trifles' (4.3.24–6). Here he alludes to the maternal grandfather of Homer's resourceful wanderer Odysseus, who was also named Autolycus, and who according to myth was fathered by Mercury himself. The god Mercury, as we have noted in our Introduction, was the new patron of Renaissance artists. He was also the patron of poets and thieves. Accordingly, Shakespeare's Autolycus is a shape-shifting and ambivalent figure, imaging a potentially darker side of art.[62]

Another element in Shakespeare's complex construction of Autolycus concerns Elizabethan social mobility in relation to the arts. Autolycus traces his own former career trajectory from a 'servant' of Prince Florizel who was dismissed for just cause through 'many knavish professions', including a theatrical exhibitioner of apes and puppets (4.3.85–98). At last we see him first as a high-handed pretended courtier (4.4.712–827), and then as the fashionably spoken courtly companion of new-made 'gentlemen born' (5.2.125–73). The linking of Autolycus' mercurial, dishonest and amoral artistic occupations with parodies of a newly-minted courtier's pretentious language and behaviour casts an oblique light – perhaps satiric of King James often selling honours – on the points we have been making about the 'mediation' between social ranks afforded by the Elizabethan fascination with art, and especially the art of music.[63]

Next, let us consider some Shakespearean musical jollity that is less morally ambiguous than that of Autolycus.

The case of English 'three-men's' or 'freemen's' singers[64]

Elizabethan semi-professional musicians were less dubious figures than Shakespeare's criminally inclined singer of bawdy ballads, yet they still attracted adverse legal interest. They were certainly numerous. Following a survey of over a thousand early modern working musicians, Christopher Marsh gives details of part-time musicians who were mainly tailors, basket-makers and weavers, or else husbandmen, carpenters, smiths, bellows-makers, butchers, lime-burners, millers, shoemakers, wheelwrights and sailors, thus demonstrating that many 'regarded music as one of several potential sources of income'.[65] That situation alarmed the London Guild of Musicians (or Fellowship of Minstrels), which in 1554 persuaded the Court of the Corporation to issue an Act intended to prevent 'foreign competition' which was causing 'hindraunce of the gaines and profitts of the poore minstrels being freemen of the Cytie'. The Act explained that: 'because many Artificers and Handimen such as Tailors, Shoemakers and such "leaving the use of their crafts and manual occupations and giving themselves wholly to wandering abroad . . . do commonly use nowadays to sing songs called 'Three Mens Songs' in the Taverns etc. of the City, and also at weddings 'to the great loss of the poor fellowship of minstrels' it is enacted that such conduct is to cease under penalty for disobedience".'[66] The 1554 Act was, however, ineffectual, even when re-enacted in 1562 by the Lord Mayor. The reason, according to H.A.F. Crewdson, was because music 'is a profession singularly unsusceptible to control'.[67] Nor did the 1563 Elizabethan Statute of Artificers, which required a specific apprenticeship in any occupation before it could be practised professionally, effectively protect the City musicians. The musicians again petitioned the Corporation regarding a monopoly on apprentices and again received scant relief following yet another Act in 1574. Neither did a further petition in 1601 bring effective relief to their complaints about lax control.[68]

The 1554 London ordinance that prohibited musicianship as a secondary occupation made an exception concerning the popular format known as 'three men's songs', allowing that these may be 'sung in a common play or interlude'.[69] Thus actors were licensed to sing them both on public stages and for more exclusive entertainments. Christopher Marsh remarks that 'Three-mens songs, although associated with lowly artisans, [were] fashionable in the Henrician court and prominent within Tudor interludes'.[70] A three-men's song once even played a part

in a diplomatic manoeuvre: during a mission to Rome in 1517–
18 Thomas Cromwell gained access to the passing-by Pope Leo
X by surprising him 'with a performance of an English "three
man's song"'.[71] In 1607, at a grand Merchant Tailors' Company
feast attended by King James and Prince Henry, a freeman's song
for three mariners was performed (other music was provided
by the combined forces of the royal musicians and the city
waits).[72] That same song was soon after published among a
group of 'Freemens Songs' in Thomas Ravenscroft's 1609
musical anthology *Deuteromelia*.[73] Linda Austern shows that
Ravenscroft's *Deuteromelia* and three other music collections
made by Ravenscroft contain between them songs used in eleven
stage plays, and notes that many of these were popular songs,
which 'were widely known in London, did not originate as
theater music and were undoubtedly gathered independently by
Ravenscroft, Beaumont, Shakespeare, and the other collectors'.[74]
Here again popular music crossed cultural divides.

Many Elizabethans, including artisans, were capable of
singing three-men's songs: for instance, in Thomas Deloney's
The Gentle Craft the shoemakers agree that each must be able
to 'bear his Part in a Three-man's song' or else pay a forfeit.[75]
Shakespeare's plays repeatedly allude to this. During the
festival in *The Winter's Tale*, the trio of Mopsa, Dorcas and
Autolycus performs a song 'to the tune of "Two Maids Wooing
a Man" . . . in three parts' (4.4.287–94). Although there are
structural differences between such a three-voiced part-song,
called a 'three-men's' or 'freemen's' song, and a 'catch' (which,
as mentioned above, was a kind of round), Christopher Marsh
shows that the terms for these two formats were often conflated
in Shakespeare's time.[76] In *Twelfth Night*, Sir Toby, Feste and
Aguecheek perform a raucous three-part 'catch' (2.3.68). In
The Tempest 3.2.119–29, Caliban, Stephano and Trinculo
begin an even wilder 'catch' (but the more musical of the three,
Caliban, has to tell the others 'that's not the tune', and Ariel
must correct them).

Although according to the sole surviving text of the play
(the Folio) they never sing, the most intriguing Shakespearean

three-men's singers are those described by the Clown in *The Winter's Tale* 4.3.40–4. He mentions them when his budgeting for the upcoming festival identifies the need for 'four-and-twenty nosegays for the shearers – three-man-song-men, all, and very good ones – but they are most of them means and basses, but one Puritan amongst them, and he sings psalms to hornpipes'. It is apparently intended that these (mean and base?) shearers will perform their three-men's songs at the pastoral festival – where the audience will eventually include a prince, a princess, a king and the king's chief counsellor. However, the Folio text of the play calls for an alternative performance by a band of male 'saultiers'.[77] Regarding these, a servant reports that 'One three of them, by their own report, sir, hath danced before the King, and not the worst of the three but jumps twelve foot and a half by th' square' (4.4.325–7). There is evidence that professional actors from Shakespeare's company were available to present this dance during a 1611 court performance of the play,[78] but in other performances the promised three-men's songs might well have been heard instead.

It would not have surprised Elizabethans when rustic shearers are described by the Clown in *The Winter's Tale* as 'very good' three-men's singers, but his remark that there is 'but one Puritan amongst them, and he sings psalms to hornpipes' would have surprised and amused many of them. Here Shakespeare's remark about Puritans is, as is usual, only moderately derisive.[79] Nevertheless, the ridiculous notion of a dour Puritan singing psalms to hornpipes is telling in ways related to our concerns in the next two sections.

Was performing music degrading or disgraceful in Shakespeare's world?

Music-opposing, self-important, Malvolio stands stiffly on his dignity until gulled into smilingly wearing cross-gartered yellow stockings. His grinning disgrace may lead us to question how self-display during artistic performance matched up with Elizabethan notions of social decorum. In particular, was it considered befitting, or degrading, for men or women to be seen making music? As we shall see, despite some vehemently expressed contemporary views to the contrary, there are indications that Shakespeare did not in general think it lowering for well-born or high-status men or women to perform music.

In at least one place Shakespeare reduces objections to music-making to mere snobbery. This is when his Hotspur, a choleric guardian of his own social standing, accepts his wife's refusal when he asks her to sing in public by reflecting that singing may be 'the next way to turn tailor' (*1 Henry IV* 3.1.255). Hotspur's remark alludes to artisans singing at their work and also traditional mockery of tailors. When Shakespeare presents Hotspur's denigration of musicianship he does not necessarily validate it, any more than he does Hotspur's denigration of poetry and poets.[80]

On the contrary, Shakespeare presents Princess Marina in *Pericles* and Lady Mortimer in *1 Henry IV* as admirable musical performers.[81] Additionally, according to Tiffany Stern, *Twelfth Night* 'seems to bear the leftovers of a voice-revision' in that, originally, 'the role of Viola is written for a singing heroine'. If Viola did sing to Orsino, as she promises to do in 1.2.53–4, and is bidden to do in 2.4.2–7, would she have been disgraced had it not been for her disguise as a boy?[82] Probably not, for the upper-echelon Shakespearean fathers Baptista, Brabantio, and Cleon happily train their daughters in music, not fearing disgrace, and most likely mirroring typical Elizabethan practice (although statistical proof of this is elusive).[83] Castiglione's Count also agrees that both male and female courtiers should possess musical abilities.[84]

Thomas Morley famously describes a social gaffe made by an imagined Elizabethan gentleman who could not sing from a score.[85] Elizabethan books of part songs were published formatted so as to be sight-read and performed convivially by families or guests seated around a table (Figure 12). Despite these very well-known circumstances, many modern critics have

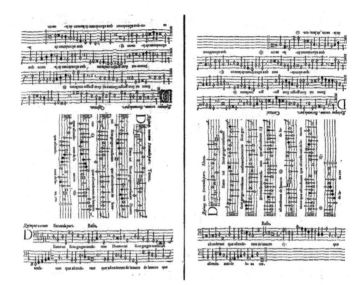

FIGURE 12 *Pages from Thomas Morley,* A plaine and easie introduction to practicall musicke set downe in forme of a dialogue, *1597, sig. Bb6.*

expressed opinions along the lines that 'Rosaline's transgressive indecorum would have been increased by her singing in public'.[86] Others extend this to high-status men as well, as in 'A lord cannot be displayed as a singer.'[87] But even if some Elizabethans observed rigid inhibitions concerning performance, would Shakespeare have wished to promote them? He was after all himself a performing artist, and yet was active in procuring a family's coat of arms with the motto 'Non sancz droict'.

Moreover, the dedications of many music books of the period, like one to the Earl of Hertford,[88] fulsomely praise their noble dedicatees' personal musical skills. It is also known that very high-born children were trained in music: for example, Mary Sidney, who 'was taught to play the lute as early as 1571', and her brother, Robert Sidney, who 'was taught to sing ... as early as 1576'.[89] In addition to this, all the Tudor

FIGURE 13 *Nicholas Hilliard, miniature of Queen Elizabeth I playing a lute. © Bridgeman Art Library.*

sovereigns from Henry VIII onwards played music. Queen Elizabeth was painted by Hilliard holding a lute (Figure 13), and she even contrived to have her virginal playing overheard and admired.[90]

Although authors of educational manuals and conduct books diverged regarding the suitability of musical education for middling and higher status Elizabethan children,[91] one very notable educator of such children, Richard Mulcaster, put the matter thus: 'I dare be bould therefore to admit yong *maidens* to learne, seeing my countrie gives me leave, and her *custome* standes for me', where the visible and acceptable accomplishments he refers to included learned abilities to 'sing and playe: and both passing well'.[92]

Yet, although Elizabethan aversion to displaying musical abilities was evidently not nearly so universal as has been claimed, it is still true that 'in Shakespeare's drama almost all performed songs are rendered by professionals or servants'.[93] However, that most likely did not mirror societal norms, but rather playhouse practicalities. For there is evidence that Shakespeare's company employed only one or a few specialist musicians who performed onstage in the stead of the company's major players, who themselves were not especially trained to do so.[94] This explains why several prominent Shakespearean characters are said to have musical training or accomplishments and yet are not called upon to demonstrate their abilities. Those unheard musicians include Viola, Laertes, Marina, Imogen/Fidele, Perdita and possibly even Hamlet.[95]

Another argument maintaining that Shakespeare mirrored social restrictions on public musical performance rests on the expressions of self-abnegation before they sing made by Balthazar, Amiens and Pandarus, all of whom protest that they possess scant musical abilities.[96] But this overlooks an analogously insincere convention of expressing extreme modesty in the prefaces of books where Elizabethan authors repeatedly mock-dismiss their trifling literary efforts. Thus, when Pericles is praised as 'music's master' by King Simonides he protests, only politely, 'The worst of all her scholars, my good lord' (9.23–8). Seeing through Balthazar's self-deprecation in advance of his own singing, Don Pedro says, 'It is the witness still of excellency / To put a strange face on his own perfection' (*Much Ado* 2.3.45–6).

This is not to say that all music-making by Shakespeare characters is virtuous. Some is self-deceiving, or self-serving, or even deliberately fraudulent. Thus, as noted, Hugh Evans in *The Merry Wives* attempts to sing in order to beguile himself from terror at the prospect of a duel. The wedding musicians in *Romeo and Juliet* seem wholly unconcerned that they have been hired to help celebrate the forced marriage of the very young girl, although such a marriage would certainly have seemed abusive to many of Shakespeare's contemporaries.[97] The seducer, deceiver and would-be rapist Proteus in *Two Gentlemen of Verona* (probably) sings the beautiful song 'Who is Silvia? What is she',[98] while the betrayed Julia, listening, says 'The musician likes me not' (4.2.38–55). In *All's Well that Ends Well* the married Bertram lustfully besieges the virginal Diana: 'Every night he comes / With musics of all sorts' (3.7.39–40). The revolting Cloten in *Cymbeline* also hires serenading musicians, hoping that 'horse hairs and calves' guts' and 'the voice of unpaved eunuch' (2.3.28–9) will help him to 'penetrate [Imogen] with your fingering . . . we'll try with tongue too' (2.3.13–14). Pandarus sings an obscene lyric in *Troilus and Cressida* to spur on lust (3.1.111–23), Iago sings drinking songs in *Othello* to undermine Cassio (2.3.63–7, 82–9), and Autolycus sings in *The Winter's Tale* to divert attention from his purse-cutting (4.4.219–30, 313–21). None of these cases, in which music is used for deception rather than honest expression, gains Shakespeare's approval.

In relation to musical honesty in a Shakespeare play, W.H. Auden makes a peculiar distinction between a 'called-for song', which is 'sung by one character at the request of another who wishes to hear some music', and an 'impromptu song', where the singing serves to 'relieve [the singer's] feelings in a way that speech cannot do'.[99] Very oddly, it seems to me, Auden holds that 'An impromptu song is not art but a form of personal behaviour'. That exclusion cannot be accepted here, because several important Shakespearean female musicians use musical *art* to give vent to intensely felt emotions. We will turn to those women presently, after a preparatory discussion of music and sex.

Music, sex, scandal and three Shakespearean women singers

The third unlawfull Concomitant of Stage-plays,
is efeminate, delicate, lust-provoking Musicke

The epigraph above heads a section of William Prynne's 1632 anti-theatrical *Histrio-Mastix* that proposes as the major premise of a syllogism, 'That which is always accompanied with lascivious, amorous, voluptuous Musique, is doubtless inexpedient and unlawfull unto Christians', and as the minor premise, 'Stage-plays are always accompanied with such Musicke.'[100] The conclusion, that stage plays are unlawful, still left Prynne space to accept the virtues of religious music, which he did approve. However, other authors in Shakespeare's age who have received a great deal of attention from modern critics express a belief that all music effeminizes men and is lust-provoking.[101] The purpose of this section will be to show that Shakespeare's work does not support that belief.

Anti-musical notions are, however, expressed by some Shakespearean characters. These are for the most part immature, thuggish or swaggeringly militaristic men. Thus in *Richard III* the tyrant-to-be laments 'this weak piping time of peace' (1.1.24). When compelled to peace-making, the misguided young Coriolanus sarcastically invokes a spirit he finds at once whorish, unmanning, musical, feminine and maternal: 'possess me / Some harlot's spirit. My throat of war be turned, / Which choired with my drum, into a pipe / Small as an eunuch or the virgin voice / That babies lull asleep!' (3.2.111–15). Shakespeare's bellicose Hotspur derides Glendower's claims to have 'framed to the harp / Many an English ditty lovely well' (*1 Henry IV* 3.1.120–1). In addition to rejecting music and poetry, Hotspur also shuns his loving wife's bed when anticipating battle (2.4.37–9).

We must bear in mind that Shakespeare consistently favours humanistic and irenic attitudes over militaristic ones, and

disapproves of those seeing war and violence as manly.[102] Thus
a comeuppance follows the would-be hyper-masculine Benedick
lamenting the changed state of his 'in love' friend Claudio: 'I
have known when there was no music with him but the drum
and the fife, and now had he rather hear the tabor and the pipe'
(*Much Ado* 2.3.12–14). However, Shakespeare shows a more
amused tolerance when the two adolescent princes in *Cymbeline*
fear that to sing about emotions is feminizing or unmanning.
First the elder brother dismisses the younger brother's beautiful
spoken 'obsequies' for the supposedly dead Fidele/Imogen,
saying 'do not play in wench-like words' (4.2.231). Then, when
the younger brother proposes that they sing for her the lovely
lyric 'Fear no more the heat of the sun', the elder brother insists
that they only 'word', or 'speak', or 'say our song' (4.2.241–
55). So these young lads, striving to be more 'mannish',[103]
attempt to avoid the 'wench-like' and fall headlong into comic
gender stereotypes.[104]

Prynne's complaint that stage-play music is 'lust-provoking'
may seem to be supported by Linda Austern's observation that
on the Elizabethan stage 'many of the most beautiful and
intricately set songs are assigned to courtesan characters or
other lovers in seduction scenes'. Austern reminds us that this
derives from precedents in classical theatre where skilful
courtesans often play music.[105] But here Shakespeare disregards
the precedents and prostitution has nothing to do with the
virtuous Desdemona being 'an admirable musician' (*Othello*
4.1.184), or with fastidious Benedick desiring a wife who is not
only 'Rich', 'Wise', 'Virtuous' and 'Noble', but also 'an excellent
musician, and her hair shall be of what colour it please God'
(*Much Ado* 2.3.29–34). In *Pericles*, Marina is actually sold to a
Bawd, but then reverses the association of musicianship with
harlotry to win fame by singing professionally 'like one
immortal' (20.3).

Thus Shakespearean practice largely thrusts aside Prynne's
views of stage music. It also fails to conform to associated
generalizations such as that in Elizabethan drama 'the musician
is evocative most often of the negative effects of his practice,

associated with drunkenness, popular festivals, prostitution, and most basically, madness'.[106] Such views are belied in Shakespeare's work when sober and virtuous Prince Pericles is praised as 'music's master' (9.28), which typifies how numerous high-placed Shakespearean characters show deep appreciation of, and sometimes skill in, music.

Thus, broadly-based assessments of how music or musicians were 'most often' presented on Elizabethan stages may not be fully applicable to Shakespeare's work. Very helpfully, some critics have carefully differentiated Shakespeare's views of music-making from those of other Elizabethan dramatists. For instance, David O'Neill shows that, in contrast to John Marston's allusions to music, Shakespeare's do not generally raise images of 'lust', nor of 'discord and strife ... harsh revenges ... ugliness of all kinds'.[107] Also, a wide-ranging comparative study by Rochelle Smith finds that Shakespeare's contrary practice actually altered the norm whereby 'Female singing in late sixteenth- and early seventeenth-century drama most often serves as a clear and unambiguous expression of a licentious female sexuality'. According to Smith, 'In the plays that follow *Othello* ... the rejected but faithful lover becomes almost as popular a singing character as the promiscuous courtesan'. She concludes that Desdemona, although sexually vital, is the diametrical opposite of any benighted male's 'subtitle whore', and 'Her singing ... becomes an expression of her love for Othello, the fullest expression of her chaste and mature sexuality'.[108] Of course, this interpretation of the much-debated (Folio only) Willow Song scene contrasts with other ones. The deciding factor must be how Shakespeare presents his three main female musicians.

These women are Desdemona, Ophelia and the Jailor's Daughter in *The Two Noble Kinsmen*. Although their circumstances differ widely,[109] all three reveal through their singing what custom and propriety would have them conceal: their erotic sorrows. The erotic element in their songs raises, I think, much more significant questions of decorum than the issue of where and to whom these women sing. However, those lesser matters may be discussed first.

Some observe that Desdemona sings in the privacy of her bedchamber and solely in the presence of a female companion, and this has seemed acceptable or admirable to some recent critics.[110] Similarly, Peter Seng notes that Ophelia sings only to an 'intimate' audience – first before just two and then before four auditors – and proposes that her singing would not have scandalized any but a very 'puristic' courtier.[111] However, many other critics repeat the view that singing inherently disgraces Shakespeare's women. Let me start with Desdemona, arguing that this may not be correct.

The 'Duke' of Venice appears in two Shakespeare plays as a figure more similar to an English town's mayor than the *Serenissimo Principe* that he was addressed as, and was, in reality. So in *The Merchant of Venice* he presides over a 'law-merchant' tribunal in a dispute over a debt.[112] In the course of the trial Shylock says should his bond not be honoured, 'let the danger light / Upon your charter and your city's freedom' (4.1.37–8), making Venice equivalent to an English city subordinate to the Crown. The Venetian Duke in *Othello* sits in judgement on a domestic dispute brought by an outraged father, which again would have been absurd in historical Venice.[113] So, Shakespeare's Republic of Venice has a distinctly citizen, even a domestic, aspect. Such a view is tonally embedded in *Othello*, where the tragic hero is a man of only middling station (an alien soldier, only temporarily a governor).[114] Othello's downfall is not, moreover, a dynastic tragedy but rather a domestic one, and correspondingly the play progresses inexorably into increasingly enclosed spaces, from a street, to a council chamber, to an island camp, and finally into the private bedchamber of a marriage. Also, the prominence of Desdemona's patrician origins continually diminishes through the play as her isolation from her city and family increases. Although she was educated in music-making when the daughter of a senator, her later singing may be judged by other standards – and the song she sings derives from her mother's maid, Barbary.

If we consider citizen-class Tudor and Jacobean women, we find something very surprising: that they could be made free of

the London Companies of Minstrels or Musicians. The
regulations of the Brotherhood of the King's Minstrels, which
was granted a charter by Edward IV in 1469, allowed the
Company 'to receive, to admit and to accept as brothers and
sisters of the said Brotherhood or Guild, whatsoever persons,
both men and women, adhering to them with loyal intention'.
The London Company of Musicians, a descendant of that
guild, was chartered in 1603. It issued bylaws in 1606 with
the main aim of restricting competition in an overcrowded
profession and also empowering the Company to suppress any
'evening or morning' playing of music 'under any nobleman,
knight or gentleman's window' (such as is played in the early-
morning *Othello*, as will be discussed in the next chapter).
Those bylaws also allowed for women members of the
Company, referring to matters 'concerning . . . any brother or
sister of the . . . fellowship', and 'the burial of a brother or sister
of the said fellowship'.[115] We do not know precisely who these
Elizabethan 'sisters' were, or how many of them there were
(because unhappily the membership records of the Company
have been lost[116]), but see, nevertheless, that professional female
musicians were countenanced in Shakespeare's England.
Clearly, Shakespeare's female musicians are not modelled on
the renowned professional female singers of contemporary
Italy,[117] or on the 'sisters' of the London Company of Musicians
either. Yet the very existence of the latter suggests that we
should discard an often-repeated blanket notion that all
Elizabethan women musicians were inherently disgraced.[118]

This brings us to the question of whether Shakespeare's
three singing women were degraded not on account of the fact
that they sang, but on account of what they sang. One study
alleges that 'Christian theology' maintained belief in 'a broad
gulf between humanity and the base Nature that guarded
incomprehensible secrets, leaving civilized society surrounded
by a threatening universe full of uncontrollable passion and
animal instinct'. Music, as opposed to rational language, was
therefore aligned with 'the wild sensuality of animal pleasure'.[119]
In my opinion, Shakespeare rejects such dire views of sensual

pleasure by dramatizing them as characteristic of his dire Angelo, Pandarus, Iago and Thersites. These scabrous, hypocritical or destructive characters *do* relegate human sexual drives to the animal realm, and by inversion their author commends toleration of those very drives.

Moreover, despite their evident erotic contents, the songs sung by Shakespeare's three desperately unhappy young women are not in any way comparable with, for instance, Autolycus' bawdy 'love songs for maids . . . with such delicate burdens of dildoes and fadings, "jump her and thump her"' (*The Winter's Tale* 4.4.194–6), or with the unpleasantly obscene lyrics that Pandarus sings for Helen in *Troilus and Cressida* (3.1.111–23). Rather, for all three of Shakespeare's singing women erotic life is a serious topic, neither risible nor abhorrent, and their songs give us access to this seriousness. As Inga-Stina Ewbank says, Shakespeare's songs are 'dramatically functional, and one of their functions . . . is to say what could not be said in the plays where they occur'.[120] Heather Dubrow likewise proposes that in Shakespeare, 'Even as song participates in the spectrum of various types of heightened or lyricized speech, it often insists on its difference from other registers and on its ability to authorize new types of insight and to write a new set of rules.'[121]

Indeed, the otherwise unsayable, as well as new types of insight, are uncovered when Shakespeare's unhappy women sing. Ophelia's first song is of a true love's death, possibly conflating her loss of Hamlet with that of her father. She then sings about St Valentine's Day, when a 'maid' willingly loses her virginity, and next of a girl who complains, 'Before you tumbled me. / You promised me to wed', to which the male reply is, 'So would I 'a done, by yonder sun, / An thou hadst not come to my bed' (4.5.35–65). She sings several more snatches of songs imaging loss, betrayal and frustrated sexual desires. These include the line 'For bonny sweet robin is all my joy' (4.5.185) – commentators have pointed out the traditional phallic overtones of 'robin' in verse and song.[122] Such images are not derived from the virginal Ophelia's experience, but, dream-like, track her unconscious emotions.

Just after shockingly being struck by Othello in public, Desdemona finds that the Willow Song 'Will not go from my mind' (Folio text only, 4.3.30).[123] The Willow Song, however, does not concern marital abuse *per se*, but rather a breakdown of trust and commitment. Desdemona learned it from her mother's maid, Barbary, who was forsaken in love and then died (4.3.25–32). Ernst Brennecke carefully analyses Desdemona's rendition of this song and concludes that she sings it 'as if in a dream or a deep reverie, thereby revealing more of her subconscious awareness than any spoken words could indicate'.[124] Indeed, as if a dream, the Willow Song exhibits a mixture of parallels, inversions and displacements. Desdemona has been unjustly accused of infidelity, while inversely the man who rejects the woman in the song is the unfaithful one, a 'false love'. Yet in parallel, Barbary's beloved has 'proved mad', as apparently Hamlet has also. A further inversion of Desdemona's circumstances arises when Barbary's 'false love' becomes a libertine and declares, 'If I court more women, you'll couch with more men' (4.3.53–5). By contrast, Othello is overcome by sexual revulsion (3.3.401). As Freud explained, taking examples from Shakespeare, the unconscious often substitutes opposites for one another.[125]

Ophelia and Desdemona die, one by suicide and the other by murder, but the Jailor's Daughter in *The Two Noble Kinsmen* lives thanks to a wise physician. He determines that the Daughter has become 'distracted' on account of unrequited passion and sexual frustration; her songs include the phrases 'O for a prick now, like a nightingale, / To put my breast against. I shall sleep like a top else' (3.4.25–6) and 'O let me have your company / Till I come to the sound-a' (3.5.65–6). The Doctor's prescription for healing the erotically addled girl is to instruct her spurned suitor to 'Lie with her if she ask you ... in the way of cure' (5.4.19–20). The Daughter does ask, saying, 'And then we'll sleep together' (5.4.111), and is duly cured.

Such compassionate understanding by a Doctor who correctly reads the erotic cause of a mental breakdown would have been in accord with the Elizabethan norm if his patient had been male.[126] Shakespeare and Fletcher's Doctor is most unusual in proposing a cure for a female musician and sufferer.

Shakespeare's most 'hands-on' musician

Finally, let us consider the female musician addressed and apotheosized in Shakespeare's Sonnet 128 as 'my music'.

Her naming as such is a supreme compliment that draws on the famous doctrine that musical harmony sets the pattern for all the harmony in the cosmos, the state, the family, the soul and the human body. The difference between such *musica speculativa* and *musica practica* has been much discussed in the Renaissance as well as by modern scholars. As we have noted, it is seen from an unusual perspective by the practical Thomas Whythorne who identifies 'musicians that be named speculators' as those who have nothing at all to do with making audible music.[127] Nevertheless, Sonnet 128 wittily jumps the gap between idealizing a woman as 'my music' and very practical matters, including hearing music audible to the 'eare'. It begins:

> How oft when thou my musike musike playst,
> Upon that blessed wood whose motion sounds
> With thy sweet fingers when thou gently swayst,
> The wiry concord that mine eare confounds . . .

In the first line above the topic of a schism between *musica speculativa* and *musica practica* is engaged immediately via a rhetorical *antistasis* in which two differing meanings of *music* are juxtaposed: 'my *musike*' meaning the basis of all harmony for me, and '*musike* playst' referring to music that can be heard. In the doubling up '*musike musike*' the typically contrasted territories of audible and ideal music collide, or collude, in a most unusual way that may subvert their conventional hierarchy. This certainly demands investigation.

Shakespeare's take on the doctrines of speculative music is most complex. For instance, he several times slights *musica speculativa*, or, more exactly, its subcategory *musica mundane*, when he alludes to the music of the spheres in jocular or erotically charged contexts.[128] Yet he also allows his redeemed Pericles to hear that music in good earnest (21.215). In Sonnet 8, the two kinds of music are conflated as one, for the octave criticizes a young man for resistance or insensitivity to the pleasures of audible 'Musick to heare' and then the sestet merges this into a *musica humana* metaphor in which 'speechless' (silent) music represents the harmonies of marriage and fatherhood:

> Marke how one string sweet husband to an other,
> Strikes each in each by mutuall ordering;
> Resembling sier, and child, and happy mother,
> Who all in one, one pleasing note do sing:
> Whose speechlesse song being many, seeming one,
> Sings this to thee thou single wilt proue none.

The seamless equivalence made in this sonnet between music that is heard and the music that is the basis of all human harmonies seems to be a witty gesture, rather than a philosophical one. By Shakespeare's time discourses of speculative music (although still omnipresent) were becoming threadbare from overuse, and were being increasingly displaced by affective and scientific theories of musical power. So in common with other scholars Erin Minear claims that 'The connection between earthly music and heavenly harmony ... was on the verge of breakdown at the end of the sixteenth century.'[129] Imagery of heavenly harmony is in fact traduced when the preposterously vain Jaques in *As You Like It* is described as 'One who the music of his own vain tongue / Doth ravish like enchanting harmony' (1.1.164–5), and when Hortensio in *The Taming of the Shrew*, having claimed allegiance to 'The patroness of heavenly harmony' (3.1.5), enters with his lute broken over his head.

Nevertheless, there is no sense that Shakespeare mocks the old doctrines when his speaker in Sonnet 128 addresses a woman as 'my musike'. Rather, this phrase associates her with perfect harmony no less than do the first thirteen lines of Sidney's *Astrophil and Stella* Sonnet 71, which offer a thoroughly Platonizing description of *Stella*. The famous conclusion of Sidney's sonnet, however, suddenly recalls the earthy and material in relation to Stella: 'So while thy beautie drawes the heart to love, / As fast as Vertue bends that love to good. / "But ah," Desire still cries, "give me some food".' As we shall see, Shakespeare's Sonnet 128 also reintroduces the material and physical following a Platonizing gesture. However, it does this more subtly and using more unconventional imagery than does Sidney's sonnet.

By means of the *antistasis* in line one the woman in Sonnet 128 addressed as 'my musike' is promptly identified as someone who *oft* plays audible 'musike', no doubt excellent Elizabethan keyboard music.[130] The question we must ask in order to understand this sonnet is 'when does she play it?' The answer, as we shall see, is that she plays at some time other than the time of the encounter referred to in the sonnet. The first hint of this comes in the striking oxymoron in line 4: 'The . . . concord that mine eare confounds'. This is extremely paradoxical, for Shakespeare often uses the word 'concord' in contexts where it is opposed to a contrary notion of a musical discord.[131] Yet to 'confound' means at least to surprise and confuse,[132] and possibly also to ruin, defeat utterly, destroy, spoil, corrupt or waste.[133] So, confounding 'mine eare' must mean by discord. How, we must ask, can musical 'concord' confound the 'eare'?

Despite the misapprehensions of some scholars, this and several other riddles of the poem are resolved by the realization that the lady in the sonnet is not described as playing music, but rather as preparing to do so by tuning her instrument. This realization was arrived at long ago by E.W. Naylor but has been noticed only sporadically since, with many still assuming that the encounter in the poem has her playing music.[134] It seems that Naylor and the few who have noted him do not explain themselves sufficiently to be generally understood, and indeed they do not precisely identify all of the many aspects that make the connections between the poem and the description of tuning proposed by Naylor. Here a focus on the activities of a musician prompts us to reveal those connections in detail.

It is first necessary to note that the mention of 'Iackes' in line 13 of Sonnet 128 proves that the lady is dealing with a 'virginals', which word signified in Shakespeare's England 'any jack action instrument'.[135] (In Elizabethan parlance, 'harpsichord', 'virginal', 'virginals' and 'spinet' were interchangeable terms.) A second crucial point is that considerable irony attends the above-mentioned oxymoron 'concord . . . confounds' if we understand it to represent 'concord/discord'. For then it would allude to the ancient trope of *concordia discors*, which involved a *conceptual* notion of creating harmony out of disharmony, of finding 'the concord of this discord' as Theseus puts it in *A Midsummer's Night's Dream* (5.1.60). The poem's great joke is that while making this allusion the speaker is not being conceptual at all. Rather, he describes his 'eare' actually being physically confounded by particular discordant sounds. The poem's opening phrase, 'How oft . . .' refers only to a *recollection* of having heard being played the wonderful English keyboard compositions of the likes of Bull, Byrd, Wilbye, Farnaby or Morley.

This is possible and rational because a very particular and literal sort of *concordia discors* is very precisely described in Shakespeare's poem. Discord is made into concord in the scene described in Sonnet 128 through the physical act of regulating (adjusting the mechanism of) and tuning the strings of a discordant virginals, thereby *preparing* it for the playing of concordant music.

The poem makes its radical turn to detailed physical description in lines 3 and 4: 'With thou sweet fingers when thou gently swayst, / The wiry concord that mine eare confounds'. What is *wiry* are the wire strings of the virginals; the *swaying* is the careful adjustment of their tension back and forth to bring them into tune, or 'concord'; the *confounding* of the ear is due to the sounds heard when out-of-tune strings are *gently* corrected.

Matters even more physical are described in the second quatrain, which names the 'Jackes' of a virginals or harpsichord. Some technical background is required to explain this.[136] Harpsichord jacks are light wooden assemblages that are thrown upwards when the player strikes a key. The keys are simple levers that pivot around their balance pins and at their far end push up the jacks. Each key-propelled jack carries with it a hinged mechanism, called a tongue, from which a projecting part, called the plectrum, protrudes. The flexible plectra are made from thin pieces of crow or raven's quill, and each plectrum is positioned so that on its jack's upwards journey it will catch and pluck the string corresponding with the key pressed. 'Jack' has a root implying suddenness, and also shares a root with 'javelin'. Indeed, when being kicked up, a jack might fly out of the instrument like a javelin,[137] but normally this is prevented by the placement of the 'jack rail', a single padded bar of wood that crosses the instrument in a position above the upwards path of all the jacks. When a key is released its jack (in larger instruments sometimes multiple jacks for each key) descends again. It is necessary that when the plectra pass by the strings on their downward journeys they do not pluck them a second time. This is enabled by a mechanism whereby each plectrum and its tongue swings away from its string when its jack falls downward. That mechanism is an escapement-like hinging of each tongue, using a very light spring made of boar's bristle. Its proper operation requires the careful tapering of the underside of each plectrum.

Fine tolerances are involved in such keyboard mechanisms, and wooden virginals or harpsichords often require adjustment, for instance when temperature or humidity changes, or when parts wear or relax after playing. Then some strings may need to be retuned or some plectra trimmed with a sharp blade to ensure good and equal sound across the keyboard. Even very experienced players require considerable time to complete the 'voicing', as it is called, of a virginals or harpsichord. As they test and adjust an instrument they make a good deal of noise, which takes us back to Shakespeare's sonnet.

As mentioned, a well-padded jack rail prevents the jacks from excessive upwards movement. However, 'voicing' an instrument requires the removal of the jack rail so that its jacks may be taken out and adjusted. With the jack rail removed and the keys struck to test notes, the thrown-up jacks are free to continue their upward motion and can exit the instrument. To prevent this, the lady in the poem cups the palm of her hand above the jacks while striking keys with her other hand, thus catching any light jack that attempts to fly away. Shakespeare's narrator observes this, noting how the jacks 'leape / To kisse the tender inward of thy hand', while the lady's fingers 'walke with gentle gate' as she moves along the keyboard, adjusting each note in turn. Thus the 'chips' referred to are the 'Iackes', which are 'blest' and 'happy' because they kiss her hand. The speaker would like to do the same, and begs for even more: 'thy lips to kisse'. The sonnet therefore turns from idealization of a woman to the erotic and corporeal, just as Sidney's sonnet does, but it goes by a quite different route, using unique and surprising physical imagery.

The physicality of the sonnet's imaging of a harpsichord's inner working is, I believe, even more significant than the sexual innuendoes in the language of the poem that some critics have detected.[138] The leaping jacks imaged in the poem are quite accurately described as 'nimble', 'sausie' and 'dancing'. The poem's structure also seems nimble and dancing as each of its themes greets the others in turn; a dancing syncopation of themes would seem a fair description of its organization. Thus the woman described in this poem is a very practical artist, and yet one bridging multiple worlds. Intensely involved in a complex physical activity required *before* the production of art, she also prepares to play a kind of musical repertoire that bridged the distinction now made (but not then) between lively 'dancing' art and serious high art. For most of the great complex Elizabethan keyboard music was based on dance measures. Finally this woman, the artist, is seen as a worker in the world of material things, whose efforts will make life and vigour shine out of 'dead wood'.[139]

A segue

Paving the way to our next chapter, let us further consider certain Shakespearean reactions to Elizabethan musical culture. The circulation of musical manuscripts and frequent republication of editions indicates the widespread popularity of what might be called Elizabethan art music. I have argued elsewhere that John Dowland-like sophisticated music was likely heard on Shakespeare's stage.[140] Some of Shakespeare's plays may also have alluded to Dowland's famous songs.[141] If so, this contradicts one critic's contention that Shakespeare failed to 'record the [contemporary] pressure toward a conscious art of music'. Part of the evidence offered for that claim is the assertion that Shakespeare was 'either unaware of or uninterested in' the Elizabethan madrigal.[142] However, Christopher Wilson gives better reasons why no madrigals were performed on Shakespeare's stages: these are that madrigals subordinate their texts to the music, and also typically require multiple voices, 'involving soprano, alto, tenor and bass pitches', whereas 'Shakespeare's company contained at best one adult singer and no females'.[143]

The advanced music of John Dowland and his peers was more suitable for drama, and also more avant-garde, than madrigals.[144] Dowland's professional persona was advertised in the titling of one of his consort pieces: 'Semper Dowland, semper dolens'.[145] Although some of Dowland's songs are sprightly,[146] the most famous among his Ayres is 'Flow my Tears', which epitomizes the Elizabethan vogue for melancholy.[147] Dowland's style of music, written for stringed instruments and/ or highly adept singers, is properly described as structurally and harmonically advanced, emotionally deep and sophisticated, and even intellectual.

Although Dowland's music may have been alluded to by Shakespeare, and possibly even heard during one of his plays, it is just the sort of music that is explicitly rejected by Benedick in *Much Ado*: 'Now, divine air! Now is his soul ravished. Is it not strange that sheep's guts should hale souls out of men's bodies? Well, a horn for my money, when all's done' (2.3.57–60). Benedick's humorous preference (albeit punning on cuckoldry) for the wind-instrument music of warfare or hunting over the string-instrument accompaniment to a love song alerts us to the blaring, unrestrained sort of music played on loud wind instruments that was thought appropriate for Elizabethan military, processional or festive occasions. The use of such raw, attention-grabbing kinds of music is indicated in numerous Shakespearean contexts that call for hautboys, cornets or trumpets,[148] and its purveyors sometimes appear as minor Shakespearean characters, such as the trumpeter addressed in *Troilus and Cressida* (4.6.7–10), or the town waits who, it is implied, are the impoverished musicians hired in for Juliet's aborted wedding. Indeed, if we attend to certain mythological allusions, deliberately loud, even honking, musical players can be seen to be crucially important in some Shakespeare plays. To these we turn next.

6

Shakespeare's Mythical Musicians

Myths operate in men's minds without their being aware of the fact

CLAUDE LÉVI-STRAUSS[1]

The oboe is an ill-wind that nobody blows good

OLD MUSICIAN'S GAG

Prospectus

Applying a principle of *cherchez l'artiste*, this chapter will identify two mythological musicians. These two are never explicitly named by Shakespeare, but it will be argued that their presence is strongly felt in two of his plays.[2] Thus I will argue that the famous story of the musician Marsyas has complex ramified connections with the text and main themes of *The Merchant of Venice*, and that an anecdote about the mythical musician Babys (Βαβυς) helps to untangle certain textual and structural conundrums in *Othello*.

More specifically, the world of *The Merchant of Venice* is full of raucous noises corresponding with insubordination, prejudice, jeering and spite. Examining the myth of the defiant and tragic pipe-playing satyr Marsyas alongside that raucousness will produce new perspectives on the play. The very odd provision of a failed serenade in *Othello* may likewise be better understood if we consider the reputation of the mythological musician Babys (who was said to be Marsyas' brother).

The satyr Marsyas' contest with the musician god Apollo was very frequently represented and elaborated upon by classical and Renaissance writers and visual artists. Their fascination with this loudly insubordinate satyr probably owed to the fact that his claim for pre-eminence in music over a god recklessly foregoes the usual tactics used by artists who intended to expose the flaws or weaknesses of the powerful. When challenging authority, Shakespeare in common with other artists deployed modes of indirection, such as displacing narratives to remote times or places, shielding topicalities under genre conventions, or using comic types to enunciate dangerous points.[3] Marsyas does none of that, and is horribly punished for his *hubris*, thereby attracting many artists' pity and possibly also their veiled admiration.

Before turning to Shakespearean adumbrations of the skilled but defeated Marsyas, and the unskilled but equally unashamed musician Babys, let us review briefly some other more explicit Shakespearean allusions to musicians in classical myth. In several cases their stories reveal the vulnerability of artists to indifference or to violence, a topic that will have continuing interest in this chapter.

Vulnerable mythical musicians alluded to by Shakespeare

Shakespeare mentions the musician god Apollo, the rival of Marsyas in the myth, more than twenty times.[4] In *Love's Labour's Lost* (4.3.318–19, 5.2.13–14) and *The Taming of the Shrew* (Induction 2.23), Apollo is a golden-voiced singer descanting on the themes of love or luxury, but in *The Winter's Tale* (4.4.25–31) the disguised Prince Florizel foolishly brackets his own wooing with that of 'Golden Apollo' and other lustful deities self-transformed into lesser beings or beasts. Thersites in *Troilus and Cressida* (3.3.293–4) contemptuously refers to 'the fiddler Apollo'. Renaissance visual artworks to be discussed presently sometimes depict Apollo as a fiddler, while several writers represent him in his musical encounter with Marsyas as prideful, underhanded and cruel.

Shakespeare names Orpheus, or invokes him as 'the Thracian poet' or 'Thracian singer', six times. On five of those occasions his musicianship is said to be a miraculous tamer of gross matter, wild nature or ravening beasts.[5] However, in the sixth instance Shakespeare refers to the very violent myth in which Orpheus is dismembered by a band of enraged followers of Dionysus who cannot hear him. Thus Theseus in *A Midsummer Night's Dream* expresses sophisticated distaste for 'an old device' that 'was played / When I from Thebes came last a conqueror', a portrayal of a 'riot of the tipsy bacchanals / Tearing the Thracian singer in their rage' (5.1.48–51). The insensitive Theseus is jaded about this 'device', yet Shakespeare may expect us to be appalled by the brutal killing of a musical artist.

In *The Tempest* Sebastian and Antonio derisively allude to the Orphic myth of Amphion raising the walls of Thebes by playing his harp. Thus they ridicule Gonzalo's remarks about Dido's Tunis, bandying between them: 'His word is more than the miraculous harp'; 'He hath raised the wall, and houses too'; 'What impossible matter will he make easy next?' (2.1.91–4). While deriding the old counsellor, these two cynics also label the powers of Amphion's music 'impossible'.

The musician god Mercury, or his Greek model Hermes, is named sixteen times by Shakespeare. He is most often referred to as a swift and cunning messenger, but is also mentioned jocularly or wryly in connection with music-making. Thus the musicality of Hermes' 'pipe' is referenced in the course of a *blazon* of a horse in *Henry V* (3.7.17–18), while two of Shakespeare's professional musicians, Feste in *Twelfth Night*

(1.5.93) and Autolycus in *The Winter's Tale* (4.3.25), identify Mercury as their patron – Mercury being the patron of poets, performers and thieves.[6]

When Thesus in *A Midsummer Night's Dream* arranges for Queen Hippolyta to join in a hunt and hear 'the music of my hounds ... the musical confusion' (4.1.105–9), Hippolyta replies, 'I was with Hercules and Cadmus once / When in a wood of Crete they bayed the bear / With hounds of Sparta. Never did I hear ... / So musical a discord, such sweet thunder' (4.1.111–17). Both captor and captive thus suggest that the bloodthirsty 'confusion' or 'discord' of hunting dogs can be 'musical'. Of special interest to us are Hippolyta's references here to the heroes Hercules and Cadmus, for both are participants in stories connecting unfortunate musicians with violence. In one, Hercules as a youth becomes annoyed by the demands of his music tutor, Linus, and kills him using his own lyre as a weapon.[7] Force and resistance to art thus destroy an artist.

The story of Hippolyta's hunting companion Cadmus also involves music and violence. As related by Nonnos in his *Dionysiaca* (early fifth century), Cadmus disguises himself as a shepherd or goatherd playing the panpipes in order to help Zeus to recover from being vanquished by the monster Typhon, and then to help Zeus overcome Typhon. Nonnos identifies the guileful Cadmus, or his musicianship, as 'counterfeit', 'mindbefooling', 'guileful', 'deceitful' and 'deluding'.[8] Typhon is entranced by Cadmus' playing and is lured into a musical competition with him. He agrees: 'Let's have a friendly match, if you like. Come on, you make music and sound your reedy tune, I will crash my thundery tune. You puff out your cheek all swollen with wind, and blow with your lips, but Boreas is my blower, and my thunderbolts boom when his breath flogs them' (1.439). Next, wily Cadmus claims to have bettered Apollo in a stringed-instrument contest: 'I matched myself against Phoibos with his heavenly quill, and beat him with my own harp.' He adds that if he had Zeus' sinews, which Typhon has confiscated, to use as strings he would sing surpassingly of Typhon's (future) great victory: 'when you strike Zeus and the gods with your thunderbolt ... I and Phoibos may have [another] match, and see which will beat which in celebrating mighty Typhon!' (1.486–506). Book One of the *Dionysiaca* ends with Typhon yielding up Zeus' sinews. Book Two then begins with Zeus recovering his sinews and his thunderbolts, thanks to the 'turncoat herdsman' Cadmus, and then annihilating Typhon. Thus Cadmus' musical skill seeds destruction, because 'all the Giant wanted was, to hear more and more of the mind-bewitching melody with its delicious thrill. When a sailor hears the Siren's perfidious song, and bewitched by the melody, he is dragged to a self-chosen fate too soon' (2.1–19).

Multiple elements in these stories about Hercules and Cadmus – including Hercules' extreme reaction when bettered artistically, Cadmus' puffed-out cheeks 'all swollen with wind', a contrasting of wind and stringed instruments, a musician seizing victory by stealth, and a musical contest with Apollo – are echoed in the Marsyas myths to which we turn next.

Introducing Marsyas

The oft-retold story of the musical contest between the god Apollo and the satyr Marsyas begins when Marsyas finds and becomes expert on Athene's newly invented double-reeded pipe, or *aulos*. Heedless of the god's power, he then challenges the lyre- or *kithara*-playing Apollo to a musical contest, and when he loses the contest he has to pay the forfeit of being flayed alive. It is easy to access hundreds of repetitions of this story by classical authors.[9] There is also evidence that the voluminous production of depictions of Marsyas by classical and Renaissance visual artists peaked in the sixteenth century.[10] According to Maria Rika Maniates, Marsyas is 'the theme of hundreds of [classical] written accounts and visual representations – certainly more numerous than any other single figure, with the possible exception of Orpheus'. Maniates even claims that Marsyas' story is 'one of the fundamental myths of ancient culture'.[11]

In many classical and Renaissance versions of the myth, Marsyas is the superior musician and Apollo cheats in order to be judged the winner of the contest. Thus in the sixteenth century Natale Conti's *Mythologiae* presented a corrupt or pettifogging Apollo:

> Marsyas is supposed to have picked up the flute that Minerva had thrown away; and when he blew into it he thought he had become a very skilled musician. And so he challenged Apollo to a musical duel, agreeing that the winner could order the loser to do anything he wanted him to do . . . As the contest progressed, Apollo first played on the cithara, and then sang a song. But all that Marsyas could do was play the flute . . . Those writers who wanted to be a little more precise about what happened pointed out that during the period when Marsyas was competing with Apollo, Nysian judges were elected to their offices.[12]

Conti continues that in the second round of the contest Apollo sang at the same time as playing his lyre, and dared Marsyas to do the same. Marsyas then complained to the judges that his challenge concerned one instrument only. Apollo trickily countered that 'both [contestants] should abide by the same rules, i.e. either both of them or neither of them should use their mouths in the contest, or else they should both show how good they were by using only their fingers'. So Conti implies that Apollo exerts undue influence on the judges, twists the rules of the contest, and deploys logic-chopping arguments. Several other classical authors suggest similar chicanery.[13]

Pseudo-Hyginus says that when one judge of the contest, King Midas, grants victory to Marsyas, the angry Apollo gives him a pair of ass's ears (like those of the unmusical Bottom in *A Midsummer Night's Dream*). Renaissance artists often represent Midas in that plight.[14] This may seem merely comic until we remember Marsyas' notoriously cruel punishment. Marsyas' suffering is made hideously vivid in Ovid's *Metamorphoses*:

Another of a satyr straight began to make report
Whom Phoebus, overcomming on a pipe (made late ago
By Pallas), put to punishment. 'Why flayest thou me so?
Alas! he cried, It irketh me. Alas, a sorry pipe
Deserveth not so cruelly my skin from me to strip.'
For all his crying, o'er his ears quite pulled was his skin.
Nought else he was than one whole wound. The grisly
    blood did spin
From every part; the sinews lay discovered to the eye;
The quivering veins without a skin lay beating nakedly.
The panting bowels in his bulk ye might have numbered
    well,
And in his breast the sheer small strings a man might easily
    tell.[15]

Shakespeare, always highly sensitive to cruelty, would no doubt
have reacted strongly to this account in Golding's English
translation, and perhaps even more so to Ovid's original verses
which spell out the outrageous treatment of Marsyas in even
greater anatomical detail. Between howls of pain, Ovid's
Marsyas cries out, 'quid me mihi detrahis', 'Why do you tear me
from myself?'[16]

Marsyas and the disgrace of playing wind instruments

Although evaluations of Marsyas could be complex,[17] there
was one mode in which he was repeatedly held up for dispraise
from classical times onwards solely on the basis of his choice
of musical instrument. In this mode Renaissance conduct
books and many classical texts raise Marsyas' name at the
same time as they condemn the playing of a wind instrument
as unseemly, or unbefitting for freeborn citizens or gentlemen.
It will be shown that Shakespeare responded strongly to such
views, especially in *The Merchant of Venice*.

Backtracking slightly on the legend of Marsyas, we find a myth in which Pallas Athene invents the *aulos*, then while playing it either sees her contorted face reflected in water or else is mocked at a banquet for her distorted facial appearance. Athene then casts her instrument aside and Marsyas takes it up, leading on to his contest with Apollo.

Shakespeare certainly encountered accounts of Athene's acquired distaste for her *aulos*. For instance, Ovid's *Fasti*, although not yet translated, was almost surely a main source for *The Rape of Lucrece*.[18] Ovid's Athene explains:

> among my inventions is also the guild of flute-players. I was the first, by piercing boxwood with holes wide apart, to produce the music of the long flute. The sound was pleasing; but in the water that reflected my face I saw my virgin cheeks puffed up. 'I value not the art so high; farewell, my flute!' said I, and threw it away; it fell on the turf of the river-bank.[19]

Here Ovid maintains that the flute's 'inventress and foundress' rejected it because playing it marred her appearance.

Athene's unwanted instrument and its adoption by Marsyas feature in an allegorical 'fable' about bridling anger in Plutarch's *Moralia*, another text known to Shakespeare.[20] Philemon Holland's 1603 translation says that pipe playing resulted in Minerva's 'puft ... paire of cheekes', and so she eschewed it. Yet, because

> [the] art and skill of playing well upon the pipe, yeeldeth some comfort and maketh amends for the deformitie of disfigured visage, with the melodious tune and harmonie that it affoordeth ... Marsyas the Minstrell (as it is thought) devised first with a certaine hood and muzzle fastened round about the mouth, as well to restraine and keepe downe the violence of the blast enclosed thus by force, as also to correct and hide the deformitie and undecent inequalitie of the visage.[21]

Indeed, so familiar was the link between the stories of Athene rejecting her pipe and of Marsyas adopting it that Plutarch's 'Life of Alcibiades', a text used by Shakespeare when writing *Timon of Athens*, refers to the connection without even naming Marsyas. According to North's 1579 translation:

when [Alcibiades] was put to schoole to learne, he was very obedient to all his masters that taught him any thing, saving that he disdained to learne to playe of the flute or recorder: saying, that it was no gentlemanly qualitie. For, sayed he, to playe on the vyoll with a sticke, doth not alter mans favour, nor disgraceth any gentleman: but otherwise, to playe on the flute, his countenaunce altereth and chaungeth so ofte, that his familliar friends can scant knowe him. Moreover, the harpe or vyoll doth not let him that playeth on them, from speaking, or singing as he playeth: where he that playeth on the flute, holdeth his mouth so harde to it, that it taketh not only his wordes from him, but his voyce. Therefore, sayed he, let the children of the THEBANS playe on the flute, that cannot tell howe to speake: as for us ATHENIANS, we have (as our forefathers tell us) for protectours and patrones of our countrie, and goddesse Pallas, and the god Apollo: of the which the one in olde time (as it is sayed) brake the flute, and the other pulled his skinne over his eares, that played upon the flute. Thus Alcibiades alledging these reasons, partly in sporte, and partly in good earnest: dyd not only him selfe leave to learne to playe on the flute, but he turned his companions mindes also quite from it. For these wordes of Alcibiades, ranne from boye to boye incontinently: that Alcibiades had reason to despise playing of the flute, and that he mocked all those that learned to play of it. So afterwards, it fell out at ATHENS, that teaching to playe of the flute, was put out of the number of honest and liberall exercises, and the flute it selfe was thought a vile instrument, and of no reputation.[22]

Here Apollo and Pallas Athene are named, while Marsyas is merely alluded to by mention of his fate ('pulled his skinne over his eares').

Interestingly, North's Plutarch calls the musical instrument that Alcibiades thinks ill suited to noble youths a 'flute', although it was in the ancient myth a double-reeded *aulos*. The Renaissance habit of updating the identity of the musical instruments in Marsyas' story will be of particular interest to us presently. Of first importance, though, is Plutarch's description of Alcibiades' personal aversion spreading to his peers and then to his nation, so that his distaste for playing a wind instrument became a cultural attitude. Similar attitudes pertained in Elizabethan times. So, John Case's *The Praise of Musicke* (1586) discusses 'daintines', while defending music against detractors:

> those men, who, as if they came from some finer moulde, like well inough of musicke in others, but cannot away with it themselves. They are delighted for examples sake with the well proportioned pictures of *Jupiter*, *Juno* and *Venus*, but yet would not be *Phidias*, *Policlet* [Polykleitos] or *Praxiteles*.[23]

As an excuse for such fastidious avoidance of playing music, the author adds: 'I will speak thus much, & my speech is abetted by good authors that both a choice of musicke is to be made, and a moderation therein retained. Minerva ... cast away hir pshawime [on account of ugliness] for very shame.'[24] Immediately following this is 'And amongst us every one will not blow a bagpipe, that wil finger a Lute or Virginals'.

A concatenation in *The Praise of Musicke* of Minerva's disfiguring shawm playing and bagpipe blowing points towards a topic that will become crucial in the following discussions. For now, let us take from this passage the lesson that playing the lute or virginals is acceptable in 'men' of 'finer moulde', but playing a wind instrument is not. This was, however, deemed appropriate to the lower orders, so that, as we have noted, servants in training at Christ's Hospital were taught to play both wind and stringed instruments. Likewise, Thomas Deloney's artisan shoemakers subscribe to the following agreement regarding wind playing: 'what Journey-man . . . that cannot . . . sound the Trumpet, or play upon the Flute, or bear his Part in a Three-man's song . . . shall forfeit and pay a Bottle of Wine, or be counted for a Colt.'[25] Christopher Marsh confirms more broadly that it was acceptable for higher-status recreational musicians in England to play stringed or keyboard instruments, but not wind instruments.[26]

Given this, we may detect a weight of extra anger in Hamlet's suggestion that Guildenstern aims to 'play upon me . . . pluck out the heart of my mystery . . . sound me from my lowest note to the top of my compass' (3.2.351–60), which follows his suggestion that his erstwhile friend might be skilled in playing what he calls within a few lines a 'recorder' or a 'pipe' (3.2.332–9). For making that suggestion is a veiled insult, Hamlet knowing full well that an *au courant* university man when asked, 'Will you play upon this pipe?' must reply, as Guildenstern does, 'I have not the skill' (3.2.338–50).[27]

Hamlet's allegation that Guildenstern might play a pipe is insulting for social and aesthetic reasons, because in the Renaissance (as in antiquity) blowing a wind instrument was held to produce disgraceful disfigurement. Shakespeare shows himself aware that breath control and embouchure may produce a tensed mouth, corded neck, furrowed forehead, inflated cheeks and even protruding eyes. His crude Ajax in *Troilus and Cressida* thus demands that a hireling trumpeter:

crack thy lungs and split thy brazen pipe.
Blow, villain, till thy sphered bias cheek
Outswell the colic of puffed Aquilon.
Come, stretch thy chest and let thy eyes spout blood.

(4.6.7–10)

Such un-genteel appearances may account for the fact, noted by John Hollander, that in the graphic arts, 'the Platonic notion of the World-Soul (as well as the individual psyche) considered as a [musical] tuning, or *harmonia*, finds figurative expression in the image of the World-Lyre, or the stringed instrument of the human soul. One seldom sees, during the Renaissance or Medieval periods, any such figure employing a wind or percussive instrument.'[28] Un-genteel appearances may likewise resonate with the supposed inferiority of Marsyas' puffing into his *aulos* in a contest with Apollo's refined *kithara* playing. This notion extended through the opinion of Plutarch's Alcibiades that playing a wind instrument, like Marsyas, 'disgraceth any gentleman' and through Castiglione's crucially influential *Book of the Courtier*, where Federico explicitly endorses both Alcibiades' and Athene's rejection of 'flute' playing.[29]

Marsyas, visual imagery and *The Merchant of Venice*

Although critics have shown very few Shakespearean connections to the myth of Marsyas,[30] strong correspondences can be demonstrated between that myth and important concerns in *The Merchant of Venice*. Textual aspects of the play will become significant later, but let us begin by observing some unique iconography in Renaissance visual portrayals of Marsyas' story. If an excuse for this is required, we may recall the view of Jean Seznec that 'A myth is primarily made of images, rather than ideas'.[31] Therefore, let us first consider a shocking and forceful image drawn by Luca Cambiaso in the early 1570s which shows Apollo attacking Marsyas' breast with a knife (Figure 14). Representations of the attack on Marsyas commencing in this part of his body are frequent in the Renaissance,[32] and many depictions, like Cambiaso's, also show Marsyas having human, rather than goat-like, legs.[33] Also in common with many other Renaissance depictions, Cambiaso's drawing has a peculiarly shaped object lying on the ground directly beneath the mutilation scene, to which we will return.

FIGURE 14 *Luca Cambiaso,* Apollo attacking Marsyas.
© *Gabinetto Disegni e Stampe di Palazzo Rosso. Genova.*

Cambiaso's drawing would serve excellently to illustrate
what Shylock is about to do to Antonio before he is suddenly
stopped, his warrant being Portia's judgement that 'this bond
is forfeit, / And lawfully by this the Jew may claim / A pound
of flesh, to be by him cut off / Nearest the merchant's heart'

(4.1.227–30). Incidentally, when Shylock stoops to whet his knife in order to cut into Antonio's breast (4.1.120–5), the image of sharpening the knife in preparation resembles that seen in many Hellenistic and Roman depictions of the martyrdom of Marsyas, and also in some Renaissance ones.[34]

We are led towards other, very disturbing, Renaissance depictions of the martyrdom of Marsyas if we note that Portia's citing the 'Nearest the . . . heart' detail of Shylock's bond must be mistaken – or else the bond must have been revised after Antonio said that he was 'content' with its terms (1.3.151). For the original agreement was that if Antonio's repayment date was missed, then 'the forfeit' would be 'an equal pound / Of your fair flesh to be cut off and taken / In what part of your body pleaseth me' (1.3.147–50). What part that might be is indicated by an oft-cited possible source for the pound of flesh motif in *The Merchant of Venice*: Declamation 95 in Alexander Silvayn's *The Orator* ('Englished' in 1596).[35] In Silvayn's story a vindictive Jewish moneylender demands that a Christian merchant pay as a forfeit on his overdue bond his 'privie members, supposing that the same would altogether weigh a just pound'.[36] Thus this possible source points towards a second connection between *The Merchant of Venice* (which contains a pervasive castration motif to be examined presently) and many Renaissance graphic artists' depictions of the martyrdom of Marsyas. A powerful example is seen in Giulio Romano's design for the central figure of a frieze (now barely visible) in the Palazzo Te. Giulio's drawing shows a goat-legged Marsyas inverted for flaying with a knife pointed directly at his unprotected genitals (Figure 15).

The Merchant of Venice is filled with references to castration.[37] Shylock, having lost his daughter and his jewels, is salaciously described as lamenting the loss of 'two sealed bags' and 'two stones, two rich and precious stones' (2.8.18–20). In accordance with a peculiar congruence expressed in the play (to be discussed later) between 'merchant' and 'Jew' (4.1.171), Antonio avers, 'I am a tainted wether of the flock, / Meetest for death' (4.1.113–4), a 'wether' designating a

FIGURE 15 *Giulio Romano, detail of Apollo flaying Marsyas. Design for a frieze in the Sala di Ovidio, Palazzo Te, Mantua. Courtesy of the Louvre Museum.*

castrated ram.[38] Portia's unsuccessful suitors also lose their sexual potential, for they have sworn never to marry; thus Morocco laments, 'farewell heat, and welcome frost' (2.7.75). In addition, the caustic banter of the play's last act includes

a bawdy threat to 'mar the young clerk's pen' (5.1.237)
and a smutty joke about Nerissa's penis-harming 'ring'
(5.1.306–7).[39]

Let us now progress from noting these motifs to discovering
more precise links between the play's detailed concerns and
representations of Marsyas' story.

Shylock's disparagement of the 'wry-necked fife'

Although Shakespeare presents more than a half a dozen
characters who are unmoved or displeased by music generally,[40]
his Shylock is unique in vehemently disparaging certain
particular musical instruments. The first of two occasions on
which he expresses such a powerful antipathy arises when he
parts from his daughter Jessica, thinking this will be temporary
although in fact he will never see her again. Unaware that she
is planning to elope under the cover of festivities, he admonishes
her against hearkening to the ongoing festival's raucous 'drum
/ And the vile squealing of the wry-necked fife'. He then charges
her to 'stop my house's ears – I mean my casements / Let not
the sound of shallow fopp'ry enter / My sober house' (2.5.29–
36). The memory of her father's words may lie behind Jessica's
later admission in Belmont (of all places) that 'I am never
merry when I hear sweet music' (5.1.69), and may indeed
provoke an appalled silence when her new husband, having
just quipped about 'Jessica steal[ing] from the wealthy Jew'
(5.1.15), goes on to condemn 'The man that hath no music in
himself / Nor is not moved with concord of sweet sounds'
(5.1.83–5).[41]

That possibility aside, Shylock's aversion to 'the vile squealing
of the wry-necked fife' demands close inspection. In common
with all other Shakespearean uses of the word 'fife', the word
'drum' appears nearby, but here, uniquely, the collocation of
'fife' and 'drum' does not imply a military context.[42] Rather,

these instruments announce the celebration of a civic festival. Whatever his underlying motives,[43] Shylock frames his objection to the fife in aesthetic terms, decrying its 'vile squealing' and describing it as 'wry-necked'.

Let us focus on the compound epithet 'wry-necked'. The adjective 'wry' as seen here is a Shakespearean *hapax legomenon*, a sole occurrence.[44] Shylock's scornful application of 'wry-necked' to a 'fife' is also peculiar in that it instances the figure of speech known as *hypallage*, or misplaced epithet (called by George Puttenham 'the Changeling').[45] In senses that 'neck' and 'wry' could take in Shakespeare's time, certain musical instruments could indeed be called 'wry-necked',[46] meaning 'crooked-necked', but the fife itself was straight-necked.[47] The Folio text of *1 Henry IV* has a stage direction describing Falstaff 'playing on his Trunchion like a Fife' (tln 2093); this instructs him to hold his straight staff up to his lips, his neck turned sharply so as to mime playing a transverse flute. Thus only the *posture* of a fife player is properly described as 'wry-necked',[48] and Shylock's misplaced epithet applies to the musician who has to twist his neck to achieve the required embouchure.

In Shakespeare's time, 'wry-necked' was an uncomplimentary personal description. Thomas Overbury in his *Characters* wrote of 'A Flatterer': 'His carriage is ever of the colour of his patient; and for his sake he will halt or weare a wry necke.'[49] The 1616 extended *Characters* adds, concerning the 'Intruder into favour': 'If his Patron be given to musicke, hee opens his chops, and sings, or with a wrie necke falles to tuning his instrument.'[50] So Shakespeare, through Shylock, anticipates Overbury's distaste for someone, especially a musician, showing a 'wrie neck'.

In addition to scorning the posture of the fife player, Shylock deprecates the 'vile squealing' of his instrument. As we have noted, loud wind instruments were not chosen by Renaissance visual artists to allegorize order, harmony or decorum. Might that correspond with Shylock's demand that the 'ears' of his 'sober house' remain shut to brashness and ostentation?

The fife is loud, but not so brash in sound as the double-reeded classical *aulos* or its descendant, the modern oboe. The oboe is considered to be the most strident instrument in the symphony orchestra and tradition holds that a mistuned oboe would be unbearably audible. That is why an oboe sounds the concert A to which all the other instruments are tuned. In Shakespeare's England the oboe was called the 'hautboy' (meaning 'loud wood'), and loud hautboy sounds announce royalty or great events in a dozen Folio stage directions. According to North's Plutarch, hautboys are suited to accompany 'songes of triumphe' after a great victory.[51] However, the bright or strident sounds made by wind instruments were not to everyone's liking, and aesthetics played only one part in that. The austere Shylock is offended not just by the squealing of the instrument and the facial distortion of the fife player, but also by the insobriety of its use. And in fact, several traditions associated wind music with wanton or sinister practices. In particular, the *aulos* is said to have served practices varying from pagan initiation ceremonies to lascivious dancing by naked flute girls (*auletrides*) at 'male symposia',[52] and to have featured in the Phrygian (Anatolian) rites of the goddess Cybele,[53] which some say involved self-castration.[54]

Marsyas, Shylock and the bagpipe

The second of Shylock's vehement musical distastes is for the bagpipe. This links with the story of Marsyas via a complication in Renaissance iconography that we will consider after an analysis of Shylock's bagpipe phobia.

When offering a sarcastic explanation of his insistence on mutilating Antonio, Shylock cites what he calls his 'humour' and compares this with a range of phobias analogous to his 'lodged hate and loathing' for the merchant:

What if my house be troubled with a rat,
And I be pleased to give ten thousand ducats
To have it baned? What, are you answered yet?

Some men there are love not a gaping pig,
Some that are mad if they behold a cat,
And others when the bagpipe sings i' th' nose
Cannot contain their urine; for affection,
Mistress of passion, sways it to the mood
Of what it likes or loathes. Now for your answer:
As there is no firm reason to be rendered
Why he cannot abide a gaping pig,
Why he a harmless necessary cat,
Why he a woollen bagpipe, but of force
Must yield to such inevitable shame
As to offend himself being offended,
So can I give no reason, nor I will not,
More than a lodged hate and a certain loathing
I bear Antonio, that I follow thus
A losing suit against him. Are you answered?

(4.1.43–60)

Shylock's description of repugnance for a 'rat', 'cat' or 'gaping pig' is not surprising in a play that is saturated with references to animals, almost all tinged with disgust.[55] But Shylock's image of shaming urination provoked by the sound of a bagpipe is surprising in itself,[56] and also because it can be connected with a motif of a bagpiping Marsyas that arose in Renaissance visual art.

Renaissance writers and visual artists often updated or altered the identities of the musical instruments played competitively by Marsyas and Apollo, although always maintaining a wind instrument versus a stringed one.[57] Of particular interest to us here is the frequent substitution of a bagpipe for the *aulos* played by Athene and Marsyas, and the strange iconography associated with it. As noted, John Case's 1586 *Praise of Musicke* concatenates Minerva's disfiguring shawm playing with bagpipe blowing. By Shakespeare's time that was a connection very well established in visual art. This connection was probably first made in a woodcut illustration of the Marsyas story in the 1497 *Ovidio metamorphoeseos vulgare* (Figure 16).

FIGURE 16 *Woodcut from* Ovidio metamorphoseos vulgare. *Giovanni Bonsignori, Venice, 1497, fol. 49ᵛ. © Warburg Institute.*

Edith Wyss notes that in this widely seen image, 'the flaying of Marsyas breaks with the two-thousand-year-old taboo of depicting Apollo himself as executioner. In agreement with nearly all ancient and Renaissance literary sources, [the *Ovidio* illustrator] had Apollo perform the gruesome task himself.'[58] That innovatory detail is matched by a pioneering introduction of bagpipes into the story. Thus the woodcut shows a number of vignettes. In one, Athene plays an *aulos* (or hautboy, or shawm) at a feast of the gods, but in another she observes her reflection in water while blowing a bagpipe. In yet another vignette a seated Marsyas also plays a bagpipe, and in another a bagpipe lies on the ground below Marsyas' place of execution. (For future reference we should also note that in the upper right of the woodcut Marsyas' flayed skin is seen hanging in an open temple.)

Bagpipes often produced the shaming 'disfigurement of Athene' in artistic representations, according to the bagpipe authority Anthony Baines, because of 'the swollen cheeks and bloodshot eyes that can result from continually blowing a reed instrument with nasal inhalation to avoid breaks in the sound'.[59] Due to the need for this so-called 'circular breathing', the disgrace of wind players is maximized by drone-containing, double-reeded, bagpipes. Perhaps for that reason, the *Ovidio*'s motif of Athene and Marsyas with bagpipes was very often repeated in sixteenth-century art. Fine examples include an engraving by Benedetto Montagna showing Apollo playing a Renaissance viol in a contest with a bagpipe-blowing Marsyas wearing a countryman's hat, and a cassone painting by Andrea Schiavone showing Athene playing the bagpipe while regarding her reflection, while Marsyas, again wearing a peasant's hat, plays a double *aulos*.[60] The country attire discrediting Marsyas in these two images must have linked with longstanding associations of bagpiping with 'the lower orders of society', or 'a folk or rustic role ... lechery and gluttony', or 'simplicity, rural life, and unrestrained Bacchic festivity'.[61]

However, some artists also depicted a bagpiping Marsyas motif in refined settings. Edith Wyss identifies 'the influence of the [*Ovidio*] woodcut of 1497 extend[ing] as far as Rome' in a ceiling painting made in 1547 by Perino del Vaga (completed by Domenico Zaga) for the Sala di Apollo in the pope's Castel Sant'Angelo, in which Marsyas plays a bagpipe and Apollo is the executioner.[62] The Warburg Institute iconographic database includes a ceramic dish finely decorated by Nicola de Urbino after the *Ovidio* woodcut, on which the flaying occupies the centre and the contest and temple are around the edge (Figure 17).

A particularly striking derivative of the *Ovidio* woodcut is a complex panel now attributed to Michelangelo Anselmi which centrally shows Marsyas glumly observing a rapt Apollo performing on a fiddle-like *lira da braccio* (Figure 18).

This composition also includes vignettes showing Athene blowing into a bagpipe while regarding her image in water and a worried-looking Marsyas seated with a bagpipe in his lap (Figure 19).

FIGURE 17 *Nicola da Urbino,* maiolica *depicting myths of Apollo and Marsyas. Museo Correr, Venice.* © *Warburg Institute.*

FIGURE 18 *Michelangelo Anselmi,* cassone *painting of the myths of Apollo and Marsyas. National Gallery of Art, Kress Collection. Courtesy of the National Gallery of Art, Washington DC.*

FIGURE 19 *Detail of Figure 18.*

FIGURE 20 *Detail of Figure 18.*

Another vignette shows Marsyas being flayed by Apollo with a bagpipe lying below him (Figure 20). This last image repeats a motif often found in Renaissance visual depictions of Marsyas' punishment – a motif in which deflated bagpipes lie on the ground just beneath Marsyas' flaying, and strongly suggest the representation of male genitalia that have been detached from the mutilated satyr. That suggestion of castration has never been noted in this much-studied Anselmi panel, although as seen in the details reproduced here in one vignette a single-piped bagpipe lies on a dejected Marsyas' lap, and in another a single-piped bagpipe lies on the ground under Marsyas' groin while he is being attacked.[63]

Although less clearly so (because two pipes plus the bag are shown), a similar arrangement of a bagpipe appears in the mutilation vignette in the pioneering 1497 *Ovidio* woodcut. The same symbolism is very clearly expressed in a beautiful sixteenth-century relief carving where Marsyas' genitals are not obscured, but rather placed in exact correspondence with a discarded bagpipe just below them (Figure 21). The same arrangement appears in a mid-sixteenth-century engraving after Francesco Salviati in which a bagpipe resembling male genitalia hangs above Marsyas on the tree to which he is tied.[64]

The same bizarre iconography appears in a woodcut capital 'M' in a 1562 edition of Ariosto's *Orlando Furioso*.[65] There Apollo's knife looms centrally above a supine and horrified Marsyas, raised in such a way as to seem to menace his crotch (which is behind the letter itself). Marsyas' bagpipe appears at the bottom of the woodcut with a single prominent pipe displayed, lying on the ground just below his crotch. That image of a detached bag-plus-pipe – given a phallic and scrotal form – must indicate amputation and castration (Figure 22).

FIGURE 21 *Anon., sixteenth-century relief carving of Apollo attacking Marsyas. By kind permission of James Fenton. © Warburg Institute.*

FIGURE 22 *Initial capital letter 'M' showing Apollo attacking Marsyas, from p. 51 of Ariosto,* Orlando Furioso, *Venice, 1562.* © *Warburg Institute.*

The associations of bagpipes with half-human satyrs

Many Elizabethans would have associated phallic satyrs with bagpipes. Spenser's *Faerie Queene* (which Shakespeare studied closely early in his career[66]) does this quite explicitly. Thus Spenser's account of Hellenore preferring a hypersexual half-human satyr lover to her husband begins by describing a 'noyse of many bagpipes shrill' (III.x.63–8).

Bagpipes and bagpiping were also associated with animals. While playing a wind instrument one cannot speak or sing, as is emphasized by Plutarch's Alcibiades and also in the versions of the myth in which Apollo insists that the contestants should sing while playing, which Marsyas cannot do. Therefore, playing a wind instrument might seem to erase human capabilities and violate taboos dividing the human from the animal.[67] This may have a peculiar bearing on the *Ovidio* illustration discussed above, and on several of its derivatives in which not only is Marsyas skinned like an animal, but his pelt is also shown hanging in an open temple and filling with a breeze. Although Marsyas' flayed skin plays no part in his Ovidian metamorphosis into a Phrygian river, other classical authors report that Marsyas' skin found its way into a temple, marketplace or cave and there inspired a festival.[68] To this Pliny adds that 'the hide moved when Phrygian tunes were played on the aulos'.[69] Rika Maniates notes that a curious phenomenon mentioned by Nonnos 'was corroborated by Lucian who found it ironic that after Apollo was through with him, the only whistling sound Marsyas could make emanated from his skin dangling in the wind'.[70] All this gestures towards the fate of Marsyas' flayed skin described in Nonnos' *Dionysiaca*:

[Marsyas] fingering a proud pipe . . . lifted a haughty neck and challenged a match with Phoibos; but Phoibos tied him to a tree and stript off his hairy skin, and made it a windbag. There it hung high on a tree, and the breeze often entered, swelling it out into a shape like his, as if the shepherd could not keep silence but made his tune again.[71]

How could the arrogant piper's pelt become a Marsyas-shaped windbag, 'as if' to make 'his tune again'? In answer it has been claimed that Nonnos and Lucian suggest that Marsyas' pelt provided the bag for the first bagpipe.[72] This is at least possible, for, as we shall see, some kinds of bagpipes were played in antiquity. Moreover, Anthony Baines reports that 'In many bagpipes . . . the bag is the whole skin of a sheep or goat.'[73] Baines also claims that the 'wollen pipe' mentioned by Shylock 'was no doubt a bagpipe with the fleece of the bag showing'.[74]

Marsyas, Shylock and unfettered expression

Satyrs were phallic animals and, correspondingly, psychoanalytic commentators have interpreted phallic aspects of the Athene–Marsyas–Apollo myths.[75] Shakespeare was not squeamish about allied matters, so it is not outrageous to suggest that when Shylock posits that a bagpipe phobia causes the sufferer to void urine to his 'inevitable shame' the effects are seen in an anatomical bag, the bladder and its connected pipe. However, as we have seen, in many Renaissance pictorial representations of Marsyas' mutilation a bagpipe with a single prominent chanter resembles a scrotum and penis (rather than the internal bladder and its pipe).[76] As noted, Shakespeare uses 'bags' in *The Merchant of Venice* to indicate a scrotum when Shylock's laments about 'two sealed bags' containing 'two rich and precious stones' are mocked. Likewise, in *The Winter's Tale* the insanely jealous Leontes holds that there is 'No barricado for a belly. Know 't, / It will let in and out the enemy / With bag and baggage' (1.2.205–7). Also, sometimes in Shakespeare a 'pipe' may signify a penis, as when the ever-bawdy Nurse in *Romeo and Juliet* replies to the wedding musicians' proverbial 'we must put up our pipes and be gone' with the quibbling 'ah, put up, put up, / For well you know this is a pitiful case' (4.4.124–6).[77] So a 'bag' and a 'pipe' – and indeed a bagpipe – could signify male genitals for Shakespeare.[78] We have already noted that sixteenth-century visual artists repeatedly showed Marsyas' genitals, often symbolized by a bagpipe, under attack.

What is there about the loud[79] Renaissance bagpipe (or the other double-reeded pipes that it replaced) that makes it a fit symbol for Marsyas' particular punishment? The linked themes of blatancy and supposed shamefulness attaching to both Marsyas' and Shylock's behaviour require an explanation going beyond Emanuel Winternitz's comment that Pallas Athene rejected her *aulos* because 'as a goddess of reason [she] could not favor an object charged with the connotation of passion, sex and inebriation'.[80] This comment adds prudery and austerity to her traditional motive of vanity for rejecting the *aulos*, but does not explain an oft-heard suggestion that Athene placed a curse on her discarded pipe and on any future adopter of it.[81]

Athene's curse most probably links to objections to wind instrument playing which are more profound than aesthetic distaste for awkward facial expressions or bodily postures, and which also go beyond disapproval of hedonistic uses of music. Instead, they entail long-established hostility to the ostentation of skilled performers. Thus George Sandys interpreted Ovid's account of Marsyas: 'Marsyas, the inventor of wind instruments, may resemble ambition and vaine-glory, which delight in loud shouts and applauses: but virtue and wisdome have a sweeter touch, though they make not so great a noyse in popular opinion.'[82] A similar hostility is expressed in a sarcastic comment, probably about Nero, by Dio Chrysostom (*c*. 40–115 CE): 'They say he can write, carve statues, play the *aulos* both with his mouth, and also with the armpit, a bag being thrown under it, in order that he might escape the disfigurement of Athene. Was he not a wise man?'[83] This refers to a special sort of bagpipe that was inflated by arm-driven bellows. Although Nero avoided being disfigured by blowing into the bagpipe, he was not 'wise', but rather dishonoured by making a spectacle of himself.[84]

The basis of such attitudes is more clearly expressed by Aristotle than by Plato. In Plato's *Gorgias*, 'flute playing' is said to typify activities 'pursuing our pleasure only' (501e). In the *Republic*, when 'preferring Apollo and the instruments of Apollo to Marsyas and his instruments', Plato also refers to hedonism when he disallows 'flute makers and flute players' in order to 'purge' his ideal city of the 'luxurious'

(Book III, 399d–e). However, near the end of Aristotle's *Politics*, Book VIII, anti-hedonism takes second place to an ethical emphasis demanding that only that which is seemly be included in the education of 'freemen who are being trained to political virtue'.[85] So Aristotle objects to musical education that may have a 'vulgarizing effect', adding that:

> it is quite possible that certain methods of teaching and learning music do really have a degrading effect . . . The right measure will be attained if students of music stop short of the arts which are practised in professional contests, and do not seek to acquire those fantastic marvels of execution which are now the fashion in such contests, and from those have passed into education . . . From these principles we may also infer what instruments should be used. The flute, or any instrument that requires great skill . . . ought not be admitted into education. Besides, the flute is not an instrument which is expressive of moral character; it is too exciting. The proper time for using it is not when the performance aims at instruction, but the relief of passions . . . There is meaning also in the myth of the ancients, which tells how Athene invented the flute and then threw it away. It was not a bad idea of theirs, that the Goddess disliked the instrument because it made the face ugly; but with still more reason we may say that she rejected it because the acquirement of flute-playing contributes nothing to the mind, since to Athene we ascribe both knowledge and art.
>
> (1341a–b)

The doctrine that the artistic activities of the freeborn must not be showy or professional is further expounded in Castiglione's *Book of the Courtier*, where Sir Fredericke holds (in Hoby's translation):

> I would have our Courtier [perform any skilled activity] beside handling his weapon, as a matter that is not his

profession: and not to seeme to seeke or looke for any
prayse for it. Nor will I have him be acknowen that he
bestoweth much studie or time about it, although he do it
excellently well.[86]

Fredericke adds, concerning performing music:

The like judgement I have to Musicke: but I woulde not our
Courtier should doe as many doe, that as soone as they
come to any place, and also in the presence of great men
with whome they have no acquintance at all, without much
entreating set out them selves to shew as much as they
know, yea and many times that they know not, so that a
man would weene they came purposely to shew themselve
for that, and that is their principall profession. Therefore let
our Courtier come to shew his musick as a thing to passe
the time withall, as he were enforced to doe it, and not in
the presence of noble men, nor of any great multitude. And
for all hee be skilfull and doth well understand it, yet . . . let
him make semblance that he esteemeth but litle in himselfe
that qualitie . . .[87]

Defying such doctrines, Shylock in *The Merchant of Venice*
publicly and ostentatiously flaunts his forensic skills when
attempting to defeat Antonio. He also does this in the presence
of Venice's greatest man, just as Castiglione says he should not
do. Moreover, when going to law against Antonio, Shylock
exhibits what Hoby's Castiglione scorns as 'curiousitie',[88]
meaning socio-political audacity.

It is as if Shylock thinks that entering a Venetian law
court equates with standing in that protected corner of the
ancient Roman forum near the statue of Marsyas where
citizens were permitted to post anonymous complaints or hold
'protest meetings'. Interestingly, that statue showed the musical
satyr hefting a wine skin.[89] Many scholars describe this statue
of Marsyas in Rome (and its duplicates in Roman colonial
fora) as a symbol of liberty, as a 'guarantor of civic freedom',

or an 'icon . . . of libertas and rule by law'.[90] Such protection was not available to either Marsyas or Shylock – hopes for the rights of expression and a fair trial led to disaster for both.

It is also arguable that neither of them actually received a fair trial, even by the standards of those they challenged. We have noted that in Conti's Renaissance retelling and in various classical accounts Apollo was accused of employing chicanery or jury-rigging. Maniates, in common with other scholars,[91] holds that Apollo wins his contest with Marsyas by means of duplicity (dolos), rather than merely resourceful stratagem (metis).[92] She reflects that 'it does not seem to have occurred to Marsyas that the Muses', who were often said to be the judges in the contest, had a 'connection . . . indeed subservience' to Apollo, so that 'these divine ladies could hardly have been expected to give an unbiased verdict'.[93] Likewise, Shylock is unaware that the hair-splitting argument that defeats him is delivered by a supposedly unbiased legal expert who is in fact connected by marriage to his adversary's closest friend. Portia's mere pretence at being a lawyer would have been a serious crime in Elizabethan England.

Maniates next quotes a dialogue by Lucian in which Hera asserts, ironically, 'what a laugh! Truly admirable is Apollo whom Marsyas would have flayed after prevailing over him in a musical competition, had the Muses chosen to judge fairly'.[94] Hera thus comments that Marsyas might have been the knife-wielder himself had he not been cheated. Other classical and Renaissance sources also suggest that Marsyas might have done to Apollo what Apollo did to him.[95] This symmetry of a satyr and a classical god may be compared with Portia asking in *The Merchant of Venice*, 'Which is the merchant here, and which the Jew?' (4.1.171). For in both cases the blindness of even-handed justice is a sham and there is no doubt as to who will be the winner. In both cases, too, a false symmetry raises other quandaries. For instance, Portia's sham objectivity overlays a truth that mercantile activity and risk capital are inextricable, despite the merchant's snobbery.

The outcome for both the underdog challengers, Marsyas and Shylock, is abject failure followed by enormous anguish. Shylock initially imagines that he can be wholly outspoken (so, for instance, he cites scripture to the Christians at 1.3.70–89), and he then triumphantly sharpens his knife. But finally cut down, he is left wholly defenceless and deprived of the protection of his social skin. Shorn of his identity, the very 'means whereby I live' (4.1.374), like Marsyas, he too could cry out, 'why do you tear me from myself?'

Babys and the playing of wind instruments in *Othello*

Marsyas is a highly skilled player, but loud wind instruments can be played very badly as well. Double-reeded wind-blown instruments – such as the *aulos*, shawm or hautboy – are notoriously hard to control in terms of intonation, and so Marsyas puts himself at considerable risk in the contest, for the possibility of technical failure is present. I am told that there is no middle ground with such double-reeded modern instruments as the oboe, English horn or bassoon: players who are not at the top of their form tend to play badly. Hence the musician's joke, 'the oboe is an ill wind that nobody blows good'.

A not dissimilar musician's joke from antiquity introduces the unskilled mythical *aulos* player Babys (Βαβυς is said by some to be Marsyas' brother).[96] The ancient jest runs to the tune of 'the more Babys plays the worse he gets'.[97] This inspired a pun in the 1586 *Praise of Musicke*: 'There are infantes in all arts, & I grant none so very a babe in Musike as was *Babys*'. This passage continues to the effect that Minerva interceded with Apollo on Babys' behalf so that he would not have to undergo the punishment of Marsyas: 'Cast not away such chastisement upon so base and unexpert a person.'[98]

A more detailed account of the quip 'Babys plays the flute even worse' appears in Erasmus's *Adages*:

This adage was used as a familiar jibe against those whose performance always tends to deteriorate. Some speakers are like that: the longer they go on, the worse they speak. They attribute this to a story on the following lines. Babys, they say, was a brother of Marsyas, the man who was not afraid to challenge Apollo himself to a musical contest. When he was defeated, he was suspended by Apollo from a pine-tree upside down, and flayed. Then, when Apollo was preparing to destroy Babys too, Pallas interceded for him, saying that his flute-playing was so unsuccessful and unskilful that clearly he was quite negligible; 'Babys' she said 'plays even worse.' Apollo was impressed by her words, and treated Babys with such disdain that he did not even think him worthy of punishment, but judged it better to abandon him to his incompetence.

The adage will also be useful in comparisons; after speaking of an incompetent teacher, if asked about one of his pupils, one might reply 'Babys plays even worse.' Nor should I object if anyone were to take 'worse' here in the sense of more pitiful, giving the meaning that Babys is more to be pitied for the way in which his incompetent playing makes him a general laughingstock than he would be if he were dead.[99]

Let us turn now to a crucial but often overlooked and sometimes unperformed episode in *Othello* in which wind instrument players displease their intended audience (3.1.1–29). Just after Michael Cassio hires a band of musicians to play 'Good morrow general' under Othello's and Desdemona's bedroom window Othello sends down a loquacious servant, called a 'Clown' in both the Folio and quarto texts, to quell this objectionable early-morning music. Othello's Clown pays the musicians to desist, and adds several comments of interest, including: 'But masters, here's money for you, and the general so likes your music that he desires you, for love's sake, to make no more noise with it', and 'If you have any music that may not be heard, to 't again; but, as they say, to hear music the general does not greatly care' (3.1.11–13 and 15–17). The inverted logic and syntax of the Clown's remarks echoes the structure of, and contains the gist of, the 'less is better' logic in the classical quip about Babys: 'the more he plays, the worse'.

That Othello likes these musicians' music more the less it is heard might mean that he is not keen on music generally, and some take it that way.[100] But that seems unlikely because, speaking retrospectively, Othello describes Desdemona as 'an admirable musician. O she will sing the savageness out of a bear!' (4.1.184–5). The meaning must be, therefore, that Othello dislikes the music played *particularly* at this time. Many commentators have suggested that the Clown's bantering remark that Othello would prefer 'music that may not be heard' alludes to the unheard music of the universe, or 'the spheres', here placed in opposition to the musicians' nocturnal 'noise'.[101] However, that need not imply that the music heard at the start of scene 3.1 is less than raucous – and the text of the play suggests rather that it is precisely that, and that it is, moreover, music played on loud double-reeded wind instruments, as is Babys' unpalatable music. Thus the Clown initially confronts Cassio's musicians with a remark that their instruments 'speak i'th' nose', referring to the nasal tone of loud double-reeded *aulos*-like wind instruments such as were played by Elizabethan town waits (as well as by Babys).

Critics have diverged widely on the nature of the music played in this scene,[102] but if we read the Clown's 'quillets' (3.1.23), his quibbling sallies, in the light of the deplorable *aulos* playing of Babys, insight may be achieved. The Clown's sallies, or the second half of them, are obviously ribald:

CLOWN
    Are these, I pray you, wind instruments?
MUSICIAN
    Ay, marry are they, sir.
CLOWN
    O, thereby hangs a tail.

MUSICIAN
  Whereby hangs a tale, sir?
CLOWN
  Marry, sir, by many a wind instrument that I know.

                                                    (3.1.6–11)

When glossing the quibbles here almost all recent editors note
an allusion to wind = flatulence, and some also note that the
Latin for 'tail' can be 'penis'. Problems arise, however, in the
interpretation of the Clown's opening remark to the musicians:
'Why, Masters, have your Instruments bin in Naples, that they
speake i'th' Nose thus?'[103] Two hoary glosses for this have
been cited for centuries: the Furness *Variorum Edition* traces
the first to Cowden-Clarke and the second to Samuel
Johnson.[104] These are, side by side: 'The Clown may mean that
the music has an ugly nasal twang like the Neapolitan accent,
but there is probably also a reference to venereal disease, which
attacked the nose.'[105]

Although neither repetition nor antiquity debars correctness,
I believe that both of these interpretations fail on close
examination. For one, the Neapolitan accent was not in fact
nasal, and neither was the distinct Neapolitan language.[106] It is
probably also fallacious to connect 'speake i'th' Nose' with a
venereal disease. It is true that for Elizabethans a sounding
musical instrument did 'speak', and equally true that for them
syphilis was a 'Neapolitan disease'.[107] However, Shakespeare's
more than two-dozen other references to Naples do not allude
to syphilis. Moreover, although syphilitic erosion of the nose is
mentioned in *Timon of Athens* (4.3.157–60), nasal speech is
not a typical symptom of the disease.[108]

M. R. Ridley, who is properly sceptical of the traditional
Neapolitan accent and venereal disease interpretations, points
out that bagpipes have a nasal sound. So do other odd-harmonic-
rich, double-reeded instruments, including the hautboy, shawm
and *aulos*. But if neither syphilis nor Neapolitan speech patterns
account for the Clown's association of nasal-sounding musical
instruments with Naples, is any reply possible to Ridley's

SHAKESPEARE'S MYTHICAL MUSICIANS

comment: 'there must be some point in the clown's remark . . . even if we have lost it'?[109] Something indeed has been identified that connects Naples with the sounds of raucous double-reeded musical instruments. This in turn carries an association with unruly and disreputable behaviour which illuminates the entire musicians episode in *Othello*. Before identifying it, however, let us review some of the very peculiar circumstances of that episode.

It has been noted that the Clown scene at the beginning of *Othello* Act Three is often omitted in performance.[110] This was done, for instance, in Jonathan Miller's almost three-and-a-half-hour 1981 BBC production, surely not in that instance to shorten the play. It seems likely that at least in some cases this cut is made because of the apparent lapse in dramatic logic, of which an explanation follows.

His dialogue with Iago at 3.1.30–1 makes it clear that Cassio has hired musicians to waken Othello only hours after he has disgraced himself in a drunken brawl and been demoted by him. On that occasion Cassio's violent drunken behaviour brought first Othello and then Desdemona from their marriage chamber, so that Othello had to say to his new wife, 'All's well now sweeting / Come away to bed', and then 'Come Desdemona. 'Tis the soldier's life / To have their balmy slumbers waked with strife' (2.3.246–7, 251–2). Why would Cassio repeat the same offence so blatantly, and so soon?

When he hires musicians to play loudly and raucously in the street, annoying the married pair again, Cassio is following Iago's treacherous advice to 'Importune' Desdemona to 'help to put you in your place again' (2.3.311–12). His unseemly alacrity in attempting to make contact with Desdemona might be attributed to the play's notoriously elastic (unrealistic and expressive) time scheme, but in that case Cassio's hard-to-comprehend *faux pas* would remain invisible. Rather, its ill effects are emphasized. We might even see his actions resembling those of a child who, having been rebuked for naughtiness, seeks reassurance by waking its parents.

Another explanation of sorts has been suggested in which Cassio's loud music in *Othello* 3.1 is disruptive in a manner mandated by tradition. Thus Kenneth Muir, among others, proposes: 'It was an Elizabethan custom to awaken a newly married couple with music,'[111] and François Laroque suggests that we see a 'second form of charivari', or 'Italian mattinata', played on the bagpipes here in *Othello*.[112] There may not have been an Elizabethan 'second form of charivari' (without censure), yet there were Elizabethan customs of invading the bridal chamber in friendly riotousness that are somewhat similar.[113] It is, moreover, possible that Othello and Desdemona's bridal night is delayed until they reach Cyprus thanks to the elastic time scheme of the play, as well as its repeated tendency to disturb its hero in his marital bed.

Crucially, however, when Cassio hires wake-up musicians he is in no position to do so. He has been cast out of office and has lost Othello's regard. Yet he seems to ignore his new standing, and still claims a familiarity that licenses annoying a newly married pair (of the sort that today licenses best-men's rude wedding speeches). The mystery deepens because we have seen Cassio abashed and guilt-ridden about his behaviour, appalled at having ruined his reputation (2.3.256–301). This shows him possessed of refinement and sensitivity.[114]

Why would such a man deliberately set out to annoy his just-estranged friend? Surely, if Cassio remains as first seen he would avoid repeating the offence of the previous night. The only explanation possible is that Cassio has changed, or has been changed.

Here, at last, we arrive at that 'something' that connects Naples, nasal musical instruments and Cassio's misbehaviour. It was identified in a usually overlooked eighteenth-century gloss on the Clown's 'Naples' reference.[115] Partially quoted in the Furness *Variorum*,[116] this appears in full in a 1795 book by Wolstenholme Parr (albeit in a bizarre context). Parr admits that 'venereal disease first made its appearance at the siege of Naples', but goes on to contend that:

There are few clowns in Italy that know this; but every clown there knows that Pulcinella is the Neapolitan mask, and that Pulcinella speaks through the nose. He generally knows, too, that the man who plays this puppet puts into his mouth a reed similar to that which is placed in the orifice of the haut-boy.[117]

Thus Parr aligns the remark in *Othello* on Naples and double-reeded wind instruments with the *commedia dell'arte*. Interestingly, none of the more than one hundred entries indexed under '*commedia*' in the *World Shakespeare Bibliography*, nor similar items listed in two review articles, seem to take up Parr's suggestion.[118]

Parr's gloss leads us to wonder if ex-lieutenant Michael Cassio, forsaking his former conscience and delicacy, becomes the blustering Captain figure of the *commedia*, a character easily associated with Babys-like, inappropriately blaring, wind instruments. The *commedia* Captain is, moreover, closely involved in the schemes of the nasal-speaking figure of the Neapolitan Pulcinella, who is loud, unreliable, crass and offensive. When caught out, Pulcinella is always blatantly unrepentant. So too is Cassio, who follows up his sleep-disrupting overnight riot by arranging for a sleep-ruining morning ruckus.

In fact, after taking the malign advice of Iago to importune Desdemona, Cassio never again agonizes over his lost 'reputation'. He is imaged rather as a would-be self-interested interloper in Othello's marriage, and as the seducer of Bianca. Thus Cassio is transformed into a *commedia*-like brazen soldier-rogue who excuses his drunken excesses by shamelessly showing himself to be a man of noise and riot. Driven by a burning envy of Cassio's grace – 'He hath a daily beauty in his life / That makes me ugly' (5.1.19–20) – Iago succeeds in making Cassio's behaviour coarse and ugly.[119] Thus the hyper-subtle Iago, whose own pretence is to be a rough, unable-to-be-politic, plain soldier, projects a swaggering spirit into Cassio. In parallel, transmogrified Othello displays a brutality that 'would not be believed in Venice' (4.1.242) when overwhelmed by an Iago-like paranoid sexual jealousy elicited by Iago's cunning projections.[120] The Iago function is to instil hateful parts of himself into others, His success, in the case of Cassio, is immediately shown by Cassio's choice of crude, incompetent musicians.

Two musical artists, the brothers Marsyas and Babys, both play boldly and loudly. Apollo favours neither, but only the more skilful and stronger of the two, and the more rebellious, attracts his vicious chastisement. Nevertheless, the Renaissance was fascinated by the figure of Marsyas. Sometimes, as we shall see next, it even viewed his excoriating punishment as the badge of artistic liberation.

An Afterword, Considering Joyousness in Art

There is much, much more to explore regarding Shakespeare's artists than the foregoing has even touched upon. In that one respect, at least, I have fulfilled an initial promise, which was to produce a study that neither intends to be nor pretends to be totalizing.

It may be that the observations and speculations here have usefully broached selected aspects of some Shakespearean depictions of artists – for instance Shakespeare's representations of the virtual interiority of certain fictional artists, or his expositions of the transactional aspects of artists' activities, or his demonstrations of the embedding of artists' productions in cultural and social matrices. Readers must decide if these attempts have been helpful; this afterword is perhaps better focused not on topics already discussed, but rather on aspects of our subject which have been treated only partially here and that may reward further investigation.

For instance, much might be said concerning Shakespeare's appreciation of a late Renaissance understanding of the artist as a mercurial craftsman, or *maker*. The actual word 'maker' was sometimes used in Shakespeare's time to denote a poet. This recalled the etymology of the term 'poet' from the Greek *poiein* meaning 'to make', as Philip Sidney explains in his *Apology*. Sidney also explains that the Latin term for a poet is *vates*, meaning a 'Diviner, Fore-seer, or Prophet',[1] and this may seem to align with the notion of the saturnine or inspired artist. Shakespeare, as has been briefly noted, was sometimes satiric of that latter notion, but perhaps sometimes was not.

Again, we have supplied only a limited account of the impact of genres on the treatments of various artists by Shakespeare. We have seen that lyric poetry, narrative poetry and drama allow for quite different kinds of exposition of artists' interiority as well as of their work. One might ask if similar differentiations apply to the (often mixed) genres of Shakespeare's theatrical histories, comedies, tragedies and tragicomedies.

Additionally, I have perhaps too scantily discussed the transaction whereby an artist's work may evoke delight. A small attempt to atone for this will conclude this afterword.

The wild *aulos* music of the unfortunate artist Marsyas sometimes received extravagant praise. For instance, at the climax of Plato's *Symposium* Alcibiades compares Socrates' personal allure with the wisdom, wit and irresistible charm of Marsyas (215b ff.).[2] Edgar Wind thinks that, although drunken, Plato's Alcibiades does not misconstrue: 'The final note of the *Symposium* was that tragic and comic catharsis are one.'[3] Wind also holds, controversially, that Dante at the start of *Paradiso* compares the flaying of Marsyas with the great artist's release from bodily bounds.[4] This Dante passage, praising Marsyas, is very oddly echoed in Chaucer's *House of Fame* (1229–32).

Apart from high mysteries mixing Platonism with artistic pride, it is possible to view Marsyas' defiant wind-instrument playing – and in parallel, Shylock's unwise but uninhibited legal challenge – as fascinating if loud protests against a dominant order of things. Indeed, brilliant players can make wind instruments 'speak', as the Elizabethans put it, with articulation every bit as human-sounding as impassioned language.[5] They can, for instance, make the voices of their instruments fully as sardonic as the heavy sarcasm in Shylock's mid-trial 'These be the Christian husbands' (4.1.292) – whether or not that pointed remark is an aside.

Yet there is another way of attending to 'rude' wind instruments, which is from a perspective whereby such instruments and their players are perceived as sources of unconstrained joyous pleasure. Even sophisticated Renaissance tastes turned to such music for enjoyment. For instance, French music from the late sixteenth century reinvented or revived Nero's armpit-blown bagpipes, and it became highly fashionable to play a small and refined courtly-pastoral kind of bellows-blown bagpipes called a *musette de cour*. That ingenious device prevented, as Marin Mersenne put it, 'the swelling up of the cheeks which is a cause of the deformity of the face',[6] and thus was suitable for amateur as well as professional use. But despite some evidence that such face-saving instruments reached England by the late seventeenth century,[7] as noted in Chapter Five, middling or high-ranking Elizabethan recreational musicians probably confined themselves to stringed or keyboard instruments and did not perform on pipes or bagpipes. Yet refined Elizabethans did enjoy hearing them played. Christopher Marsh recounts an anecdote in which in 1574 the Presbyterian Thomas Cartwright stated, metaphorically, that Bishop John Whitgift's prose made merry 'with the bagpipe or country mirth, not with the harp or lute, which the learned were wont to handle'. Whitgift (later the Archbishop of Canterbury) replied, 'And I thank God I can be merry with the bagpipe. I am neither ashamed of the instrument nor of the country. But what divinity call you this? Alack. Poor spite at the bagpipe.'[8] In a similar vein, Thomas Whythorne relates an anecdote in which the king of France was better eased in his illness by a few shepherds playing bagpipes than by 'all the cunning masters of music within his realm'.[9]

As mentioned, perhaps the solace and pleasure in hearing music – or of attending to art generally – has received too little mention here. But we have mentioned how much the exiled Boligbroke in *Richard II* will miss hearing the music of his accustomed courtly environment (A.C. 21), and how glad

Stephano is to receive free music in *The Tempest* (3.2.147–8). Had space permitted we would have included a detailed discussion of Elizabethan fears in the 1590s that the great flourishing of poetry in their age might meet a similar fate to that of Ricardian poetry after the ending of the reign of the childless Richard II. The flourishing of poetry in England was, in the estimation of Shakespeare's contemporaries, cut off for over a century after 1400, and it is arguable that Shakespeare's second Henriad reflects this in a highly anxious manner. Those anxieties had everything to do with the great contemporary value placed on the art of poetry, a value that is also reflected in Shakespeare's sometimes-satirical treatments of the abuse of poetry.

Highly valued art does not have to be cheerful to be cheering. In Shakespeare's own art we often find an admixture of the tragic in comedies, comic elements are not infrequent in tragedies, and tragic-comedy is the ultimate achievement. Likewise, when discussing the representation of human emotions in painting and sculpture Sir Henry Wotton remarked that in art melancholy and joyousness may overlap, or even merge: 'though *Gladnesse* and *Grief* be opposites in *Nature*; yet they are ... *Neighbors* and *Consiners* in *Arte*.'[10] The denizens of such a mixed neighbourhood are celebrated in tandem in the archetypically upbeat and at the same time harshly observant choruses of a song in Shakespeare's half-pastoral and half-realistic *As You Like It*:

Hey-ho, sing hey-ho, unto the green holly.
Most friendship is feigning, most loving, mere folly.
Then hey-ho, the holly;
This life is most jolly.[11]

NOTES

Introduction

1   Shiner (2001), 38, 55.

2   Shiner holds that Shakespeare never meant to write fixed texts
    for the page, but rather only transient collaborative play scripts
    for particular occasions and acting companies (47–52), a view
    overturned by Mackinnon (1988), Cheney (2004; 2007; 2008)
    and Erne (2003; 2007) who show that Shakespeare's works were
    intended to have stability and aesthetic integrity.

3   Pettet (1950), 20, denies that Shakespeare was a theorist: 'With
    our proud native contempt for theory and speculation, it is not
    surprising that we are inclined to represent our chief poet as
    pre-eminently the practical writer.' Atkins (1951), 246–54, posits
    on the contrary that Shakespeare 'nowhere deliberately unfolds
    the secrets of his art: though hidden in his work is ample
    material for establishing a body of theory which, duly organized,
    would form a valuable counterpart to that contained in
    Aristotle's *Poetics*' (264). Kristeller (1951), 510, finds generally
    that 'contrary to a widespread opinion, the Renaissance did not
    formulate a system of the fine arts or a comprehensive theory of
    aesthetics'. Ewbank (1971), 100, holds that Shakespeare was
    'reticent about the nature of [the imaginary] process'. Yet
    Jankowski (1989) holds that Shakespeare was 'a precursor
    of modern theorists' in his ideas about art.

4   Wollheim (1971), 131 (discussed 121–32).

5   Even the painter's splendidly self-willed horse in Figure 1,
    discussed in Chapter One, is treated in an anthropomorphic
    manner. To the contrary, David Grossman's 1986 novel *See
    Under Love* turns one of its protagonists into a definitely non-
    anthropomorphic salmon, far from all the precedents of Aesopian
    fables or bestiary allegories available in Shakespeare's time.

6   For instance, Bushnell (2015), 474, reviewing Charlotte Scott's
    Shakespeare's Nature: From Cultivation to Culture (2014), says
    that this book fails to join a recent trend of work on
    Shakespeare that seeks to 'decenter the human'.

7   Wollheim (1971), 90–5.

8   That achievement is emphasized in Sokol (1994), which is
    structured around a list of characters in *WT*. It is treated
    theoretically in Sokol (1995). Today one need not blush about
    the formerly derided 'character criticism'; the trend of radical
    rejection that dominated the 1930s through the 1970s is now
    seen not to have taken into account, for instance, that 'actors
    still routinely invent "back stories" for their characters', as noted
    in Marshall and Thompson (2011), 63.

9   More than half of each of the three even-numbered chapters is
    focused on only one Shakespeare work: the *Sonnets*, *The
    Winter's Tale* and *The Merchant of Venice* respectively.

10 Jankowski, (1989), 133.

11 *OED* artist *n*. III. 6 (with citations dating from 1575). The
    definition in *OED* artist *n*. III. 6.a is 'A person skilled in any of
    the fine arts'. *OED* (second edn) artist *n*. III. 7 has 'One who
    cultivates one of the fine arts'. Both editions offer the same
    proviso and neither specifies the two remaining Muses. In both
    editions *OED* muse, *n*. 1.a, explains that originally the remit of
    some of the nine sister-goddesses was unspecific.

12 Chapter One discusses the campaign carried out in Renaissance
    Italy and the Low Countries, and reflected in Elizabethan
    England, to expand the classical curriculum so as to elevate the
    status of the plastic arts or arts of design, which had been left
    out of the gamut of the seven liberal arts. For historical context
    see Kristeller (1951), 513–15.

13 *OED* (second edn) artist, *n*. II. 4.

14 *OED* artist, *n*. I. 2.

15 *TC* 1.3.23; *AW* 2.3.10.

16 'I care not for these ladies', from Campion and Rossiter,
    A Booke of Ayres (1601).

17 As opposed to the so-called Sapir-Whorf hypothesis that the
    thoughts of language users are delimited by the structure and

vocabulary of their languages, Jakobson (2000 [1959]) holds that the lack of a term in a language will not prevent users from thinking about a concept named by the term; grammatical structures or vocabularies may force the use of awkward circumlocutions, yet 'All cognitive experience and its classification is conveyable in any existing language . . . Languages differ essentially in what they *must* convey and not in what they *may* convey' (4–5).

18 Even the doubtful Kristeller (1951), 517–18, mentions the Jesuit Jacobus Pontanus who in 1600 explicitly bracketed poetry painting and music as 'as forms of imitation aiming at pleasure'. The co-operative *paragoni* tradition discussed in Chapter One finds many affinities, and indeed the Renaissance developed several multimedia art forms.

19 Spenser (1966), 96. '*Enthousiasmos*' transliterated from the Greek.

20 Wittkower and Wittkower (1963), 103.

21 The notion that madness or melancholy may be conducive to wisdom, insight or creative genius had at least pseudo-Aristotelian origins (in *Problems* 30.1). As developed by Ficino and others this notion was very influential in the Italian Renaissance. See Radden (2000), 87–94; Klibansky et al. (1964), especially 217–77; Babb (1951); and for further discussion Sokol (2008), 191 n.97.

22 Wittkower and Wittkower (1963), 104. This continues, 'an alliance between Platonic "madness" and Aristotelian "melancholy" postulated by Ficino is echoed in Michelangelo's use of these terms, and there is reason to assume that it was this alliance that many a Renaissance artist regarded as essential for his own creativity' (105). Wells (1985) and Wells (1994), 189–207, argue that John Dowland composed music about melancholy without melancholy being the source of his genius.

23 Wittkower and Wittkower (1963), 104–7.

24 Trevor (2004), 63–86, finds that by Shakespeare's time the notion of the melancholic artist was becoming outdated not only in intellectual/aesthetic thinking, but also in medical thinking. Galenic theory was diluting Ficinian theory so that 'the positive influences' of melancholy 'are not easily separable from its negative associations . . . and the possible onset of dementia' (65–6).

25 The Doctor in *TNK* 4.2.45–7 finds a 'profound melancholy' near to 'engrafted madness'. Illnesses and malignant melancholy are placed side by side in many other Shakespeare contexts, including *R3* 1.1.137 and *R2* 5.6.20–1. In *CE* 5.1.80–1, 'moody and dull melancholy' is called a 'Kinsman to grim and comfortless despair'.

26 Wittkower and Wittkower (1963), 106–7.

27 Gellert (1968), 139 n.2.

28 Hamlet's verses are read out in *Ham* 2.2.116–19; in 2.2.542–4 he says he will write 'a speech of some dozen or sixteen lines for the player'; Lindley (2006), 126–7, 149, 159, places Hamlet among other Shakespearean characters who are said to have musical training or accomplishments and yet are not called upon to demonstrate their abilities (see Chapter Five).

29 Our interpretation of the Sonnets in Chapter Six will contradict the view taken in Faas (1986), 136–50, that in Shakespeare's Sonnets the 'poetic imagination' aligns with simply 'pathological states of mind' and that Shakespeare 'acknowledged a link between creativity and psychosis' (149). The bearing on artistic creativity of the primary unconscious processes underlying mental growth, dreams, neuroses and at worst psychoses is another matter: some of the literature on this is discussed in Sokol (1994) 78–9, 82–3, 185 n14.

30 Sonnet 98; *2H4* 2.4.265; *Cym* 2.5.12.

31 *MA* 1.3.11; *TNK* 5.6.62–3; *Tit passim*.

32 Sokol (2003), 30–47, shows that Ariel's second ditty relates crucially to the material world as well as the psychological, and suggests (178–9) Ariel may be most materially gendered.

33 In a future work I will attempt to show Shakespeare's Richard II is really a poet-king.

1 Painters and Sculptors in Shakespeare's Poems

1   Kristeller (1951), 508, describes this development. The independent visual artist neither a guildsman nor dependent on a

single patron is extolled in a long poem by Karel Van Mander introducing his 1604 *Schilder-Boeck*, translated into French in Van Mander (2008).

2   Tittler (2013), 76–7, describes such Elizabethan retail shops, and a London outdoor art market.

3   Flemish by birth (as were many Tudor artists), Teerlinc served the English court from 1545 until 1576 and was very well remunerated. See Roy Strong, 'Teerlinc, Levina (d. 1576)', *Oxford DNB* (2004). Her contemporaries included the Italian painters Lavinia Fontana and Sofonisba Anguissola, and Catharina van Hemessen in Flanders.

4   Da Vinci (1970), I, 56. Leonardo concludes, 'The nobility of the sense of sight was shown to be three times greater than that of the other three senses' (I, 67).

5   Egan (2001), which is based on computer analysis of texts 1550–1650 in the comprehensive LION database.

6   See: Da Vinci (1970), I, 6–13; Pedretti (1977), I, 76. The manuscripts first titled *paragoni* in an 1817 edition by G. Manzi from manuscripts in *Codex Urbinas* 1270 are related to an inaccurate *Treatise on Painting* compiled by Francesco Melzi, one of Leonardo's pupils, around 1540 but that was regarded as a Leonardo original for centuries. See http://www. treatiseonpainting.org/intro.html. The phrase 'paragone of the senses' used in Dundas (1993), 54, is apt to Leonardo and others, Shakespeare included.

7   Da Vinci (1970), I, 38–9, which adds that losses of hearing or smell are trivial compared with blindness (39–40).

8   Da Vinci (1970), I, 64, stating that love 'is the main motive of the species in the whole animal world'.

9   Meek (2009), 86–8, reviews the history of such views and comments that 'at key moments' (for example when speech is demanded to confirm seen ghosts, walking statues, the risen dead), 'Shakespeare's plays display uncertainty towards the claims of the visual'.

10 Da Vinci (1970), I, 52–68 on poetry; I, 76–81 on music; I, 91–101 on sculpture. According to Pedretti (1977), I, 76–9, Leonardo also produced a text 'at the request of Lodovico Sforza, Duke of Milan, to determine which of the two arts,

Painting and Sculpture, is more noble', which survives in quotations in Lomazzo (1598).

11 Meek (2009), 12–14, which continues that the relationship is 'far more complex and ambiguous' than straightforward. Meek (13) quotes Erasmus's *De Copia*, and the 'Argument' to *The Shepeardes Calender* February eclogue: 'the olde man teleth a tale . . . as feelingly, as if the thing were set forth in some picture before our eyes'. See Spenser (1966), 19. Bender (1972) analyses how Spenser's poetry practises pictorialism. On the other hand, Spenser (1978), 342–3, proem ii to *The Faerie Queene* III, has 'Ne Poet's wit, that passeth Painter farre' can do justice to the excellence and beauty of Chastity as embodied in Queen Elizabeth, as indeed cannot any 'living art'.

12 Horace (2000), 108. Bender (1972), 12–13, holds that '*ut pictura poesis* became a dogma of Renaissance criticism' with only one 'major' dissenter, Ludovico Castelvetro. However, Platonizing beliefs in the primacy of language over imagery were widespread; Meek (2009), 88, mentions pre-Socratic antecedents.

13 *Discoveries* (1641) line 1102 in Jonson (2015).

14 Da Vinci (1970), I, 82–101. For background, see Mendelsohn (1982), esp. 55.

15 Varchi (1549), 155.

16 Varchi read a lecture to the Florentine Academy on 6 March 1547, published as Varchi (1549), in which Michelangelo's sonnet is interpreted as equating the work of a sculptor with a lover's idealization of the beloved. See Carlson (2014) on Michelangelo and Varchi.

17 Michelangelo (1986), 76.

18 In Genesis 1.3–4, 1.10, 1.12, 1.18, 1.21, 1.25, 1.31, the Creator *spoke* first to create light and then the world, but then promptly and repeatedly '*saw* that it was good' (King James translation). Conversely, at the start of John's Gospel the *logos* precedes all, and vision is unmentioned; Hellenism entered Judaeo-Christianity.

19 Sokol (1994), 21–3, 68–9, and *passim*, considers *paragoni* in Shakespeare. Sillars (2015), 133–62, finds at the 'centre' of *R2* a 'parallel exploration of the identities of the visual and verbal', making the play of 'deep importance in the contemporary

discussion of the two arts' (162), which was the *paragoni* tradition.

20 Burrow (2002), 413, defends removing the parentheses in line 10 editorially by alleging that 'the chiastic relation between the *pencil* and *pen*' on the one hand and 'inward worth' and 'outward fair' on the other produces an opposition between the pen 'which describes the inward, and the pencil, which depicts the outward'. Burrow thinks that either poetry or painting must prevail in accord with 'a fundamental debate about the merits of the sister arts known in the Renaissance as "paragone"'. Although Belsey (2012), 190–1, discusses 'cooperation between the sister arts' of poetry and painting, it also supposes that one side must prevail over the other in *paragoni*, and so (190) denies that the term *paragone* is applicable to *Luc* 1457–96 because 1496–8 show that the 'two modes [verbal and visual] work together' and 'are reciprocal'.

21 Booth (2000), xi–xviii, discovers numerous syntactic and semantic ambiguities, yet insists that the 'quatrain obviously means "Thus children will give you the immortality that art cannot"' (xii) – and so the painter and poet's arts are equated. Vendler (1999), 114, similarly finds Sonnet 16 contrasting 'biological generation' with 'the inferior representational power of the graphic artist's pencil or the writer's pen', and reiterates (116) that 'rhymer and painter alike . . . cannot immortalize the young man'. Equivalence, not contrast, is indeed implied in this poem between 'my barren rime' and 'your painted counterfeit'.

22 Thus Alberti (1973), 90, advises: 'For their own enjoyment artists should associate with poets and orators who have many embellishments in common with painters.' The Shakespearean passages discussed in Dundas (1993), 49–66, 72, deny that artistic *paragoni* have single answers.

23 Michelangelo's letter is printed in Varchi (1549), 154–5, last among eight artists' opinions of painting versus sculpture. This letter is translated in Da Vinci (1970), I, 82–3.

24 Mendelsohn (1982), 165. Mendelsohn's discussion indicates that Varchi's *paragoni* arrive at equivalences, rather than oppositions.

25 Ames-Lewis (2000), 152–3, which deems this a 'careful compromise'.

26 Dolce (2000), 129. In the same dialogue Aretino denies supremacy to any single style of painting: 'there is no call to believe . . . that perfect painting takes one form and one form only' (159).

27 Lomazzo (1598), 5–7.

28 Gordon (1949), 154–5, analyses these lines, and (159–60) interprets their intellectual background.

29 The text of *Pericles* is cited from Shakespeare (2004) which numbers the play's Choruses (including a prologue and epilogue) 1–8, starting respectively on 171, 218, 271, 308, 340, 364, 394 and 405.

30 Chorus/lines 1.4, 1.41, 2.4, 2.15, 3.14, 5.22, 6.24, 7.17, 8.1, 8.3 in Shakespeare (2004) refer to visual versus aural communication.

31 Lucrece clearly hopes that spontaneous visual 'action', not artful *eloquotio* or gestural rhetorical speech, will verify her innocence.

32 Shakespearean examples of the first and second types include: *Luc* 1333–60; *H5* PR.26–7 and 3.0.3–33. Examples of the fourth include *LRF* 4.5.11–23; and *Tit* 2.3.10–29 (but Aaron sees the same scene differently). See Sokol (1994), 16–19 and Meek (2009) on *ekphrasis*.

33 The servant's muteness evidences personal deficiency rather than either of the 'two forms of mute speech' discussed in Rancière (2009), 31–42. Those are 'a speech written on the body' by overwhelming emotions requiring 'deciphering', and 'the voiceless power of a nameless speech that lurks behind consciousness' associated with a 'Schopenhauerian' abyss (41–2). The prominent unnamed unconscious process is Lucrece's undeserved shame; so Brutus': 'Thy wrenched wife mistook the matter so' (1826–7).

34 Some manuscript verses written by Shakespeare's contemporary Thomas Harriot, that may have had direct bearing on the verbal excesses spoofed in *LLL*, express parallel notions piquantly: 'A man of wordes and not of deedes is like a garden full of weedes / A man of deedes and not of wordes is like a privie full of tourdes'. Sokol (1991) discusses these lines, found in the margin of British Library, Add. MS 6786, f. 237.

35 Kemp (1987). Barolsky (2004) argues that Dante was the originator of the 'Modern Cult' in which the artist is the central culture hero, and was thus Vasari's precursor. But this argument focuses on a monotonic scale of artistic excellence, not on varieties of style.

36 Dolce (2000), 159.

37 Melion (1991) discusses Van Mander's *Schilder-Boeck* which incorporates 'large excerpts from Vasari's [1568] text' (95), and adds materials on many northern artists (78–91).

38 Sourcing a specific painting, tapestry or sculpture for a prop used in a repertory theatre may have been too costly, and sightlines in public playhouses may have made such props too indistinct. Parallel problems did not arise when poems were read out or music played onstage. Leland and Bargona (2016), 173, suggest that the casket paintings in *MV* could have been 'pieces of rolled paper', but that Silvia's portrait, noted in *TGV* 4.2.118 and 4.4.115, is 'something larger and framed' which could have been a prop (and likewise the Painter's 'piece' in *Tim* 1.1.28ff). But just as pieces of paper can simulate portrait miniatures, the backs of joined boards can simulate easel paintings.

39 The connoisseur Third Gentleman in *WT* 5.2.98–9 describes Julio thus. Sillars (2015), 236–40, discusses the 'troublesome relation between aesthetic autonomy and naturalistic representation' (240), mentioning 'one of the paradoxes of responses to painting: the more effective it is as representation, the less it is considered as a work of art' (236). Sokol, 1994, suggests that Renaissance art conveying lifelikeness (for receptive beholders) is not at all the same as art achieving illusionistic verisimilitude.

40 See Gombrich (1977), 154–244.

41 Shakespeare (2004), 272, 276 (Chorus/lines 3.11–13 and 3.58–9).

42 My fuller discussion, in relation to Shakespeare, is forthcoming in a collection of essays; see also Hunt (2011).

43 Da Vinci (1970), I, 320; Alberti (1973), 83. See Gombrich (1963), 37–41, on an experiment with deliberately distorted images.

44 See Gombrich (1963), 40, and Sokol (1994), 11–15, and *passim*.

45 'Pagan', rather than pre-Reformation, because surviving English pre-Reformation church decoration is full of vividness and vitality. Another reading would be that this reflects the Elizabethan 'iconophobia' alleged in Collinson (1988), 115–25, a theory not supported by this and the next chapter.

46 By refusing to allow viewers' imagination, this goes beyond *paragone* remarks that visual images cannot convey motion or speech.

47 Pliny is quoted in Prince (1992), 34–5, and Elizabethan accounts are named.

48 See Da Vinci (1970), I, 233–41.

49 See Alberti (1973), 89. Da Vinci (1970), I, 95, praises painting's 'miraculous' ability to make 'what is flat appear in relief'.

50 I have stood in the Room of the Giants in Giulio's Palazzo Te in Mantua and can attest that its *trompe l'oeil* effects are not at all irresistible or overwhelming, as alleged in Vasari (1996), II, 132 (in the Life of Giulio Romano): 'whoever enters that room . . . cannot but fear that everything will fall upon him . . . that room, which is not more than fifteen braccia in length, has the appearance of open country'. Far from it – from most vantages the perspective of this fantastic room is 'out', and neither is the modelling convincingly realistic. However, the room is very beautiful and impressive; the forms and facial expressions of the (very human-like) falling giants depicted there cause one to *imagine* frightening possibilities, although not to experience them as actually present and immediately perilous.

51 The story of Zeuxis painting Lucina is recounted in Alberti (1973), 93. Ames-Lewis (2000), 190, comments on Alberti's disapproval of 'the early painter Demetrius' who was 'more devoted to representing the likeness of things than to beauty'.

52 Doebler (1988) discusses the history of horse imagery in relation to *VA*, mentioning that Philip Sidney was 'almost persuaded' in his *Apology for Poetry* 'to wish himself a horse' (72). However, Thomas (1983), 38–9, 94–117, 118–19, 134–5, makes clear that there was intense early modern anxiety connected with any violation of an insecure yet crucial line of division between humans and other animal species.

53 Tudeau-Clayton (2000), 21.

54 On the polysemous word 'rein' used by Shakespeare and his
    contemporaries see Sokol (1994), 236 n.28.

55 The account of the horse in *VA* contrasts with the hilarious
    word painting in *TS* 3.2.48–55 of an anti-ideal one. *H5* zanily
    parodies Petrarchanism when to cap a long blazon of his 'palfry'
    Bourbon asserts, 'I once wrote a sonnet in his praise . . . my
    horse is my mistress' (3.7.3–43).

56 Donaldson (1972), 123–4.

57 Astley (1584), 4.

58 *OED* object, *n.* I. 1.a., 2.a.

59 These paintings are illustrated in Doebler (1988), and discussed
    in relation to *VA*.

60 See Alberti (1973), 95. See Melion (1991), 100, on how Van
    Mander's similar views echo Pliny's and contrast with Vasari's.

61 Alberti (1973), 89.

62 See Dolce (2000), 159; Mendelsohn (1982), 137.

63 Alberti (1973), 23–4. Here Spenser comments that 'the concept
    of *istoria* dominates the whole [of Alberti's] treatise', and that
    Alberti 'puts it at the pinnacle of artistic development'.

64 Gombrich (1977), 176–7, and see also 176–86 which traces this
    tactic from a classical description by Philostratus through the
    Renaissance and up to modern times.

65 Gombrich (1977), 167.

66 Horace (2000), 108.

67 Quoted from Henry Wotton's *The Elements of Architecture* in
    Martinet (1975), 267, and related there to the aesthetic of *WT*,
    immediately after quotation of a 1598 letter from Wotton to the
    Earl of Salisbury stating that a portrait was 'done truly and
    naturally, but roughly, *alla Venetiana*, and therefore to be set at
    some good distance from the sight'. There may have been
    draughts of Wotton's *Elements* circulating by 1608. See Sokol
    (1994), 207 n.34.

68 Ever since Aristotle recorded his remarkable observations about
    children and *mimesis* in *Poetics* 1448b, note has been taken that
    imitation, and also 'reading' imitation, is instinctual in human
    beings. It has been increasingly understood that extracting

meaning from seeing and hearing is enabled and mediated by creative extrapolation, for sensory data is typically beset by lacunae and noise. Similar capabilities apply when filling in sensory lacunae and when 'reading' imaginative works, and this may partly explain instincts for engaging with *mimesis*. So I think that an observation in Meek (2006), 65, about the unavailability of 'an ideal, visual mode of interpretation' is not sufficiently countered by the following remark that 'Lucrece herself emphasises the fact that one's state of mind can alter what one sees'. Meek here accurately depicts the interaction of Lucrece and the groom, but on a basis somewhat open to question. Meek (80) concludes by remarking that Shakespeare 'suggests that both visual and verbal works of art are incomplete, and reminds us that there is no representational ideality', and yet that *Luc* 'is also an implied defence of the imagination and its ability to fill in the gaps left by an artwork. It insists on the limitations of art, yet simultaneously champions the power of the imagination to piece out these imperfections.' I accept that but question if 'incomplete', 'limitations' and filled with 'gaps' doesn't also describe sensory perception.

69 The conveying by an artwork of such impressions is not identical to it possessing either of the *energeia* and *enargeia* that are distinguished and discussed in Bender (1972), 8–11.

70 Dolce (2000), 157.

71 Quinn (2004), 22–3, adopts the minority view that Lucrece's 'piece / Of skillful painting' work' is a tapestry.

72 Plausible falseness was a major topic for many Renaissance writers, following a lead in Plutarch's *Moralia*; for an excellent discussion of this in relation to Iago in *Oth* see Evans (2001).

73 Virgil's shepherds are rough with their captive Sinon, and some of his Trojans at first jeer at him, but in *Luc* 1501–2, the 'bound' Sinon evokes only pity, making him even more ungrateful and treacherous.

74 *Tit* 5.3.84; *3H6* 3.2.190; *Cym* 3.4.59.

75 Burrow (2002), 322 n., identifies the source of this story in Livy 1.53–4 and *Fasti* 2.690–710, and discusses the likelihood of Shakespeare knowing this, quite possibly through Paulus

Marsus' edition of *Fasti* which makes the connections to Livy and between Sinon and Tarquin explicit (48–50).

76 Prince (1992), 65 n., has: 'Baldwin showed that Shakespeare, in writing the Argument, had before him an annotated edition of Ovid's *Fasti* and a text of Livy's *Historia*'.

77 Burrow (2002), 45–54, reviews how literary/political sources had bearing on *Luc*.

78 *Tit* 4.1.20–1; *Ham* 2.2.504–21 and 559–62; *TC* 5.3.56–7 and 86; *Cym* 4.2.15.

79 Da Vinci (1970), 53, which states, regarding a writer portraying a battle scene, 'the painter will be your superior, because your pen will be worn out before you can fully describe what the painter can demonstrate forthwith . . . and your tongue will be parched and your body overcome by sleep and hunger before you can describe with words what a painter is able to show you in an instant.'

80 Rosenberg and Klein (2015) is an up-to-date account of research into fine art viewing using eye-tracking devices.

2 Painters and Sculptors in Shakespeare's Plays

1 *Luc* 1367, 1499ff describe the Troy painting as admirable, and *Tim* 1.1.91–3, 1.1.159–61 refers to paintings as valuable or valued. Elsewhere paintings are ridiculed, in, for instance, 'your hands in your pocket like a man after the old painting' in *LLL* 3.1.18–19 and a 'reechy painting', in *MA* 3.3.129–30. Paintings are misleading in 'are you like the painting of a sorrow / A face without a heart' in *Ham* 4.7.91–2 and 'This is the very painting of your fear' in *Mac* 3.4.60.

2 For instance, words derived from 'to paint' appear eleven times in *LLL*, only once in a positive context, and three of those times refer to the falsity of rhetoric. The falsity of cosmetic 'painting' is referred to in *LLL* 4.3.257; Sonnets 67, 82, 83, 146; and *Cym* 3.4.50. Ambiguities hover over approval when Coriolanus refers to the blood of battle on his face as 'painting' (1.7.68), or when women sweating in their heavy costumes at the pageant of the

Field of the Cloth of Gold are said to be red in the face as if
'painting' (*H8* 1.1.23–6).

3 A 'picture' serves as a love icon in *LC* 134; *TGV* 4.2.117;
   4.4.113–15; *LLL* 4.1.83–4; *MA* 2.3.51. Pictures are described in
   detail in *Luc*; *VA*; *LLL* 5.2.38; *Per* 16.91; *Cym* 5.6.175. They
   are mentioned jocularly in *LLL* 4.1.84, 5.2.38; *CE* 4.3.13;
   2H4 4.2.47; *TN* 1.3.122, 1.5.223–6, 2.3.16; *Tem* 3.2.129.

4 *Paragone* objections that visual artworks lack voice, argument,
   or motion are echoed in *VA* 211; *MV* 1.2.69–70; *Ham* 2.2.483;
   TC 5.1.6; and *Cor* 1.3.11. In *Ham* 4.5.82–4 Claudius refers to
   'pictures'' lack of reasoning abilities: 'poor Ophelia / Divided
   from herself and her fair judgement, / Without the which we are
   pictures or mere beasts', and Lady Macbeth speaks similarly in
   2.2.51–2. Iago calls women false 'pictures' in *Oth* 2.1.112.
   'Pictures' are talismans of ill will in *1H6* 2.3.36 and *LRF* 2.1.80.
   Erotic pictures are mentioned in *TS* I.1.45–8; *LC* 134; *TGV*
   2.4.207, 4.2.117–18, 4.4.85, 4.4.113–15; *MW* 2.2.86;
   TC 3.2.46; *Per* 16.91; *Cym* 2.2.25, 5.6.204; *TNK* 4.1.1ff,
   5.5.41ff.

5 Collinson, 1988, 115–25, holds that post-Reformation
   'iconophobia' robbed a generation of Elizabethans of all
   acquaintance with visual art.

6 These include *1H6* 4.7.83; *MV* 2.7.48 (the 'picture' is called
   'Fair Portia's counterfeit' in 3.2.115); *MA* 2.3.251; *Ham*
   2.2.367, 3.4.52; *WT* 5.1.74, 172. See Dundas (1993), 55–63, on
   Shakespeare's Sonnets imaging painting or painters.

7 Portraits, full-length or otherwise, focus on faces. Hulse (1986)
   maintains that Shakespeare often represents faces as maddeningly
   misleading. But undetectable dissimulation in faces does not
   feature in the portraits described by Shakespeare, for falsified
   portraits give themselves away by being lifeless. An exception to
   this rule appears when Lucrece at first does not detect the
   dissimulation of the hypocrite Sinon when viewing his portrayal:
   'Such signs of truth in his plain face she spied . . .' but she revises
   that to 'It cannot be . . . / But such a face should bear a wicked
   mind' (*Luc* 1532, 1539–40).

8 The exceptions are *MV* 2.9.53, where Aragon finds 'The portrait
   of a blinking idiot' in the silver casket, and *Ham* 5.2.79 where
   'portraiture' is mentioned figuratively.

9   See Strong (1983), 65–136, on Hilliard. Sabatier (2016), 176–7,
     agrees concerning perspective, quoting Hilliard's *Treatise
     Concerning the Arte of Limning*: 'For perspective . . . is an art
     . . . to deceive both the understanding and the eye.' Strong
     (1983), 142–85, finds Hilliard's pupil Isaac Oliver contrastingly
     a wholly Renaissance artist, as sophisticated as any in Europe
     and abreast of all new developments. This view of Hilliard may
     be unfair. His *Treatise* shows him fully aware of both aerial and
     linear perspective: thus Hilliard (1911–12), 20, describes
     perspective effects involving both 'forshortning' and 'shading'.
     Hilliard relied more on his eyes and hands than mathematics
     when obtaining perspective and other subtle effects 'cuningly
     drawne with true observations, for ower eye is cuninge, and is
     learned without rulle by long usse' (27). Yet he understood that
     perspective is a means 'by falshood to express truth in very
     cunning of line, and true observation of shadoing' (20), and
     it was in that sense that he wrote about deceiving the eye.
     Hilliard's miniatures have shallow depths of field and lack
     receding background images, but that may have been a
     sophisticated choice of expressive gestures as 'mannerist' in
     their way as was Oliver in his.

10   Mercer (1962), 190.

11   Reynolds (1964), 284. This continues: 'It was matter-of-fact to
     the Elizabethans because they learned to accept it and to us
     because we have acquired the historical imagination to do so.
     Our disappearing sense of how strange, how unnatural Hilliard's
     style is can be restored by recalling the reactions of eighteenth
     and nineteenth centuries to the costumes which he painted so
     well.' Amusing examples follow.

12   In 'Ode to Himself' in Jonson (1980), 283.

13   Nicholas Hilliard and Isaac Oliver were both born into
     goldsmiths' families. Portrait miniatures were often enclosed in
     jewelled containers, as seen in *TN* 3.4.203: 'Here, wear this
     jewel for me, 'tis my picture'. The historical account of the rise
     and decline of English limning given in Mercer (1962), 191–216,
     is modified in Strong (1983), *passim*, which charts an uneven
     course of development beginning with the arrival in England in
     the 1520s of the Hornebolte family of illuminators of the
     Ghent-Bruges school (including the daughter Susanna), reaching

an early highpoint in the work of Holbein and later maturity in the work of Hilliard, followed by Oliver. For a broader overview of limning see Coombs (2009).

14 Strong (1983), 95, and see 92–136.

15 Hilliard (1911–12), 37. On the wider impact of 'Albertus Dure' on Hilliard, see 19–20 and 26–7.

16 Strong (1983), 68.

17 Strong (1983), 68.

18 Thus a remark on why Holbein's portraits 'excel' made in Strong (1983), 52, may be applied to Hilliard as well. Such a capacity is more important for us than Strong's conclusion that 'Hilliard had an enormous impact on the aesthetic of his age' (136). Shakespeare rarely shows interest in art history except in his allusion to painted statues in *WT* and in the accurate description of extreme uses of linear perspective in anamorphic painting in a simile in *R2* 2.2.16–20.

19 Lomazzo (1598), 13. Hilliard (1911–12) was self-confessedly 'written at the request of R. Haydocke who publisht in English a translation Paulo Lomazzo on Painting' (18), and it praises Lomazzo's work (18, 21). Strong (1983), 136, is doubtful of the 'mediaeval' Hilliard's relation to the 'late Renaissance' Lomazzo, but the above perhaps undercuts that.

20 Mary Edmond, 'Hilliard, Nicholas (1547?–1619)', *Oxford DNB* (2004). This would have been their price without jewelled settings.

21 Tittler (2013), 72–7; 74, explains that English-born painters could usually charge on average only up to a few pounds for their work, with the costs of materials possibly paid separately.

22 According to Tittler (2013), 56, 'panel portraits remained surprisingly inexpensive' until a new 'virtual craze' for owning artworks by past and present masters hit England in the 1610s and 1620s.

23 Quoted from the text of the royal entertainment at Mitcham, most likely by John Lyly, in Cooper (2013), 19 n.1. The entertainment is discussed in Cooper (2013), 11, 19 n.1, and Cooper (2012), 2.

24 On portraits of other artists see Cooper (2013), 172–83. See also Cooper and Hadfield (2013) on verifiable artists portraits. There is of course much debate about Shakespeare's likenesses.

25 Although said to be 'raised', these two statues are somehow also typical prone burial effigies, for Romeo's statue will 'by his lady's lie' (*RJ* 5.3.302).

26 Kelleher (2007), 217, 223–4, suggests that the value of the ducat was between five and ten Tudor shillings.

27 It might have struck some of them as an irony, as well, revealing the under-valuation of visual artists. Hilliard himself was often in financial straits and forty pounds was the most that he was ever promised from the royal purse for a year, with evidence that he rarely received all of it. See Mary Edmond, 'Hilliard, Nicholas (1547?–1619)', *Oxford DNB* (2004).

28 Merchant (1959), 12, suggests that when Viola describes Olivia's complexion: ''Tis beauty truly blent, whose red and white / Nature's own sweet and cunning hand laid on' (*TN* 1.5.228–9), 'the tribute is in terms of the limner's technique, an almost literal echo of Hillyard's method of achieving "carnation" or flesh tones'. Hilliard (1911–12), 34–5, describes the handling of 'carnation' in detail.

29 Whall (1994), holds that Hilliard did not use sophisticated continental techniques, and argues that the closet scene in *Ham* '"conserves" Hilliard by parodying him', and that 'Shakespeare's own ironic treatment of the Prince reduces him, caricatures him in and as a miniature' (308). But, as Strong (1983), 146, points out, from about 1587 Isaac Oliver produced miniatures 'responding to the work of a new generation in the person of Hendrik Goltzius of Haarlem' (also see Strong, 1983, 151–2).

30 Reynolds (1964), 280, argues that the eighteenth-century practice of playing this scene with miniatures was in accord with Shakespeare's intentions.

31 Reynolds (1964), 282, adding that 'the miniature was a fetish', which in its alienating distortions 'reflects the emotion of the lover, the sense he has of a pale face seen too close and too feelingly for normal understanding' (284).

32 Mercer (1962), 195; and see 195–201, where Mercer counterpoises English miniature painting (before its supposed decadence) against 'the increasingly State and public nature of oil-painting'.

33 Hilliard (1911–12), 16, which appears just before a mutilation of the MS.

34 The general weirdness of the sexual relations in *TGV*, culminating in the intended rape and then transfer of Silvia in 5.4, is discussed in Sokol and Sokol (2003), 113. Noting Silvia's words – 'your idol', 'worship shadows and adore false shapes' – Hunt (2004), 9, connects the picture in *TGV* with contrasts between Catholic and Protestant viewpoints, which pervade the play (1–17). This, however, does not explain Silvia's action.

35 *TGV* 2.1.1–8, presents symbolic exchanges (including an exchange of rings, handfasting, and a mutual kiss), echoing a marriage by *spousals* as described in Sokol and Sokol (2003), 15, 17–18 (see also 13–29, 83–4, 93–116).

36 'Portraiture', according to Strong (1983), 26, as it 'emerged under the Tudors was exclusively royal portraiture. The usual incentives for the production of pictures were that they were needed in marriage negotiations.' Silvia's portrait might be associated with the stereotyped lifeless 'costume piece' paintings described in Mercer (1962), 171.

37 Elizabethan easel portraiture is thus harshly described in Mercer (1962), 157, which continues: 'In a dialogue from yet another "Entertainment" to Queen Elizabeth in 1598 a poet is made to say to a painter "so shallow are we both, that the Painter must spend his colors in limning attires, the Poet in commending the fashions".' Strong (1970) largely concurs. Cooper (2012), 199, suggests that portraits 'strove towards an often elaborate decorative accuracy and credible likeness rather than an illusory presence' on account of 'post reformation anxieties'. Cooper (2013), 14–17, finds Elizabethan portraits naive and avoiding 'embodying the essence of the person' (17). For more admiring views see Hearn (1995), 9–10. Leslie (1985), 21, holds that 'Elizabethan neomedievalism' in portraiture is not unsophisticated or unaware of contemporary Italian developments, but rather 'a self-conscious stylistic development, by no means unparalleled in continental art'.

38 Quotations are from Strong (1983), 111.

39 Hilliard (1911–12), 24.

40 If Portia's lively portrait is a miniature and Silvia's stereotyping one is 'in large' this accords with repeated remarks in Mercer (1962), 145–216, on the qualities and functions of Elizabethan

easel portraits versus miniatures, but, as mentioned in Note 36, such views may be outdated.

41 Shakespeare and Fletcher (2005 [1634]), 62: tln 2359.

42 Hearn (1995), 107, transcribes the inscription and points out that the miniature self-portraits made by Hilliard and Oliver did not show them as painters, which makes Gower's painting doubly unique. See also Cooper (2012), 20–1; Karen Hearn, 'Gower, George (d. 1596)', *Oxford DNB* (2004).

43 See the old spelling edition Whythorne (1961), 305–6, on the portraits.

44 Whythorne (1962), 11–12, 116, describes the mottos and verses Whythorne had inscribed on his portraits, and also (38) records other verses he intended to have written on a third portrait, although he was dissuaded from this.

45 See Whythorne (1962), 175–7 (the first quotation is from 176, the others from 175).

46 Blunt (1939), the first serious discussion of a possible echo of the *paragone* in *Tim*, finds painting and poetry compared only in 'More pregnantly than words' (1.1.93). Neither Hunt (1988) nor Sillars (2015), 234–40, find more.

47 Alberti (1973), 90. Aretino in Dolce (2000), 129, asserts that a painter should be 'versed in historical narrative and the tales of poets'.

48 Adair (1998), 354.

49 Perhaps such an upwelling shows in the curtness of the Poet's 'Nay, sir, but hear me on' (1.1.78), or the Painter's equally short 'Ay, marry, but what of these?' (1.1.84) or ''Tis common' (1.1.90). When considering the 'thousand moral paintings' remark Hunt (1988), 51, finds that the 'latent antagonisms of [the Painter and the Poet's] very first social exchange ("good day, sir" answered by "I am glad y' are well") suddenly surface . . . and the rivalry of the verbal and visual artists is revealed: exactly the *paragone* that Blunt diagnosed'. However, Hunt thinks that this alleged hostility does not prove them, or the play itself, 'embattled in *paragone*' (57). Hunt's essay refers to cooperation between the arts rather than rivalry (59, 61), but does not detect it between the Painter and Poet in *Tim*.

50 Nuttall (1989), 8; Sillars (2015), 239.

51 Nuttall (1989), 15.

52 For instance, Hunt (1988), 56, labels the Poet and Painter in *Tim* 'sycophantic time-servers'. Sillars (2015), 234–40, interprets the Poet's phrase 'artificial strife' partially in terms of 'hypocrisy and overreaching', and presumes that the Painter and Poet betray (presumably unwarranted) 'social pretensions' (237). Both artists are also accused of being 'hypocrites in their approach to Timon' and wholly deficient in their 'knowledge of the traditions of their arts' (239). The many citations of others in this section of Sillar's valuable book show that tendencies to half-despise the two artists are in no way exceptional.

53 The inscription is transcribed in Hearn (1995), 107.

54 On the influx of foreign painters, especially from Antwerp and later from Amsterdam, see Brown (1995); and on competition between foreign and native painters, see Cooper (2012), 52–5.

55 Wilson (2005), 23.

56 Sidney (1961), 8.

57 Nuttall (1989), 6, writes that the Poet speaks 'precious tumid verse', which is perhaps more harsh than his tendency towards speaking with circumlocutions and flowery diction deserve. Sillars (2015), 235, judges that the Poet's inflated language does not seek to draw together 'disparate elements to offer a new truth' (like other late sixteenth-century poetry), but is 'simply waywardly complicated'. However, we should remember that the Poet is not here composing poetry, but rather speaking through the dramatic medium of blank verse – a distinction that will be addressed at the start of the next chapter. It is therefore necessary to compare the Poet's diction with that of other dramatic characters in courtly situations, and unwarranted to judge it as 'verse'.

58 *Tim* 5.1.30–1, 36–8, 46–53. Apemantus anticipates just this disgust at 4.3.353–6, when he pre-announces to Timon, 'Yonder comes a poet and a painter', expresses fear of catching the plague, and departs.

59 Unless otherwise noted the text and paratexts of *The Spanish Tragedy* are cited from Kyd (2013).

60 Stevenson (1968), 308, traces discussions of the additions back
    to Lamb and Coleridge, and adduces strong internal evidence
    that Shakespeare was 'the person most likely to have written the
    Additions to *The Spanish Tragedy*'.

61 Kyd (2013), 319–28, reviews the question of the authorship of
    the additions to the 1602 quarto and concludes that 'there are
    sufficient grounds to link the author of the fourth "addition"
    [which is the Painter scene] with Shakespeare'. Bruster (2013)
    presents new evidence supporting the same conclusion
    concerning all four additions; Nance (2017) argues for
    Shakespeare's authorship of the Painter scene, and Taylor (2017)
    for Shakespeare and Heywood's authorship of the additions.

62 Alberti (1973), 77.

63 Dolce (2000), 159.

64 Young (1985), 453–4. This article describes Elizabethan
    practices of keeping *imprese* in the Shield Gallery at Whitehall,
    and traces likely sources for the six *imprese* detailed in *Per*.
    Imprese are discussed in Sokol (1994), 19–21.

65 Leslie (1985), 28, stated in connection with *Tim* having an
    impresa-like structure.

66 See Leslie (1985), 25–7. This asserts that William Drummond of
    Hawthornden's *A Short Discourse upon Impresa's* [*sic*], 'besides
    conveying the peculiar pleasures and excitements of these word/
    image games, reminds us of the crucial point in the discussion of
    imprese . . . an essential role is that of the reader: ordering,
    relating, interpreting, understanding, evaluating . . . The process
    of comprehending the interrelations of the various elements,
    whereby the indeterminate becomes fixed and redolent of
    meaning, takes place within the reader as is at the heart of the
    form.'

67 Castiglione (1975), 77–8.

68 Hilliard (1911–12), 22. I quote more of Hilliard's long sentence
    than other commentators have done, truncating only its
    conclusion about a single person having a 'variety of looks and
    countenance'. Leslie (1985), 22, quotes separately in two
    different paragraphs the first and last parts of this Hilliard
    sentence, skipping over the middle portion of the sentence
    beginning 'of all thinges the perfection is to imitate the face of

mankind'. Strong (1983), 98, quotes the passage only up to
'device whatsoever', in order to support a discussion of Hilliard
and *imprese* (95–101); this is followed by a discussion of
Hilliard's work in areas other than limning (112–36).

69 Another possibility is seen in Hilliard (1911–12), 28, 'Forget not
therefore that the principal parte of painting or drawing after
the life consiste[t]h in the truth of the lyne', which might suggest
that excellent draughtsmanship can render a kind of
truthfulness, even in formalistic genres.

70 See the documents reproduced in Chambers (1930), II, 153.

71 Unnamed painters or carvers are alluded to (sometimes only
facetiously) in *VA*; *Luc*; *LLL* 5.2.636; *TGV* 4.4.184; *RJ* 1.2.39;
MV 3.2.121; *LRF* 2.2.57; *Tim* 1.1 and 5.1 *passim*; *TNK*
1.2.122.

72 Although Hamlet shows concern for the economic plight of the
players and the future careers of their child-actor rivals
(2.2.346–52), he does not recall the name of a single actor and
rather addresses them in terms of the roles they typically play, as
if they were mere functions. The Lord in *TS*, 1.1.84–7, heartless
as he seems, at least acknowledges that one player has a name,
when he is reminded, 'I think 'twas Soto that your honour
means.' A topical joke seemingly overrides the improbability that
the Lord in *TS* should have more regard than Hamlet for such
underlings.

73 McCarthy (2013) makes a strong case for the Shakespearean
authorship of *Arden*. *Arden* is included in the 2016 New Oxford
Shakespeare; the analyses in Elliott and Greatley-Hirsch (2017)
support this attribution.

74 See King (2012) for the background to *Arden*. The murder story
appeared in Holinshed's first edition of 1577 and second edition
of 1578. *Arden* is cited hereafter from White (2000), as is the
1578 version of Holinshed (reprinted there 104–20).

75 See White (2000), 104, 111.

76 A marginal note to Holinshed in White (2000), 110.

77 *OED* clerk, *n.* 1, 2. *OED* shows 'cleric' as a noun from
the 1620s, although 'clerical' as an adjective was in use
by 1592.

78 *OED* clerk, *n.* 6.b.

79 All citations of *Arden of Faversham* will be from the edition
    White (2000) which uses scene numbers and has no act
    divisions.

80 See Mendelsohn (1982), 98, 104, on Benedetto Varchi's reading
    of this doctrine in Michelangelo's Sonnets.

81 The ancient extramission theory holding that the eye projects
    beams to enable sight was gradually displaced, a significant
    turning point in Europe being Kepler's 1604 *Paralipomenes a
    Vitellion*.

82 In Holinshed's account Alice Arden, and not Mosby, initiates the
    murder plot. No occult painting is in question, only the painter's
    provision of poison for Arden's food. Tassi (2005), 133–43,
    provides background to the notion of a poisonous portrait made
    by a cunning magician in *Arden*.

83 Whythorne (1962), 115–16. Whythorne (1962), 11, 38, 115–17,
    discusses each of the portrait commissions except the 1569,
    revealing Whythorne's motives ranging from youthful
    exuberance to *momento mori* including an attempt to win
    over a widow he was courting.

84 The danger was not just of insulting Catholics, for Queen
    Elizabeth used the least 'reformed' version of the Prayer Book in
    her private chapel, and was observed to have a crucifix there. See
    Sokol (2008), 200 n.78 and Lord (2003), 77–8.

85 For recent studies of this motif see Wilson (2013), Karim-Cooper
    (2006), Tassi (2005), especially 134–6, and Pollard (1999).

86 This conjunction is explored, together Elizabethan
    antitheatricalism, in Pollard (1999). Elizabethan attitudes to
    cosmetics reflected in drama are discussed in Tayler (1964),
    14–15, Dolan (1993) and especially Karim-Cooper (2006). See
    also Sokol (1994), 59–60 73–5, 206, 210, 211 and 232, and on
    cosmetic painting 76–7, 138–40.

87 Pollard (1999), 199–200, cites records of paying a 'paynter' to
    apply stage cosmetics and remarks on Renaissance etymological
    speculations connecting playing with painting that imply the
    latter means 'makeup'.

88 Lomazzo (1598), 129–33. In his introduction to this translation
    (3–4) Richard Haydock explains that he has suppressed
    Lomazzo's 'large discourse of the use of Images . . . because it

crosseth the doctrine of the reformed Churches'. On how the fraudulence of Haydock's Puritan sermonizing in his sleep was exposed by King James, see Sarah Bakewell, 'Haydock, Richard (1569/70–c. 1642)', *Oxford DNB*, 2004.

89 Ben Jonson is scathing about female cosmetics in *Epicoene*, *Cynthia's Revels*, *Sejanus*, *The Devil is an Ass* and the poems 'To Fine Lady Would-bee', 'A Satyricall Shrub' and 'An Epigram: To the small Poxe'. The 'Famous Whore' in Markham (1609), B2^v, confesses that 'The womans great art (painting) was in me / So compleat, I could blinde the choicest eie'. Among nearly sixty Shakespearean passages linking women's face painting with corruption are 'The harlot's cheek, beautied with plast'ring art, / Is not more ugly to the thing that helps it / Than is my most painted word' (*Ham* 3.1.53–5), and 'whore still; / Paint till a horse may mire upon your face' (*Tim* 4.3.147–8).

90 Guilpin (1592) C6^v–C7^r. See also B5^r, Epigrams 57, 61, 62 and 65. A 'Jubily' is a year of indulgence.

91 This play is known only from a MS containing Buc's annotations and additional slips of paper. *The Second Maiden's Tragedy* (1964) reproduces portions of the MS including a final leaf written on in an early hand, containing 'By Will Shakespeare', with the other names 'Thomas Goff' and 'George Chapman' crossed out. The current consensus is that Thomas Middleton was the author.

92 Discussion of this in Sokol (1994), 78–84, draws on the psychoanalytic insights of Melanie Klein, Hanna Segal, Donald Meltzer and Janine Chasseguet-Smirgel.

93 This stage business combines the poisoning of an object that will be kissed (as in *The Revenger's Tragedy*) with the onstage application of destructive makeup (as in Barnaby Barnes's *The Devil's Charter* and the Red Bull droll *The Humour of John Swabber*).

94 Compare *WT* 5.3.35–6, 66, 109 and see Sokol (1994), 82.

95 For instance, Duffin (1994) amusingly argues for an Italian singer known as 'Julio Romano'.

96 Martinet (1975), 261, 267, 268 (my translations).

97 See Sokol (1994), 92–6.

98 Hilliard (1911–12), 22.

99   Stone (1979), 253.

100 Private spaces could facilitate libertine as well as conspiratorial
     or heretical activities. The Lord in *TS* Induction 1.44–5 orders
     his 'fairest chamber' is to be hanged around with 'all my
     wanton pictures', according with classical precedents described
     (in another context) in Talvaccia (1997), 82–4, 100, and echoed
     as well in Jonson's *Alchemist* (1610), 2.2.41–8. The Tyrant
     takes the Lady's corpse to his 'owne privat chamber' with lewd
     intent in *The Second Maiden's Tragedy*.

101 Plutarch (1579), 723, tells the story of Olympias' husband
     being told that he will lose an eye in the 'Life of Alexander the
     Great'. Sokol (1994), 93–112, discusses this and other images
     of sexual jealousy in Giulio's Palazzo Te.

102 Sokol (1994), 117–41, sets out reasons why Perdita might be
     concerned about being wooed 'the false way' (4.4.147–51),
     mentioning implications of the classical figure of Flora and
     contemporary attitudes to royal concubines. Polixenes only
     becomes enraged about what he assumes is a sexual liaison
     between his son and Perdita after their marriage by handfasting
     has taken place.

103 This is in Jonson's Epigram 77, 'To the . . . Lord Treasurer' in
     Jonson (1980), 225. In addition, Jonson's prose *Discoveries*
     (1641), 1125–7, has 'here lived in this latter age six famous
     painters in Italy, who were excellent and emulous of the
     ancients: Raphael de Urbino, Michelangelo Buonarota, Titian,
     Antonio of Correggio, Sebastian of Venice, Giulio Romano,
     and Andrea Sartorio'.

104 See Sokol (1994), 104–6, for discussion of references to
     Aretino's supposed pictures in Jonson's *Volpone* and *The
     Alchemist*, and in satires by Markham, Marston and Donne.

105 Vasari (1996), II, 86–7, in 'The Life of Marc' Antonio
     Bolognese and of Other Engravers of Prints'.

106 Talvacchia (1999), 66, explains that Aretino's 'name became a
     password for obscene art and literature, a usage developed in
     part from the circulation of the illustrated editions of *Sonetti
     lussuriosi*'.

107 The letter is translated in Lawner (1988), 8–9. In it, Aretino
     also expresses his wish for the phallus to be more on view than

hands or mouths, and his liking for 'handsome boys and beautiful women'.

108 Talvacchia (1999), 199–227.

109 See Lawner (1988) and Talvacchia (1999). The fragments are London, British Museum, Prints and Drawings, 1972.u.1306–1314.

110 Freud (1977), 69–70, lists three criteria for perverse scopophilia, which are that it is 'restricted exclusively to the genitals', or 'is connected with the overriding of disgust', or 'instead of being *preparatory* to the normal sexual aim, it supplants it'.

111 Marcus (1966), 286.

112 A range of earlier condemnatory views are summarized in Young (1964), 89–90. Few are as censorious as Adams (1989), which in a review of Lawner (1988) labels Aretino 'pimp, pornographer, parasite . . . scum'. As befits its era, Young celebrates Giulio's designs as a neo-pagan 'high water mark of humanism' (82, 95).

113 Quoted in Gurr (1982), 58, from an essay in *Essays and Studies* in 1977 by T.S.B. Spenser.

114 Gurr (1982), 60.

115 Gurr (1982), 57. The language is not only modern: Guilpin (1592), C1^r, refers to '*Rabelais* with his durtie mouth', and associates this with '*Aretines* great wit' and other famous erotic poets and painters.

116 Gurr (1982), 58, which also associates with *I Modi* the Clown's reference in *WT* 5.2.172 to 'the Queen's picture'. Again, the word 'picture' is unlikely to be intended as a sexual innuendo here.

117 Talvacchia (1992), 168, states that aside from in *WT* 5.3.23, 'the word "posture" . . . appears only six other times in the corpus of [Shakespeare's] plays', and rightly identifies the 'salacious overtones' of its appearance in *AC* (5.2.217). However, none of the five other instances of postures, graceful or otherwise, carry any salacious or sexual implications. See *JC* 5.1.33; *Cor* 2.1.18; *Cym* 3.3.94, 5.6.165; *H8* 3.2.19.

118 Elam (2014), 138.

119 Elam (2014), 133.

120 Elam (2014), 135.

121 Talvacchia (1992), 170.

122 Both remarks in Talvacchia (1992), 168.

123 Morley's madrigal 'The Fields Abroad' has: 'The nightingale her bower hath gaily builded, / And full of kindly lust, and love's inspiring, / "I love" she sings, hark: her mate desiring.'

124 Gurr (2011), 37–8.

125 Lists appear in Elam (2014), 130–2; Talvacchia (1999), 66; Martinet (1975), 266; Talvacchia (1972), 170–2.

126 Vasari (1987), I, 323.

127 Sokol (1994), 55–84; Sokol (1989), 55–65.

128 Wotton (1624), 89–90.

129 Wollheim (1971).

130 Melanie Klein's school of psychoanalysis astutely studies the imaginative nature of inner life, especially when the repair of inner 'objects' is in question.

131 We have seen this at work in *The Second Maiden's Tragedy* as well as in *Epicoene*.

132 Sokol (1994), 32–6, 42–52, argues that Leontes is portrayed as if undergoing a paranoid nervous breakdown following from what is now known as the 'couvade syndrome'.

3 Poets in Shakespeare's Plays

1 Eliot (1957a), printing a lecture of 1951; Eliot (1957b), printing a lecture of 1953. Eliot's earlier 'The Possibility of a Poetic Drama' (1925) reprinted in Eliot (1964), 60–70, is less cogent than the 1950s essays, and contains some modernist scorn for certain writers, actors and audiences.

2 Eliot (1957a), 73.

3 Eliot (1957b), 99–100. These three voices, says Eliot, may overlap.

4   Schmidingall (1990), 121–60. Schmidingall often equates 'courting poets' with courtier-poets. He holds (103) that Boyet is a poet and speaks poetry in *LLL* 2.1.1–2 and 2.1.234–49, but there is no evidence that the fourth voice is heard there.

5   Cheney (2008), 97. Cheney (2004; 2007; 2008) all argue that Shakespeare's theatrical writing was consciously literary and emphasize tensions between dramatic and lyric poetry. Schmidingall (1990), 96–7, as well as Cheney (2008), contrast types of poetic careers, the latter arguing that Shakespeare chose to be a 'counter-laureate' poet.

6   Chenney (2008), 93.

7   Dismissing former critics' doubts that Shakespeare wrote Vincentio's soliloquy, Lever (1966), 93 n., remarks that the verse formality of this soliloquy 'provides a sententious finale to an act full of surprises, and affords a much-needed point of rest'.

8   Schmidingall (1990), 89–118, holds that the court and culture in the ages of Elizabeth and James I were deeply philistine and particularly 'anti literary' (93). This runs counter to the witness of thriving literary production and consumption.

9   See B.J. Sokol 'Henry Petowe (1575/6–1636?)' *Oxford DNB*, 2004. The musician Thomas Whythorne reports in his autobiography, Whythorne (1962), that he often felt the urge to write poems, and he indeed intersperses them in his text.

10 For instance, Romeo and Juliet's two-handed sonnet (1.5.92–105) and *aubade* (3.5.1–25) do not indicate conscious poetry making. In *AW* 1.2.212–25 Helena's soliloquy comprises seven pentameter couplets, the first four setting out challenges, and the remaining three expressing resolution to overcome barriers. These fourteen lines thus match what Fuller (1978), 2, identifies as the 'essence of the sonnet's form . . . the unequal relationship between octave and sestet'. Fuller (1978), 33, identifies other sonnets in couplets, and Shakespeare's Sonnet 126 comprises six couplets plus the indication of a seventh by brackets. Skinner (2014), 175, claims that Helena here 'spontaneously composes' a 'Sonnet', implying her 'ardent' nature. This does show her ardent, but not a poet or literally 'poetical'.

11 The word 'perform', used in thirty-two Shakespeare plays, may hover between 'theatrically enact' and the senses of to complete,

finish off, discharge (a duty), or physically make, for example in *WT* 5.2.96 and *Tem* 3.3.84.

12 Sokol (1994), 146–50, notes that this is one of Camillo's self-serving deceptions that place innocents in danger, but also (161–4) that Camillo's deceptions, and Paulina's, are redeemed in the play.

13 Freud (1963), 10–11.

14 As mentioned, these include Mackinnon (1988), Cheney (2004; 2007; 2008) and Erne (2003; 2007).

15 Shakespeare's nine mentions of extemporizing include several to do with either confidence ruses or the theatrical abilities of 'quick comedians' (*AC* 5.2.212–13), while only two are concerned with poetic creativity – and in those two the would-be poets are the ridiculous Don Armado (*LLL* 1.2.174) and the ridiculed Petruchio (*TS* 2.1.257–8). On the contrary, Socrates in *Ion* 533d–535a holds that instantaneous divine inspiration, actual possession, is the sole source of artists' success.

16 Jonson (1980), 211–15.

17 Jonson (1980), 128–9.

18 McClumpha (1900), repeatedly cites *embedded* poems and *inserted* ones in *LLL* without distinction, a fusion of categories that has continued.

19 See Stern (2009), 174–200.

20 Written-down poems in *LLL* tln 1215–26, 1303–1407, 1436–57 are italicized in the Folio, but 1267–83 and 1358–75 are not. Neither are the play's concluding songs. Most poetic inserts are printed upright in the 1597 quarto (British Library, C.34.l.14.).

21 This six-lined promise of sexual violence is not italicized in the First Folio, but in the next scene the absurdly alliterative and emptily punning verses of Holofernes are (tln 1215–26).

22 Birone's and Longaville's sonnets from *LLL* 4.2.106–19 and 4.3.57–70 were pirated by William Jaggard (slightly altered) in his 1599 *The Passionate Pilgrim*, which includes also Dumaine's 'Sonnet' at 4.3.99–118; Dumaine's appears again in *England's Helicon* (1600).

23 The jingling verses of the Pageant at 5.2.547–50, 558–60, 582–87, 644–8 lead to cruel mockery prompting Holofernes', 'This is not generous, not gentle, not humble' (5.2.622).

24 Skeaping and Clegg (2014).

25 The unsolved mystery is how such lovely lyrics could have been 'compiled', as Armado says, by 'the two learned men', Holofernes and Nathaniel (5.2.872). If, as suggested in Sokol (1991a), Holofernes is modelled in part on Thomas Harriot, who wrote verses, a resolution might be found.

26 Because Romeo derives from a wealthy citizen household (unlike the County Paris), his bad poetry could have been ridiculed with propriety in accordance with the principles set down by Harbage (1973), which discusses the propriety of Shakespearean satire in relation to the social positioning of those satirized.

27 Wells (2016) lists the verse to prose ratio in *RJ* as 86.5 per cent, placing it thirteenth among thirty-nine plays.

28 See Weis (2012), 19–24.

29 Sestets at 1.2.44–9, 1.2.90–5, 1.2.96–101 are detected in Gibbons (1980), 43, and Weis (2012), 147 n. Weis (148 n.) notes that Benvolio's 'sestet' at 1.2.96–101 takes the form of three couplets, supporting a general position (20) that 'Rhyme plays a crucial role in the rhetorical texture of the play which attributes extraordinary power of control to language.' Weis (418–20) lists all of the rhymes in the text.

30 We will see that Fulke Greville paid tribute, perhaps combined with some vying, by writing a poem with an exactly parallel theme to a poem written by Philip Sidney.

31 Evans (2003), 12, which adds that Shakespeare uses 'Romeo's verbal acrobatics to foreshadow one of the central themes of the play – the ambiguous and frighteningly fragile nature of love itself.' Evans (211) finds Romeo's antitheses 'foreshadowing the course of the play'.

32 See Auden (1964), xxvi.

33 Richard Farmer, quoted in Furness (1898), 22 n., notes that 'Every sonneteer characterized love by contrarieties', and adds that earlier Provençal lyricists, and Sappho, show similar propensities.

34 Ewbank (1971), 101.

35 *AYL* appeared just when a number of Elizabethan writers were attacking one another *ad hominem* in satires and

plays. When literary satire and parody evolved into scurrilous personal attack, Shakespeare withdrew from purveying it.

36 *MW*, probably written a year before *AYL*, contrasts two rival suitors for Anne Page, elegant 'young Master Fenton', of whom it is said, 'He capers, he dances, he has eyes of youth; he writes verses, he speaks holiday, he smells April and May' (3.2.61–3), and the idiotic Slender, who laments not having to hand his 'book of songs and sonnets' (*Tottel's Miscellany*) when he goes a-wooing (1.1.181–2). I do not think the Poet in *Tim* is mocked.

37 I will argue in another place that *R2* is centrally concerned with the fate of an artist, and of the arts generally, in a time of civic upheaval, and that this was a late Elizabethan obsession.

38 In Evans (1977), 84; Jonson (1980), 140.

39 *AYL* 2.4.53, 3.3.9–12. Latham (1975), xxxiii–iv, disputes speculation that Touchstone's 'little room' was the one in which Marlowe died following a dispute over a 'reckoning'.

40 The passage from North's Plutarch is reprinted in Daniel (2006), 349–50. In Plutarch, Phaonius elicits Cassius' derision and Brutus' anger.

41 Hilliard (1910–11), 18, which adds the proviso 'and himselfe but of small meanes'.

42 The only Shakespearean texts lacking the lexeme including 'deceit', 'deceitful', 'deceive', 'deceivable', 'deceived', 'deceiver', deceivest', 'deceiveth', 'deceiving', are *STM* and *2H4*. David Crystal kindly gave me the count from the Folio, which will appear in his forthcoming linguistic dictionary of Shakespeare.

43 Cheney (2008), 92–3, counts these and comes up with well over two hundred instances.

44 *OED* feign, *v*. I. 1. Pettet (1950), 40, notes the multi-valence of 'feign' in Shakespeare's use.

45 *OED* feign, *v*. II. 2.d.

46 *3H6* 1.2.31; *AYL* 3.3.14–18.

47 Sokol and Sokol (2003), 108–11, explains that Egeus in *MND* and Brabantio in *Oth* would have succeeded in Elizabethan law

in their claims against their daughters' lovers. Brabantio dies of 'pure grief' (*Oth* 5.2.212), and Egeus is bereft of his 'will' and legal rights in *MND* 4.1.178. Both fathers, intolerant as they are, can also be seen as victims of subversion of the law against the abduction of heirs.

48 Edwards (1968), 2, 10. Asking 'how far Shakespeare himself shared in the scepticism of his characters', Edwards remarks, 'he would hardly have been human had he not, on one and the same day, had faith in his art and scoffed at it too' (3).

49 Muir (1970), 91 alleges this consensus; praises Lodowick (94–5); says the unnamed Poet in *JC* is 'comic' yet 'serious and sensible' and moreover 'determined . . . brave' (96–7), and allows the Poet in *Tim* 'sincerity' (99–100). Muir (100n.) quotes Edwin R. Hunter: 'Shakespeare thought too highly of poetry to have thought of its needing defenders, and he is just the sort of humorous man who does not mind having the jest come up occasionally against himself and his kind.' Harbage (1973), 17, suggests a potential explanation of why poets are not generally praised in Shakespeare's plays: 'a character in a play is bound to take on the coloration of the context, and to be shaped in conformity with the principle of decorum . . . We cannot determine from Shakespeare's comical or serious treatment of individual professional men just how seriously he regarded the professions they represent.'

50 Muir (1970), 95.

51 Cheney (2008), 99–100.

52 Cheney (2008), 98–9.

53 Wyatt (1975), 100–4 (101); Evans (1977), 84.

54 Muir (1970), 99, points out that 'there is no reason to doubt his sincerity'.

55 Shylock makes the same equation in *MV* 1.3.12–17, where 'Antonio is a good man' is used by him to express 'good' for the money, that is, 'sufficient' to repay a debt.

56 Thomson (1952), 280, which supports with telling examples the view that 'For the most part, patronage probably did not injure the quality of the poetry written in the Elizabethan and Jacobean periods: it did not impose falseness on the truly great' (284).

57 Muir (1953), 121. However, Muir also reads these as 'lines of self reproach'. Others think these lines of a poem being written, not self–reproach.

58 This allegory is read in a converse way in Thurman (2015), 129, which holds that the 'disloyalty' of the Poet and the Painter is 'worse than that of Timon's false friends because they have passed judgement on others' flattery; the Poet's censure is mere hypocrisy'. So Thurman claims that the Poet in *Tim* is 'One of the least likable poet-figures created by Shakespeare' (128). Muir (1953), 121, on the contrary, finds that in his 'allegory of Fortune' the Poet 'writes the truth as he sees it'.

59 Adair (1998) makes a particularly good case for adopting Pope and Johnson's emendations, based on a discovery of an echo of Horace's Epistle I.xix.

60 Pettet (1950), 34–7, concludes that this passage describes a 'largely spontaneous, and often subconscious, process of self-generation'. The phenomenology of such a process is explored in Eliot (1957b), 97–9, and in Valery (1958), 60–2. Valery adds that translating inspiration into the words of a poem is a different matter: 'The poet's function . . . is not to experience the poetic state. His function is to create it in others' (60).

61 Regarding this passage, Muir (1970), 99, comments wittily: 'It is not surprising that the Painter asks "How shall I understand you?" The general drift of the speech, however, is plain enough.' Adair (1998) applies the above-mentioned echo from Horace to this passage, connecting 'wax' with Horace's '*mella*' or honey, so rejecting a common emendation to 'tax'. and finds in the Horace epistle and in this passage 'a sophisticated metaphor . . . for the autonomy of the artist' (354). Nuttall (1989), 8–13 argues that a 'wide sea of wax' is an allusion to Icarus.

62 The accuracy of that claim is undermined when the Poet reveals, immediately afterwards, that his allegory of ingratitude will include images of the very particular figures of 'Lord Timon' and 'Apemantus' (1.1.56, 60). However, even if the irony is intended, the Poet shows the problem of understanding the poetic impulse which derives both from social 'levelled malice' in language and from 'flight'.

4 Poets in Shakespeare's Poems

1   Sloane (1991), 113, says *Copia* was written 'ostensibly at the prompting of John Colet, dean of St. Paul's School in London'. Shakespeare uses the word 'copious' only here and in *R3* 4.4.135, where it refers to abundance without connection to language.

2   Sloane (1991), *passim*.

3   *OED* tedious, *adj*. 1.a.

4   Davies's sonnets, printed in Evans (1977), 179–83, brilliantly mock rhetorical ostentation, and some deploy legal metaphors to parody strained or far-fetched poetic invention.

5   See Burrow (2002), 138–40, which also discusses the consensus that *LC* is Shakespearean.

6   The word 'sonnets' also appears in the dedication of the 1609 volume, and in *LLL*, *TGV* and *MW*.

7   *Ham* 3.2.145; a posy on a ring is also deprecated in *MV* 5.1.148–9.

8   Girard (1991) notes mimetic desire in many Shakespearean poems and plays, but not in *LC*. Love triangles or polygons involving two women appear in *MND*, *TGV*, *MM*, *MA*, *TN*, *TNK*, and even more often involve two men and a woman. The analysis of the pattern in Freud (1984 [1911]) produces concepts applied to Shakespeare by Stewart (1949).

9   Mimetic desire is described and discussed in Castiglione (1975), 125–6. Here written evidence of a woman's love for a man is seen by another woman, igniting her love for him.

10 The 'casket sonnets' and 'casket letters' may have been forgeries: see Smith (2012).

11 One holograph MS (differing somewhat from the printed version) survives – but other MSS are likely to have circulated.

12 See Bell (2015), 77–8. 'A Sonnet, to the Noble Lady, the Lady Mary Wroth', in Jonson (1980), 165–6, contains 'Since I excribe your sonnets', almost certainly referring to Jonson copying them out from manuscript. Hagerman (2001), section 13, states that Sonnet 22 in Wroth's *Pamphilia to Amphilanthus* containing 'Like to the Indians, scorched with the sun', is a 'direct reference'

to how Wroth was made up when she danced in Jonson's
Masque of Blackness in 1605. It is just possible, but not certain,
that some of Wroth's poems were known in MS before the
publication of *A Lover's Complaint*.

13 Kingsley-Smith (2016).

14 Ben Jonson knew Wroth well. The 1612 first edition of *The
Alchemist* (performed in 1610) was dedicated to her.

15 Mary Ellen Lamb, 'Wroth, Lady Mary (1587?–1651/1653)',
Oxford DNB (2004).

16 Mary Ellen Lamb, 'Wroth, Lady Mary (1587?–1651/1653)',
Oxford DNB (2004).

17 Negative descriptors in the sequence include: 'barren' (16, 76);
'scorn'd . . . stretched miter' (17); 'domb' (23); 'poore . . . bare
. . . wanting' (26); 'poore rude . . . out-strip . . . exceeded' (32);
'vulgar . . . dumbe . . . slight' (38); 'blacke' (63, 65); shaming
(72.13); 'For I am shamd by that which I bring forth'); 'decayde
. . . sick' (79); 'toungtide . . . inferior . . . worthlesse' (80); 'barren
. . . com[ing] to short . . . dombe . . . mute' (83); 'toung-tide . . .
unlettered . . . dombe (85)'; 'infeebled' (86); 'worthlesse . . .
forgetfull . . . resty' (100); 'truant . . . neglect[ful] . . . dumb'
(101); 'dull[ing]' (102); 'bare . . . blunt . . . marr[ing]' (103);
'poore' (107); 'vainely exprest' (147).

18 Burrow (1998), 47.

19 This association is mentioned in Duncan-Jones (2001), 270.

20 Muir (1979), 30.

21 Ewbank (2003), 5. See also Ewbank (1971; 1981).

22 Michelangelo (1986), 127.

23 In Brereton (1967), 74. Leishman (1961), 79, comments on the
'condescension and self-exaltation' in this sonnet. See Leishman
(1961), 57–69, and Richmond (1970), 147–54, on Shakespeare
and Ronsard.

24 In Esdaile (1908), 75.

25 See Leishman (1961) and Ferry (1975) on the eternizing theme.
It is strongly stated when Samuel Daniel's Musophilus seeks
words that 'May live' and present to 'posteritie' 'the speaking
picture of the minde, / The extract of the soule that laboured
how / To leave the Image of her selfe behinde'. Musophilus then

commends 'O blessed letters': 'By you th'unborne shall have communion / Of what we feele, and what doth us befall' (Daniel, 1599, B3ᵛ).

26 These contexts in plays include: *1H4* 3.1.124–31; *JC* 3.3.29–32, 4.2.178–90; and all of *R2*. Shakespeare's immature courtiers in *LLL* are depicted as shallow and voguish when they set out to 'hunt after' such great 'fame' that despite 'death' and 'cormorant devouring time, / Th' endeavour of this present breath may buy / That honour which shall bate his scythe's keen edge / And make heirs of all eternity' (1.1.1–7). Each then becomes a mediocre love-poet. Similar pretensions are mocked in *TS* 1.1.17–24. Foster, 1987, 48, points out that in the three places in his sonnets where Shakespeare 'uses the word eternity (77.8, 122.4, and 125.3), he expresses the sentiment that a mortal poet cannot promise eternity'.

27 See Dubrow (2015), 61–73 on uses of 'this' in Shakespeare's Sonnets. Concepts explained include 'metatextuality' (61), 'proximal diectic' in plays (62), and 'blurring . . . between proximal and distal deixis (68–9).

28 Sonnets 15, 18, 38, 54, 55, 63, 65, 78, 80, 81, 84, 100, 101, 105, 107, 108.

29 Commentators divide about Shakespearean Idealism. Faas (1986), xxii, 80, claims Shakespeare's 'basic antiessentialism', and Koskimies (1970), his Platonism.

30 The cluster of Shakespeare Sonnets from 33 through to 37 concern erotic betrayal and inconstancy (35 specifies 'thy sensuall fault'), but Sonnet 53 is highly ambiguous about constancy. It questions if the beloved *is* constant and so millions take their substance (being) from this ideal, or if they are *inconstant* and so the things that 'tend' on them are obsequious, self-interested. The word 'counterfet' is likewise ambiguous, so that the final couplet may praise faithfulness, or may bitterly condemn unfaithfulness, or may reflect an unsettled and painfully confused state of mind oscillating between alternatives.

31 One of these, a purported 'Dark Lady' sonnet, and other, a purported 'Young Man' sonnet, are equally non-idealizing.

32 Dante (1964), 73. The speakers are women acquainted with Laura, but convey no specifically female point of view.

33 Kellogg (2015), 421 n.6.

34 Astrophil shares Sidney's family connection with a Governor of Ireland (Sonnet 30) and the Sidney coat of arms (Sonnet 65). See Sidney (1962), 418, where Ringler shows that the character 'Philisides' in Sidney's *Old Arcadia* 73 describes 'Sidney's fictionalized self-portrait'.

35 Petrarch's sonnets pun on *lauro* = 'laurel' twenty-nine times, and on *l'aura* = 'breeze/air' thirty-nine times. Rime 5 plays elaborately with the name 'Laura'.

36 *Astrophil and Stella* Sonnets 3, 9, 24, 35, 37, 48, 79, and the Fifth, Eighth and Ninth Songs all pun on the name 'Rich'. For instance, 'Fame / Doth even grow rich, naming my Stella's name' (35.10–11). Sonnet 37 begins 'of my life I must a riddel tell', then puns five times on 'Rich', culminating that the married Stella 'Hath no misfortune, but that Rich she is' (37.14). Sonnet 37 locates the beloved 'Nymph' 'Towardes Aurora's Court', alluding to Penelope Rich's father the Earl of Essex.

37 See Fowler (1970), 175–6.

38 See Sidney (1962), 435–7.

39 Sidney (1962), 447.

40 See Spenser (1966), xxiv. The title *Epithalamion* is prefixed 'Epi' and many of its lines declare a concern with the likes of 'my owne loves prayses' (422).

41 The one-year natural cycle corresponding to the fruition of wooing in Spenser's *Amoretti* is symbolic rather than representational. This cycle is adumbrated as well by the 365 long lines (in twenty-four stanzas) of *Epithalamion*, on which see Hieatt (1960).

42 Bates (1910); Rollins (1944), II, 133–297; Barber (1960); Frye (1962); Kerrigan (1968), 11; Schoenbaum (1980); and Dubrow (1996) have all shown theories of the real-world persons 'behind' a supposed narrative portrayed by Shakespeare's Sonnets rest on contradictions, confusions, and, often, obsessions.

43 Gurr (1971).

44 Sonnet 57 concludes 'that in your Will / (Though you doe any thing), he thinkes no ill'. *Will* is italicized seven times in Sonnet

135, where '*Will*' is the last word and three times a rhyme word. In Sonnet 136 italicized *Will* appears twice in rhyme positions, the sonnet concluding 'for my name is *Will*'. The couplet of Sonnet 143 contains 'that thou maist have thy *Will*'.

45 The speaker in Sonnet 71.5–6 explicitly identifies as the poet of the present sonnet: 'Nay if you read this line, remember not, / The hand that writ it'. The speaker in Sonnet 72 asks to be forgotten after death and makes naught of their literary productions: 'For I am shamed by that which I bring forth'. So these sonnets deny giving names, although appearing on facing pages in the 1609 edition showing the running heads 'Shake-speares' and 'Sonnets' in large and small upper case type (sigs E3^v and E4^r). Elizabethan books and their layout were not necessarily authorial; *The Passionate Pilgrim* (1599), falsely attributed to 'W. Shakespeare', demonstrates overriding commercial motives.

46 Kerrigan (1968); Duncan-Jones (1983; 2001); and Dubrow (1996), 299, agree. Wells and Edmondson (2012) do not.

47 Wilkes (1959) claims that *Caelica* was begun early but completed late in Greville's life, and that most of Greville's work was written after Sidney died.

48 Greville (1907), this Introduction, was long admired as *The Life of the Renowned Sir Philip Sidney*.

49 Greville (1907), 150, 152.

50 This is the Warwick MS (London, British Library, Add. 54570), which Wilkes (2006), 308–9, dates to about 1619–25.

51 Unhappily, the posthumous volume Greville (1633) lists on the verso of the title page, 'Caelica, containing CIX, Sonnets'. Indeed every subsequent edition, including Greville (1945) and Greville (2006), similarly obscures Greville's numerical intentions.

52 This poem is misnumbered LVI in Greville (1633), while in the Warwick MS the correctly numbered poem contains twenty-four extra, inferior, lines.

53 The topic of Sidney's 'Second Song' is that Astrophil comes upon Stella in bed, but flees after taking only a kiss, but then regrets this. The surrounding cluster of Sidney's Sonnets 71–4 meditate on this. Greville's *Caelica* poem 54 reiterates this topic

identically, and uses the same metrical format of tetrameter couplets as does Sidney's 'Song', but it is much more cynical in its conclusions.

54 For further details, see Sokol (1980).

55 Kerrigan (1968), 12–15, 61–2. Citing Malone, Duncan-Jones (2001), 88–9, calls *Delia* 'the earliest archetype for this two part structure' also used by Shakespeare, but three parts is more accurate.

56 Duncan-Jones (1983), 165, says that John Davis of Hereford's 1605 sonnet sequence totals '152 sonnets, the same number as Shakespeare's sequence if we except the two Diana/Cupid sonnets at the end'. Cheney (2004), 208, states that over perhaps twenty years Shakespeare 'wrote 152 sonnets in the Petrarchan tradition, and they were finally published in 1609 . . . the volume includes two anacreontic sonnets (153, 154) and A Lover's Complaint, in what was then a familiar format for a printed volume of verse'. De Grazia (2007) concurs.

57 If keeping the centralized numerical structure intact during revision was Shakespeare's intention (similar to Greville's), that would answer doubts expressed in Dubrow (1996), 298: 'One of the principal limitations' to an 'assertion that the 1609 version is a coherent collection in the order its author intended' is that 'the 1609 version of the sonnets contains manifold imperfections, such as the repetition of the couplet in Sonnets 36 . . . and 96 . . . the extra line in Sonnet 99'. Dubrow judiciously allows that Duncan-Jones may have been 'right that the 1609 edition reproduces the poems in the order their author intended' (299).

58 Statistics are cited in Sokol (2011). In addition, I have applied since then the Windows findstr program that locates 'regular expressions' in all files in a directory (similarly to the UNIX 'grep' command). This shows that among the files in the Oxford Electronic Shakespeare only 0.74 per cent of the spoken lines contain words with an initial digraph 'sh' followed by words with an initial digraph 'pr' (not case-sensitive), and this proportion increases by only a tiny amount if these digraphs are allowed to be located anywhere within a spoken line.

59 Regarding Sonnet 76, Booth (2000), 265–6, claims that 'line 12 invites a reader to hunt for extra witty meanings in it' but to

no effect, and that line 12 is 'as simple and dull as its obvious surface meaning would lead us to expect any lines by this speaker to be'. Booth adds that 'telling what is told' in line 14 'also feels as if it had some witty undermeaning', but again 'a reader' following out this polyproton 'will not arrive at any extra dimension'. He judges that readers of this poem will become 'mired' in confusions, and find in it 'not quite realisable' oxymorons, 'muffled' puns, and a 'yearning but muffled wit'.

60 See Vendler (1999), 21, 488, on antagonists and rebuttals in Shakespeare sonnets. Regarding Sonnet 76, Vendler holds (344–5) that each of the three questions beginning with 'Why' in the octave repeats a 'speech-act' made prior to the poem by a 'fashionable', 'obtuse', 'fickle' and 'bored young man'; each time the poem's speaker makes a sarcastic rebuttal, flinging the accusatory questions back at the questioner. Vendler finds both Sonnets 76 and 116 reply to hostile speech acts (344), and characterizes Sonnet 116 as built on 'rebuttals' in a mini-drama where 'the speaker indirectly quotes his antagonist' to 'repudiate' an 'anterior utterance' (488–93). To support this reading, Vendler insists that 116.1–2 be stressed: 'Let *me* not to the marriage of true minds / Admit impediments: love is *not* love' (489). That spoils the charm of 116.1, which requires a subtly muted ionic double foot at its start to echo the same substitution for its final pair of iambs. For arguments that Shakespeare's sonnets are mainly not dramatic see Dubrow (1981), and for a general critique of 'speech-act' readings of Shakespeare's sonnets, see Robinson (2001).

61 The notion in Booth (2000), 265–6, that Sonnet 76 is purposefully confusing seemingly counters Booth (1969), 60, which claims that 'There is nothing in a Shakespeare sonnet that does not pattern, but there are so many patterns that in moving from one system to another the reader's mind operates similarly to the way that it operates upon unstructured experience.'

62 Sonnet 76 is not framed like John Donne's 'The Canonization' so as to indicate at the start a reply in train to an interlocutor. Shakespeare does deploy this 'third voice of poetry' structure, for instance in three succeeding scenes in *MM* as discussed in Sokol (1991b), but here he uses the first voice.

63 Evans (2006), 172, referring to Sonnets 76, 78–80, and 82–6.

64 Monosyllables signal particularly strong emotion when Prospero bitterly inserts 'all' into his pardoning of Antonio: 'I do forgive / Thy rankest fault, all of them' (*Tem* 5.1.133–4), and when the first line of Ben Jonson's 'On My First Son' includes the unexpected word 'joy' in 'Farewell, thou child of my right hand, and joy'. See Jonson (1980), 48. Jonson's monosyllable, following a very late caesura, may be heard as a catch in the breath when personal grief overcomes religious consolation. Poetic catches of breath are named in Samuel Daniel's *Delia* Sonnet 2 as 'interrupted accents of despaire'.

65 Booth (2000), 263–4. 'Barren' taking the meaning of 'bare' or 'naked' is seen in Sonnet 12: 'When lofty trees I see barren of leaves'.

66 *OED* pride, *n1*. 10.a. and *OED* pride, *n1*. 5. 'Pride' in both senses is illustrated in *OED* from the work of Shakespeare.

67 This is proposed, for instance, in Vendler (1999), 345.

68 *Astrophil and Stella* Sonnet 1 laments that poetic 'Invention' is 'Nature's child' that flees 'step-dame Studie's blowes'. On the poet's primary need for 'invention', see Gascoigne (1904), 47. The concept is discussed in Bundy (1930) and Langer (1999).

69 The poet in Sonnet 103 laments the 'poverty my Muse brings forth' and the inability of his 'blunt invention'. The poet in Sonnet 105 seeks excuse for the narrow bounds within which his verse is 'confin'de' and 'my invention spent'.

70 *OED* compound, *n1*. 2.c., which cites this very line.

71 Sidney (1961), 59–60.

72 The pair of words 'new found' in 76.4 is hyphenated in modernized editions of *Shakespeare's Sonnets* including: Ingram and Redpath (1964); Kerrigan (1968); Vendler (1999); Booth (2000); Duncan-Jones (2001); Burrow (2002); Evans (2006). Only Kerrigan (270) and Burrow (532) notice the irony. Evans (2006), 183, identifies as a first meaning for 'compounds strange' 'compound words or possibly neologisms', but also claims that 'new-found' is 'an established compound, not one of the "compounds strange" here criticised'.

73 Seventy compound words are hyphenated in Wells and Taylor (1989).

74 This proposed absence of the law of the excluded middle in
    Sonnet 76 coheres with the explanation in Kerrigan (2001), 25,
    that Sonnet 132's 'idiom has an innovative insecurity which
    comes from the dispersion of the subject in a dialectic of
    turbulent emotion'. Dubrow (1981), 64, has: 'in a number of
    ways [Shakespeare's] sonnets focus our attention on the
    speaker's chaotic reactions'.

75 Catullus 85. Catullus 75, 82 and 91 are also to the point.

5 Shakespeare's Musicians

1 For instance, Carpenter (1976) identifies many unresolved lines
   of enquiry, only some of which have been addressed.

2 That is rarely determinable with certainty, for Elizabethan play
   scripts do not specify particular musical materials (although they
   occasionally indicate well-known songs or compositions). Also,
   differing musical materials or ensembles may have accompanied
   different Elizabethan performances of the same play. Yet if we
   could know the original musical settings of songs indicated in
   Shakespeare's plays (and knew those settings were determined
   by the author) insight might be gained: Stern (2011), 320,
   reminds us that often songs in Elizabethan plays, 'whether or not
   their words are preserved', are 'sites of loss' because their
   musical settings are mostly lost, while 'Like other writers of his
   time, Shakespeare relied on the sensual properties of music to
   sophisticate and even reinterpret his lyrics'.

3 These performances could be domestic or only semi-public, as
   well as public. Nicholas Younge began the dedication of his
   Musica Transalpina (the first printed collection of Italian
   madrigals) by describing amateur musical meetings at his
   London house of 'Gentlemen and Merchants of good accompt'
   (Younge (1588), A.ii[r]). The celebrated lutenist John Dowland
   formatted his very popular *First Booke of Songes or Ayres*
   (1597, republished 1600, 1606, 1613) in such a way as to allow
   performance either by a vocal soloist or by vocal combinations.

4 Maynard (1986), 151–223, showed that the amount of song in
   Shakespeare plays varies according to genre and date, but even

in the plays with few or no songs 'trumpets sound alarms and parlays, drums indicate marches, and so on' (152).

5 Naylor (1910), 130. Naylor (1928), 89–91, adds that 'about' 224 Shakespeare passages, in thirty-three plays and four poems, 'not only speak of music, but in many cases present difficulties, or render expert assistance to the reader'.

6 Naylor (1931), 3, which analyses these stage directions in thirty-six plays (159–77).

7 Staged music in Shakespeare plays having a visible or implied source is often called 'digetic' by critics, but this usage is confusing because experts hold that 'mimesis' and 'diegesis' are contraries, the first involving *showing* something and the second *telling* about it. Music on Shakespeare stages is almost always *shown* (in the sense of made audible to the audience, even while, on occasion, it is simultaneously described).

8 See Lindley (2006), 5–6, 109, 111–12. Shakespearean music also never serves in an opera-like way as a *medium* of spoken expression in the way that verse does in verse drama. Auden (1963), 318, puts this well: 'We are thinking . . . of songs introduced into a play written in verse or prose which is spoken, not of arias in an opera, where the dramatic medium itself is song, and we forget that the singers are performers as we forget that the actor speaking blank verse is an actor.' This observation does not contradict the argument in Hopkins (1994) that the aesthetic of *Oth* is opera-like. For, as Hopkins points out, Shakespeare 'suspends the action to allow Desdemona to sing the Willow Song' (63). As unique and as crucial as that singing may be, this turn to song does not substitute for speech, but rather song is staged as actually sung, in analogy with the forth voice of poetry.

9 See Marsh (2010), 71–2; Price (1981), 173–4.

10 See Marsh (2010), 191–2.

11 For instance, Marsh (2010), 383, describes how a 'courtly vogue for country dance gathered momentum particularly during the last third of Elizabeth I's reign'.

12 Pattison (1970), 13.

13 This implies an even greater social range for the impact of early Tudor court poetry than Slender's wish to have access to his copy

of Tottel's *Miscellany* in *M W* (1.1.181–2). I will argue elsewhere that this impact is most strongly felt in the second Henriad.

14 We can contrast the indolent passengers in *Tem* 1.1 with Pericles, in parallel circumstances, 'Galling his kingly hands with haling ropes' (15.105).

15 See Crewdson (1971), 32; Lindley (2006), 55. The waits were employed by municipalities, originally as watchmen, and according to Marsh (2010), 125, were typically ill paid.

16 This remark about wild birds as court musicians appears only in the 1597 Quarto text of the play, not in the Folio text, and is reproduced in the *Oxford Electronic Shakespeare* with the lineation '*R2* A.C.21'. However, Elizabethans perceived the relations of human-made music and birdsong more complexly than that: see Austern (1998a), 18–26, 36–7.

17 Minear (2011), 58. This 'pervasiveness of music' in Shakespeare plays may relate to the cultural setting described here as much as to the psychological and artistic matters described throughout Minear's book.

18 See Naylor (1931), 6, 17; Woodfill (1953), 203. The practice serves in a metaphor in the 1601 quarto *Every Man in his Humor* 2.3, Jonson (1601), F1^r.

19 Martin Butler, 'Robert Armin (1563–1615)', *Oxford DNB* (2004). Touchstone in *AYL* was likely Armin's first Shakespearean role.

20 McGee (1995) charts this decline and attributes it to changes in taste regarding musical style and format (especially the rise of polyphony).

21 McGee (1995) proposes that theatrical players took over the storytelling roles and some of the musical roles of the minstrels.

22 Whythorne (1962), 193–4.

23 Whythorne (1962), 203–4.

24 Whythorne (1962), 194.

25 See Marsh (2010), 104–5; Woodfill (1953), 64–7, for examples.

26 Whythorne (1962), 203.

27 Surveying both Protestant and Recusant households, Price (1981), 167, declares that 'the desire for music and its

refinements coloured the whole atmosphere of educated society by the late Elizabethan period'. Price comments on competition in the upper echelons for the services of boy servants skilled in singing (173–4).

28 Marsh (2010), 115–30, and *passim*, confirms this.

29 See Lord (2003), 73–92.

30 Whythorne (1962), 46.

31 Whythorne (1962), 201.

32 Ferne (1586), 51, 53–4, 55, 50. *The Blazon of Gentrie* appeared soon after Whythorne's autobiography was written.

33 Whythorne (1962), 206, 193, 205, 205–6.

34 Brennecke (1939) discusses possible connections between Morley's music and the songs 'It was a lover and his lass' of *AYL* and 'O mistress mine' of *TN*.

35 Wilson (2011a), 119, differentiates this 'catch' from the less bawdy 'round' and the more sophisticated 'canon'.

36 *2H4* 4.2 and 4.7; *MND passim*; *MW* 5.1.22; *H8* 1.2.34; *TNK* 3.2.52. Weavers are associated with psalm-singing by Falstaff in *1H4* 2.5.132–3.

37 See Woodfill (1953), 11; Crewdson (1971), 35.

38 Thus Marsh (2010), 58, cites Roger North (1651–1734) who reports on the household of his grandfather.

39 Marsh (2010), 193–5, describes Lant's MS.

40 Marsh (2010), 168. I restrict my mention to Marsh's Elizabethan examples.

41 Quoted from John Howes in 1578, in Pattison (1970), 11.

42 Pattison (1970), 11–13; and see Price (1981), 173–4.

43 Marsh (2010), 169, 163, 164–8.

44 Woodfill (1953), 63.

45 Musical art also links the diverse ethnicities of Caliban, Stephano and Trinculo in *Tem*.

46 Marsh (2010), 383.

47 Sidney (1961), 32.

48 Montaigne (1942), I, 215–29; 228.

49 Sternfeld and Chan (1970) give details of this episode in *MW*, including the history and place of the lyric, and textual differences between Q and F.

50 Lathrop (1908), 1, says this remark was made by Shaw 'at a meeting of the Browning society in London, when someone had quoted the hackneyed lines from *Twelfth Night* so often pressed into service to prove Shakespeare's surpassing love for music'.

51 *TS* 3.1.62–79. Nelson (2012) cites real-life examples of seduction of female pupils by music teachers, and of love affairs and even marriages between them. Marsh (2010), 202, gives a contextual reading of such encounters, noting the 'feigned social inferiority of the teachers' to their female students.

52 Whythorne (1962) contrasts his honourable position as resident music teacher to the children of a 'man of worship' with the low 'estate' of an itinerant 'minstrel' (203–4). Nelson (2012), 18–19, commenting on Whythorne elevating the standing of his nine positions as domestic music tutor, claims there are 'hints of the same attitude in the biographies of other music tutors' of the age.

53 Nelson (2012), 18. This refers to only one of Whythorne's widows-as-pupils, but argues that a similar erotic ambiguity applied whenever music tutors had female pupils.

54 More will be said in the next chapter about contrasts between wind and stringed instruments. Boenig (1988) indicates that in later Elizabethan times the 'broken' consort was not an ad hoc collection of different instruments at hand, for 'composers began to specify which instruments were to play which lines' (65). Boenig also indicates that some wind instruments were likely excluded from consorts, and that George Herbert in particular played only stringed instruments.

55 Despite the fact that Tilley (1950), 345, lists 'put up ones pipes' as proverbial for 'give over' or 'give up', if the hired musicians in *RJ* do not 'put up' actual 'pipes' into a 'case', the evident bawdy equivocations made by Juliet's Nurse cannot function (these will be detailed in the next chapter). Moreover, 'put up your pipes in your bag' is said in *Oth* 3.1.19 where 'wind instruments' are specifically named in 3.1.6. Lindley (2006), 50, claims that the musicians in *RJ* must be 'players of stringed instruments' because Peter names them as Simon Catling, James

Rebec and Hugh Soundpost. However, the quartos and Folio are
a mess at this point, on which see Wells and Taylor (1997),
300–1; indeed, 'Q2 has prefixes "Musi<tion>," "Fid<ler>", and
"Min." or "Minst<rel>"'.

56 Marsh (2010), 115–30, details the town waits' ill pay, and
indicates that they 'often played at weddings' (125). Lindley
(2006), 55, says waits were hired in *RJ*.

57 Petronella (1972), 55, argues that, 'Peter is not merely a
reflection of the short-lived Mercutio, for his witty exchange
with the musicians involves important references to three of the
four archetypal metals that are traditionally associated with the
ages of civilization: gold, silver and iron. These references help
to create a scene that acts as a comic transition between the
love-lyricism of earlier portions of the play and the harshness
of a money- or gold-oriented world depicted in the play's last
scenes.'

58 Fabry (1982) analyses this banter, which we will consider further
in the next chapter.

59 See Marsh (2010), 109.

60 Autolycus cons the charitable Clown (4.3.79–117), pretends to
be a courtier (4.4.712–827), and will steal but fears 'Gallows
and knock . . . Beating and hanging' (4.3.28–9).

61 That realm is evoked by the peddler's refrain, 'Though all my
wares be false / The heart is true', in John Dowland's song 'Fine
Knacks for Ladies', on which see Poulton (1982), 266–7.

62 This topic is treated in Sokol (1994), 167–82.

63 Shakespeare himself seemingly avoided the opportunity taken up
by some of his colleagues (Spenser, Jonson) to become court-
based poets. See Cheney (2008) on Shakespeare's 'counter-
laureate' authorship.

64 Duffin (2002), 532–8, discusses confusions between three-men's
songs and freemen's songs, and suggests that the second
nomenclature referred to men made 'free' of the City (in livery
companies) singing such songs. Iselin (1996), 138, suggests
that a punning relation between the two terms may be relevant
to *Tem*.

65 The quotation is from Marsh (2010), 71, and the specifications
of the first and second groups of semi-professionals from 71–2,

75–6. Marsh also describes salaried musicians who doubled up as 'parish clerks, alehouse-keepers . . . weavers, dyers or barbers' (109).

66 Crewdson (1971), 36–7.

67 Crewdson (1971), 37.

68 See Crewdson (1971), 37–40, with the 1574 act partly transcribed (107–9). See also Woodfill (1953), 12–13.

69 Only the transcription and paraphrase of the Act in Woodfill (1953), 14–15, shows this provision.

70 Marsh (2010), 193.

71 Howard Leithead, 'Cromwell, Thomas (b. in or before 1485, d. 1540)', *Oxford DNB* (2004), corrects John Foxe's anecdote, which names the wrong pope. Stevens (1979), 268, tells the anecdote but mistakenly names Richard Cromwell in place of Thomas Cromwell.

72 Duffin (2002), describes the event, adding that the wonderful three men's song portraying war veterans drinking on credit, 'Wee be souldiers three / Pardonez moi je vous en prie: / Lately come forth of the low countrie / With never a penney of mony' (no. 3 in Ravenscourt's *Deuteromelia*), was very likely also performed at that 1607 entertainment (538).

73 Duffin (2002), 531.

74 Austern (1985), 238, 240. The plays include *The Knight of the Burning Pestle*, *Twelfth Night*, and nine other stage plays performed around 1600, including six in the repertory of the particularly musical Children of Paul's company.

75 Deloney (1690?), 14.

76 See Marsh (2010), 191, which cites in support the *Mask of Flowers* staged at Gray's Inn in 1614. Naylor (1931), 82–3, cites the conflation of the two terms in both Florio's *Italian Dictionary* and Cotgrave's *French Dictionary* (both 1611).

77 The servant takes his word from 'sault' meaning to 'leap, dance' (*OED* sault. *v.* 2.), but may also reference satyrs, since the dancers were possibly shared with Jonson's masque *Oberon* – see next note.

78 Hosley (1980), 45, 48, suggests the same King's Men dancers were shared between *WT* and the performance at court on

1 January 1611 of Ben Jonson's masque *Oberon, the Fairy Prince*. See also Pitcher (2010), 70–1, 92–3, 394–6, 402–3.

79 Puritans and Papists are equally mocked in *AW* 1.3.51–5 in a context discussed in Sokol (2008), 103–8. Malvolio is not counted a puritan by witty Maria: 'The dev'l a puritan that he is, or anything constantly but a time-pleaser, an affectioned ass that cons state without book and utters it by great swathes' (*TN* 2.3.141–3).

80 Hotspur denigrates 'mincing poetry' in *1H4* 3.1.130, and Mortimer's wife's singing in 3.1.232. In *2H4* (also set in a militaristic age), Falstaff is said to have disparagingly compared King Henry to 'a singing man of Windsor', provoking Hal's violent response (2.1.91–3). Special meanings of 'singing man' may apply there: see Brennecke (1951).

81 Shakespeare's fiction thereby contradicts Trudell (2014), 20, which holds that Elizabethan men 'were advised to restrict their musicianship to private leisure', but 'women were liable to suffer a much more vehement reaction to public performance [than men], including accusations of harlotry'.

82 Stern (2004), 71–2. Stern further remarks: 'whether because the boy playing Viola lost his voice or was replaced with a worse singer (or whether the company wished the new fool, Armin, to sing the songs instead), Viola's songs are given to Feste'.

83 See Nelson (2012), 15, 24n.; Woodfill (1953), 61–5.

84 Castiglione (1975), 75. This will be discussed in more detail in the next chapter.

85 Morley (1597), 1 (sig. B2ʳ).

86 Lindley (2006), 145–6, which adds that, if sung, this verse might introduce the 'impropriety of admitting low-life song into courtly word-play'. See next note.

87 Maynard (1986), 189. Maynard further comments on 'the unseemliness of Pandarus singing at all, as a lord, and an old one' (206), and opines that 'Men or women of high rank would rarely be heard to sing in real life, and it was not expected of such characters in drama, especially tragic drama' (161).

88 Price (1981), 167; also Wilson (2011a), 119–20.

89 Price (1981), 171, 172.

90 Collinson, 'Elizabeth I (1533–1603)', *Oxford DNB* (2004), says
    that Elizabeth 'was not above exploiting her femininity. When the
    Scottish ambassador, Sir James Melville, surprised her playing the
    virginals, she stopped, pretended to slap him, and said that "she
    was not used to play before men, but when she was solitary, to
    shun melancholy".' Lindley (2006), 87, 252 n.133, adds that she
    was also overheard by Lord Hunsdon, and that she was 'keen to
    know' from Melville 'whether she played better than her rival
    Mary Queen of Scots'. However, Elizabeth did not openly
    perform in public. According to Price (1981), 190, 'From the
    early part of the sixteenth century onwards it was made clear in
    "courtly" and educational literature that, although private
    performance and even composition [of music] were socially
    tolerable, performance or publication for an audience not made
    up of one's peers was certainly not a sign of breeding.'

91 Starr (2010), 195, considers nearly 100 such books, finding a
    wide variety of views.

92 Mulcaster (1581), 168. This reiterates that the customs of
    England call for education of girls, and somewhat wryly
    describes their musical education at the behest of their parents
    becoming less valued by themselves 'when the yong wenches
    become yong wives' (178).

93 Lindley (2006), 8.

94 Auden (1963), 318–19, suggests that Shakespeare's company
    would have had 'to hire at least one person as a singer, rather
    than as an actor' in order to be able stage such roles as
    Balthazar, Amiens and Feste. Stern (2004), 70–1, discusses the
    probable necessity of switching over singing roles when boy
    actors' voices broke, and notes that the talent of one particular
    singing boy actor 'probably relates to the fact that major
    Shakespearean heroines sing between 1601 and 1604'. Wilson
    (2011a), 119–20, holds that 'Shakespeare's company contained
    at best one adult singer and no females'.

95 See Lindley (2006), 126–7, 149, 159.

96 *MA* 2.3.43–4, 78; *AYL* 2.5.14; *TC* 3.1.53. Lindley (2006),
    170, attributes this to 'the conventional reluctance of the
    courtly male about performing in public'. Sternfeld (1959),
    57–8, also attributes their reluctance to conduct book strictures
    concerning music.

97   See Sokol and Sokol (2003), 38–9, 196.

98   Maynard (1986), 176, points out that the actor playing Proteus in *TGV* must play music and it is best if he can sing it.

99   Auden (1963), 318, 232.

100 Prynne (1632), 273, 274.

101 So Austern (1993), 343, indicates that 'feminine nature' was considered 'a literal inversion of the positive, direct qualities associated with the eras masculine ideals' and therefore 'Because of perceived affective similarities between music and femininity, many English writers of the late sixteenth and early seventeenth centuries discussed one in terms of the other'. This continues (351): 'Even the power of Orpheus over the finality of Death and over all earthly objects and beings was clearly secondary in the English imagination to the implicitly sexual and feminizing capacity of his music'.

102 See Sokol (2008), 27–56, and notes.

103 Their fears have to do with the newness of their manhood, for the younger brother goes on to say that they should sing despite the fact that 'now' (presumably recently) 'our voices / Have got the mannish crack' (4.2.236–9).

104 Inverse and equally comical gender stereotyping by a young woman appears in *AYL* 3.2.392–408.

105 Austern (1985), 260. Austern explains concerning 'the literate and accomplished courtesan' that 'On the English stage, her direct antecedents are to be found in the wise and witty courtesans of dramas patterned after those of Terence and Plautus, and not in the real activities of the contemporary native whore' (259–60). There are no such characters in Shakespeare, but of course the singing seductress also has antecedents in the mythology of the Sirens, mentioned in *CE* 3.2.47, *Tit* 2.1.23, and Sonnet 119.

106 Iselin (1988), 29 (my translation). A few of Shakespeare's singers are drunk or deranged, but most are not. None are whores or rowdies, and the mentally distressed are treated with sympathy.

107 O'Neill (1972), 409, 410. Wong (2013), 168, concludes a wide-ranging survey of music and gender in Elizabethan plays acknowledging that her examples are of 'male and female

characters, most of them non-Shakespearean', and that even among these some deviate from 'social stipulations of musical practice'.

108 Smith (1994), 315, 316, 320.

109 Ophelia is bereft of her king, her father, her lover's affection and her brother's protection. Desdemona has an insanely jealous husband for whom she has renounced her family and former life. The Jailor's Daughter suffers from an unrequited passion. All sing to express sexually-oriented grief, about which, I will contend, Shakespeare was compassionate rather than condemnatory.

110 Thus Austern (1994), 99–102, approves of the Willow Song, and Austern (2006), 452–3, claims that 'the circumstances of its performance help to emphasize Desdemona's chaste propriety' because in marriage musical performance 'could stand for the harmonious bond between husband and wife'. Hopkins (1994), 65–6, proposes that singing 'at all in such a situation indicates [Desdemoma's] imperviousness to habitual considerations of decorum'. But the author kindly wrote to me that Desdemona's singing is not indecorous in itself, but rather: 'that a woman who sings, particularly about sexual experience (even someone else's), when her own sexual conduct is being called into question is being inadvertently or deliberatively provocative. She is not explaining her innocence; she is not maintaining silence; she is engaging in an act that seems as though it must be communicating something but at the same time she is refusing to specify what is being communicated, instead veiling it in a song.' It is true that the medium of song does diffuse meanings, but as we shall discuss presently, that may be its advantage in relation to what needs to be uncovered.

111 Seng (1967), 133. Seng quotes with approval another critic's view that 'the presence of a lute means that Ophelia, like any Court lady, is a musician and will play and sing like one' (132). On the contrary Maynard (1986), 159–60, says of Ophelia, 'The very fact that she, a court lady, sings in the presence of the queen, and the king, shows that the controls of reason and social propriety have snapped'. It is true, at least, that her courtly audience do not understand her, for as Wong (2013), 133, explains, quoting Robert Burton, female 'melancoly' is often incomprehensible: 'Singing is documented as one of the "most ordinary symptoms" melancholic women display since, Burton argues, many of these women "cannot tell how to express themselves in words, or how it holds them, what ails them, you cannot understand them, or well tell what to make of their sayings".'

112 See Sokol (1992) on the role of mayors in merchant tribunals in relation to *MV*.

113 In reply to my enquiry, Carol Chillington Rutter very kindly reported that it is wholly 'fanciful that Brabantio could have hi-jacked the council deliberations for domestic concerns'.

114 It was often commented that to protect its constitution Venice prohibited its patrician families from military command and instead used foreign mercenaries; see Sokol (2008), 133–5.

115 Crewdson (1971), 101, 129, 122.

116 See Crewdson (1971), 179–81. Crewdson adds (123) that a 1606 by-law of the London Musician's Company demands 'every brother or widow of the same art or science [e.g. music] shall pay for quarterage at every of the said quarter days . . . sixpence', suggesting that allowance for 'sisters' of the London Company may have had mainly to do with guild traditions in which 'widows' were allowed to carry on their late husbands' occupations. But some unmarried women were members of London livery companies, on which see Brodsky (1986), and Laurence (1994), 125–43. For an example, see Kreps (2003).

117 The renowned Marina in *Per* may be an exception. The famous Italians include the *concerto delle donne* of Ferrara, for whom much music was specially written, and the singer Rachel of Venice.

118 For one instance out of many, Trudell (2014), 20, holds that 'it would have been out of the question for a woman to be employed as a musician at court, in the Chapel Royal, or even as a common minstrel'. It seems, however, that a woman could have been a licensed minstrel.

119 Austern (1998a), 5, 6.

120 Ewbank (1971), 105. Brennecke (1953), 37, similarly says that 'Shakespeare uses music to tell us what his characters could not communicate by any other means.'

121 Dubrow (2011), 227.

122 See Seng (1967), 151–2.

123 This suggests that the song was a familiar one, but according to Austern (2006), 451, it had a unique aspect when heard on Shakespeare's stage in being sung by a woman: 'During the sixteenth century and early seventeenth there were so many English laments for lost love with refrains evoking the willow tree as to constitute a distinct genre, of which Shakespeare clearly took advantage in Othello – though his is the only known example in which the lamenting lover is a woman.' Brennecke (1953), 36, also notes that Desdemona's song has many ancestors and suggests it is adapted to a female persona from a male one.

124 Brennecke (1953), 37.

125 See Freud (1958a; 1958b). On English songs showing reversed genders of the persona, see Trudell (2014).

126 Austern (1998a), 615–20, describes long traditions of treating love-induced illness (with music): the sufferers cited are all male.

127 Whythorne (1962), 205. Finney (1959), 43–4, mentions non-communication between those who produced audible music and those who saw music as an emblem of 'all harmony', noting that 'composers' techniques for ordering sound were largely ignored by the lay philosopher.'

128 Jocularly in *MND* 2.7.5–7; erotically in *MND* 2.1.148–54; *TN* 3.1.109; *AC* 5.2.82–3. The music of the spheres is also treated jocularly when the witty Clown in *Oth* mentions preference for 'music that may not be heard', as discussed in the next chapter. On the other hand, the 'music of the spheres' is taken seriously in *Per* 21.215.

129 Minear (2011), 2, which adds that it still 'continued to exert a powerful influence over the seventeenth-century imagination and world-view'. See also Finney (1953); Finney (1959); Finney (1962), 126–38; Hollander (1961); Smith (1979). See also Lindley (2006), 17–18, 21, 32, and 48–9.

130 This would be the sophisticated music that is found in many late sixteenth-century English keyboard manuscripts and was later collected in the anthologies following from the *c.* 1612

Parthenia; or, The Maydenhead of the First Musicke that Ever Was Printed for the Virginalls.

131 *Son* 8; *TGV* 1.2.95; *MV* 5.1.84; *MND* 4.1.142, 5.1.60; *R2* 5.5.47; *AW* 1.1.168; *Mac* 4.3.99.

132 *OED* confound, *v.* 4, 5.

133 *OED* confound, *v.* 1.

134 Naylor (1928), 91–3, realized that the lady is not yet playing, but rather adjusting her instrument preparatory to playing it. His discovery is discussed in Kitson (1987), which correctly describes her need to press each key repetitively while tuning and adjusting her instrument. Kerrigan (1968), 355–6, notes 'it is sometimes suggested' that the poem's 'dancing chips' may be 'jacks', but makes nothing of this. Trillini (2008), 10 n.63, cites Kitson, and Moore (1985) credits Naylor, yet both hold that some music is played. Vendler (1999), 544–8; Booth (2000), 438–9; Burrow (2002), 636, all think the lady is currently playing music; Kerrigan (1968), 355–6 and Duncan-Jones (2001), 370, both hold that the poem's 'dancing chips' are the keys being played.

135 Koster (1980), 45. Koster thinks early English-made harpsichords were 'important', contrary to Hubbard (1965).

136 See Russell (1973), 13–17, for a brief account.

137 Currently, this is described at the beginning of 'Elaine Comparone tuning' on YouTube.

138 Sexual innuendoes arise in Sonnet 128 concerning a woman and her 'virginal', although not as significantly as elsewhere. In *WT* 1.2.127–8, sexualized insanity causes Leontes to perceive his wife's courteous gesture to his friend as obscene 'virginalling / Upon his palm'. See Sokol (1994), 126, 165, 177–9, on the imagery of hands in the play. The title of the first printed book of English keyboard music, *Parthenia* (1611), puns on 'virginals'. 'Virginal' is punned on sexually in *TNK* 3.3.34 and often in Elizabethan drama, as shown in Williams (1994), III, 1485, which adds that virginals' 'jacks . . . acquire a phallic sense' in Dekker's *Northward Ho* 1.3.42 (*c.* 1605). Williams also asserts that 'jack' in the drama most often implies 'penis' (II, 727–8), and, that in Dekker's *1 Honest Whore* 5.2.265 (1604), 'his Iacks leap up' means to 'have an erection' (I, 278).

Writing in relation to Shakespeare's Sonnet 128, Trillini (2008), 8 n.56, asserts that in *2 Honest Whore* sig. H4^r, 'the word "jack" not only denotes vulgar men but also an erect penis'. Ripin (*Grove Music Online*) explains that 'The derivation of the term "virginal" remains in dispute, the association with the Latin *virga* ("rod") being unproved.' If we do take the suggestion that virginals jacks are associated with the Latin *virga*, then there is a further possible pun via the French cognate noun '*verge*'. This means both a rod and a penis, according to Cotgrave (1968), a French–English dictionary of 1611 which includes among the translations of '*verge*' the English word 'yard',

139 On the symbolism of 'wood' in *Tem* see Sokol (2003), 179–80.

140 Sokol (2014) proposes that when the charitable Cerimon in *Pericles* calls for 'the rough and / Wofull Musick that we have', he demands a new and startlingly sophisticated kind of music just emerging in Italy and England.

141 The jacket notes to the Alfred Deller and Desmond Dupré recording (Angel 45016) suggest that allusions to Dowland pieces appear in the quarto only text of *2H4* A.C. 4–5, where Falstaff remembers Justice Shallow singing 'his fancies or his good-nights', and in *TGV* 1.2.80–3, where a request for "a tune . . . a note' is answered by 'As little by such toys, as may be possible'. These Dowland pieces are 'A Fancie' and 'The Shoemaker's Wife – A Toy'. See Wilson (2011a), 120, on Dowland's Ayres on Shakespeare's stage. Duffin (2004), 162–3, 179, 257, also finds possible connections between Shakespeare and Dowland's work.

142 Welch (1922), 511–12, which adds that Shakespeare also failed to take notice of the genre of the musical 'fancy'. But Falstaff remembers Shallow singing 'his fancies or his good-nights' and Madrigals are named in *MW* 3.1.17.

143 Wilson (2011a), 119–20.

144 On the development from the late 1590s of the English Ayre see Pattison (1970), 113–40; Fischlin (1997). Alfonso Ferrabosco imported the madrigal from Italy from the 1560s. Younge published his very popular collection of Italian madrigals, *Musica Transalpina*, in 1588, and an English

madrigal school developed featuring Thomas Morley and his fellows.

145 The contending positions that Dowland's famed melancholy was artistic/philosophical, artistic/conventional, or personal and embittered are suggested respectively in Rooley (1983); Wells (1985); Poulton (1983).

146 We have mentioned one such sprightly Dowland song, 'Fine Knacks for Ladies', above. On the other hand, his deeply melancholic through-composed ayre 'In darkness let me dwell' must rank among the world's great art songs.

147 Dowland's famous song 'Flow my Tears' (published in his *Second Booke of Ayres*, 1600) was derived from one of his solo lute pieces. Illustrating what Watkins (2010), 56, calls a trend towards 'instrumental performances of vocal music . . . common throughout the Renaissance' the same material was reworked by Dowland into his groundbreaking instrumental suite *Lachrimae* for a 'broken' consort of 'Lute, Viols, or Violons', on which see Poulton (1982), 126; Holman (1999); Holman and O'Dette (2009), and the notes, seemingly by Thurston Dart, to the L'Oiseau Lyre recording of the *Lachrimae* suite (OLS 164).

148 See Wilson (2011a), 123–5, on how tuckets and sennets played on varied wind instruments introduced plays and characters in the Elizabethan theatre.

6 Shakespeare's Mythical Musicians

1 Lévi-Strauss (1983), 12. Using Lévi-Strauss's terminology, a binary opposition embodied in myth central to this chapter is between the raucous Marsyas' 'raw' and the constrained Apollo's 'cooked' kinds of music.

2 Nuttall (1989), 8–13, offers justification for this kind of argument (when claiming an allusion to an unnamed Icarus in *Tim*) in terms of 'a Shakespeare play' being 'an indefinitely recessive, progressively more and more intelligible object'.

3 More subtle means were also available. In a paper read at the 2015 RSA convention in Berlin, Clark Hulse explained how

Holbein was able to portray without danger the increasing corpulence of Henry VIII. Sokol (2008), 103–11 discusses how in *AW* and *TS* Shakespeare addressed dangerous controversies concerning the *Book of Common Prayer* where any but a highly indirect approach would have attracted censure and very probably punishment. Shakespeare also avoided the penalties of law when implying that the culture of the realm of the ageing, childless Queen Elizabeth stood in a similar danger to that of his tragic King Richard II – a topic I will address elsewhere.

4   In addition, the Latin appellation for Apollo, Phoebus ('bright'), appears in fifteen Shakespeare plays but always referring to the sun, not the artist.

5   These appearances are in *Tit* 2.4.51; *TGV* 3.2.77–80; *Luc* 553; *MV* 5.1.80–82; *H8* 3.1.3–13. See Rooley (1990) on Orpheus in English Renaissance thinking regarding music. Another similar myth about the benign influence of music over beasts is mentioned in *Twelfth Night* (1.2.14–16), when sea rescue by the music-loving dolphins of the music-playing god Arion is compared to the salvation from shipwreck of Viola's spar-grasping brother. Allusions to the same sea rescue by dolphins may arise in *MND* 2.1.148–54, on which see Brooks (1989), lxvii–lxviii, and in *AC* 5.2.87–9. Bate (1993), 138–9, 267, 314, connects the story of Arion with *MND*, *TN*, and *Tem*. Iselin (1996), 138, suggests that Zethus, Arion's 'pragmatic' twin brother, may be connected with Caliban in *Tem*.

6   Shakespeare's treatment of Arion, Orpheus, Mercury and Amphion – the three same mythical musicians that Wells (1994), 4–5, 7, 67, 144, 146, 196, brackets as miraculous creators of the lyre, or of human language, or of civilization – is far from idealizing.

7   The story is told in Apollodorus (1921), 2.4.9, beginning 'Hercules was taught . . . to play the lyre by Linus.' The version in Aelian (1576), sigs L3ʳ–L3ᵛ (3:32), records that Hercules, when 'but a boy', is taught to play the 'violyn' by Linus, 'whome Linus reprehending, because he handled his rebecke somewhat rudely, Hercules swelling with poyson of anger, smote his master Linus with his bowe, and harmed him is such sorte, that he dyed'. Among Shakespeare's nearly fifty mentions of Hercules,

his childhood exploits are mentioned only in *LLL* 5.1.27–34
and 5.1.584–5 – and the schoolmaster Holofernes swears by him
('*Mehercle*') in *LLL* 4.2.77.

8   Nonnos (1940–2), I, 377–409. Many of the epithets apply to the
pipes.

9   More than thirty translated Greek or Latin textual references are
provided by the online Theoi Project, and dozens more from
such authors as Xenophon, Polybius, Horace, Lucanus, Plato,
Livy and Plutarch by the Tufts University Perseus Digital Library
(all indexed under 'Marsyas'). Maniates (2000), 150–4,
catalogues 211 classical texts treating Marsyas.

10 The Warburg Institute iconographic database contains over two
hundred images of Marsyas, including thirty-two from the
fifteenth century, seventy-seven from the sixteenth century, and
sixty-three from the seventeenth century. Wyss (1996), 145–55,
catalogues 104 Italian Renaissance images of Marsyas.

11 Maniates (2000), 118, 119.

12 Conti (2006 [1581]), 520–1 (Book VI, Chapter 15, 'On
Marsyas').

13 Pseudo-Hyginus and Pseudo-Apollodorus are quoted in the
online Theoi Project. See also Lucian, quoted in Winternitz
(1959), 186 n.4, and Maniates (2000), 124.

14 This is seen, for instance, in a part of Giulio Romano's design
not shown in the detail in our Figure 15, in a painting by Andrea
Schiavone reproduced in Winternitz (1959), 194, and in a
gruesome 1581 engraving after Melichor Meier shown in the
Warburg Institute Iconographic Database, record number
23027. In the engraving, which anticipates many explicit
depictions of Apollo's sadism by seventeenth-century artists, a
Midas with ears watches Apollo holding Marsyas' skin in
triumph with the skinned corpse at his feet.

15 Ovid (2002), 188–9 (Book Six: 487–98).

16 See Ovid (1971), I, 314–15 (Book Six: 385) and the literal
translation Ovid (2004), 188.

17 For instance, Zecher (2007), 57–93, details how the myth of the
rivalry of Marsyas and Apollo, and images of their rival
instruments, were used in complex and sometimes contradictory
ways in French Renaissance literary debates.

18 On *Fasti* and *Luc*, see Gillespie (2004), 345, 395; Burrow
    (2002), 48–51, 62–3; Bate (1993), 67–82; Prince (1992),
    196–201. Bate (1993), 138–9, 267, 314 and *passim*, connects the
    story of Arion told in *Fasti* with *MND*, *TN* and *Tem*. Sokol
    (1994), 132, 229 n.60, connects the story of Flora told in *Fasti*
    with *WT*.

19 Ovid (1959), 373 (*Fasti* VI, 693).

20 Evans (2001) gives qualified support to the notion that a section
    of *Moralia* influenced the composition of *Oth*. Reynolds (2012),
    544–5, finds a source for the spider-in-a-cup idea in *WT* in
    Moralia, and Gaunt (1969) finds *Moralia* a source for *Ham*.
    Skinner (2014), 236 n.58, suggests that *Ham* echoes *Moralia*.

21 Plutarch (1603), 122. *Moralia* 456b refers to the invention of the
    phorbeia, also referred to by Simonides, according to Maniates
    (2000), 130.

22 Plutarch (1579), 211–12.

23 Case (1586), 32.

24 Case (1586), 33. The brackets enclose a translation of Greek in
    the text very kindly supplied to me by Armand D'Angour.

25 Deloney (1690?), 14.

26 Marsh (2010), 165, 175, 181.

27 In addition to a social insult, Hamlet's mock-question reflects his
    opinion of his false friend; Hamlet has stated that men who can
    be played like a 'pipe' are conformist and shallow in 3.2.68–9,
    where he praises Horatio for not being such a one.

28 Hollander (1961), 44.

29 Castiglione (1975), 101.

30 These are very few proposals of Shakespearean allusions to
    Marsyas. Poisson (1964) points out a possible onomastic pun
    whereby the name of Shakespeare's Martius recalls that of
    Marsyas when in *Cor* (1.7.22) Martius is so bloody as to
    appear 'flayed'. Levith (2007), 22–32, further speculates on
    Marsyas and *Cor*. Marsyas is not mentioned in Wilson
    (2011b), 115–35, a chapter on 'symbolic persons' related to
    music as imaged by Shakespeare. He gets parenthetical mention
    in Wilson and Calore (2005), 23–4, in an entry about 'Apollo',
    with further passing mentions (208, 304). Bardelman (2009),

cites sixteenth- and early seventeenth-century English literary references to the story of Marsyas. Smith (1979) traces the divergence of Renaissance musical thought and practice away from the classical ideas that dominated the Middle Ages, finding the myth of Marsyas of central significance (but does not apply it to Shakespeare).

31 Quoted and discussed in Kingsley-Smith (2010), 138.

32 For instance, a drawing attributed to the school of Benvenuto Garofalo (1496–1539) of a human-limbed Marsyas attacked in the breast can be viewed at the British Museum's online research collections, asset Id 231119, object Id 716302, part Id 1. Woodcut illustrations to 1557, 1563 and 1591 editions of Ovid's *Metamorphoses*, Book 6, also show a goat-legged Marsyas attacked in the breast.

33 Although, according to Maniates (2000), 132, most written and many Renaissance visual depictions of Marsyas make him a hairy satyr, he was also often depicted as fully human in form. The Warburg Institute's photographic collection is sorted on the basis of human- versus goat-legged Marsyas. When considering the animal-legged Marsyas, we should recall that Antonio in *MV* is self-defined as 'a tainted wether of the flock' (4.1.113–4); this is discussed briefly below and at length in Sokol (1998).

34 A sixteenth-century image of a knife-sharpener preparing the blade to skin Marsyas, by Angelo Falconetto, is seen in the Warburg Institute Iconographic Database, record 22987. That database contains many ancient images of knife-sharpeners preparing to attack Marsyas, indexed under 'Apollo and Marsyas . . . servant sharpening the knife'. For discussions, see Wyss (1996), 21–2, 62, 128; Winternitz (1959), 186; Adams (1988), 331; Maniates (2000), 127. Philostratus the Younger's description of a barbarian executioner sharpening a knife intended for Marsyas is quoted in the Theoi Project.

35 John Russell Brown's notes to Silvayn (1977) indicate a number of verbal correspondences with *MV*. The forensic rhetoric of Silvayn's Declamation is echoed in the play more generally.

36 Silvayn (1977), 170. The alteration of the bond in *The Merchant of Venice* so that it demands a forfeit taken from the breast, rather than the genitals, might seem to instance a classical Freudian 'displacement upwards', expressing castration anxiety.

Sokol (1995), 381–5, argues, however, that it connects more significantly with Antonio's fetishized over-generosity; the attack on Antonio's breast punishes an attempt to usurp the Great Mother.

37 See Sokol (1995). Although Elam (1996), 10, claims that 'castration might be said to be a founding trope of comedy as dramatic genre' (10), and that 'whenever comedy emerges as a genre within a given Western culture, it does so courtesy of castration' (27), and it mentions *MV* (3 n.5), it overlooks the references in *MV* to castration. Taylor (2000), discusses Shakespeare's references to eunuchs or gelding (e.g. 41), but not in *MV*.

38 *OED* wether, *n.* 1.a.

39 Sokol (1995) discusses complex psychoanalytic aspects of allied patterns in *MV*. Very briefly, the play subtly treats restrictions placed on both male and female agency, and these figure forth as sacrifices of potency to fetishization. That work is extended here in terms of mythological, art-historical, and musicological contexts.

40 Shakespearean characters are said to dislike, or say they dislike, music generally at *MV* 5.1.69, 5.1.83–5; Sonnet 8; *JC* 1.2.204–5; *Oth* 3.1.11–16; *1H4* 3.1.229–32; *TN* 2.3.83–9. As we have seen, Benedick in *MA* shows contempt for a string-instrument accompanied love song (2.3.81–5) and shows respect only for 'manly' martial music (2.3.12–14).

41 Jessica's reaction may link to a theme of prejudice in the play, on which see Sokol (1998).

42 See *MA* 2.3.14–15 (which contrasts a military fife and drum with a civilian pipe and tabor); *Oth* 3.3.357; *Cor* 5.4.50–1; Folio stage directions to *Tim* at tln 1652 and to *1H4* at tln 2093.

43 Perhaps Shylock fears that festive unconstraint may slide into civil disturbance in which, as the Jewish moneylender in Silvayn (1977), 169, puts it, 'the Christians . . . abus[e] the Jewes'.

44 However, Barton (1994), 3–30, incisively expounds the gerund 'wrying' as used in *Cym* 5.1.5.

45 Puttenham (1589), 143.

46 In the sense of *OED* wry, *adj.* 1. a. and *OED* neck, *n.* 1, 6.a.

47 Fifes were straight-necked instruments in that they lacked the crooked neck of, for instance, the Renaissance dulcian or curtal. On these ancestors of the bassoon, see http://www.dulcians.org.

48 See *OED* wry, *adj.* 1.b.

49 Overbury (1614), sig. D3ᵛ; also Overbury (1616), sig. C6ʳ.

50 Overbury (1616), sig. I4ʳ.

51 Plutarch (1579), 259.

52 See Maniates (2000), 118; Winternitz (1959), 191 n.20.

53 See Baines (1995), 54, 57. Conti (2006 [1581]), II, 520, makes Marsyas into Cybele's lover.

54 Taylor (2000), 14, and *passim*; Maniates (2000), 15 n.28. Dark aspects of Marsyas' *aulos* playing may have related to destructive aspects of Dionysos or Pan.

55 See Sokol (1995) on animal images in *MV*. Shylock's 'pig' also recalls Jewish prohibitions concerning 'pork', mentioned at *MV* 1.3.31.

56 It is surprising because it does not match up to how Shakespeare treats the bagpipe's sound as emblematic of melancholy in *1H4* 1.2.76 and *MV* 1.1.53, and as festive in *WT* 4.4.184.

57 Hollander (1961), 44–6, discusses how Renaissance translations of ancient texts often substituted more contemporary musical instruments for the *aulos* or lyre. We have seen an example in North's Plutarch above. In the visual arts there is the extreme case of a 1589 engraving by Nicolaes Clock, after Karel van Mander, in which a Marsyas-like myth is illustrated with an eclectic collection of stringed and blown musical instruments, including a lute, a viol, a lyre, two different-sized shawms and a set of pan pipes (this can be seen in the Warburg Institute Iconographic Database, record 21990).

58 Wyss (1996), 84.

59 Baines (1995), 61.

60 On Montagna, see Winternitz (1959), 193; Wyss (1966), 85. On Schiavone, see Winternitz (1959), 192 n.9, 194 figure 8.

61 Moxey (1980), 131; Wilson (1998), 8; Folkerth (2002), 89.

62 Wyss (1996), 89–91.

63 The brightly coloured bagpipe lying beneath the mutilation scene is highly visible in the image of Anselmi's painting on the National Gallery of Art website at www.nga.gov.

64 Wyss (1996), 89, points out that this engraving, made probably 1538, shows Apollo abandoning his *lira* on the ground to take up the executioner's knife, while Marsyas' skin hangs in a temple in the background, so the 'source was the woodcut of the *Ovidio vulgare*'.

65 Ariosto (1562), 51.

66 For instance, Sokol (1985) argues that the innermost structure of *TS* derives from Spenser's *Faerie Queene*, Books 2 and 3.

67 Thomas (1983), 38–9, 94–117, 118–19, 134–5, describes early modern anxiety connected with violations of an insecure yet crucial line of division between humans and other animals.

68 See Herodotus, Ptolemy Hephaestion and Aelian, quoted in the Theoi Project. See Winternitz (1959), 192 n., on visual representations of temples containing Marsyas' skin. His skin is said to have been made by Ctesippus into a comical Dionysian wine sack by Plato in *Euthydemus*, 285c–d, Philostratus the Younger (quoted in the Theoi Project), and Conti (2006 [1581]), 520.

69 Quoted in Winternitz (1959), 192.

70 Maniates (2000), 129.

71 *Dionysiaca*, 19.315, in Nonnos (1940–2), II, 113.

72 Maniates (2000), 129, discusses a controversial 1966 article by Martin Vogel (in German) that holds that the Marsyas myth represents no more than the invention of the bagpipe.

73 Baines (1995), 13. The bagpipe-maker Julian Goodacre's website states that 'The most basic bag for a bagpipe is a complete animal skin', and 'Ideally I would use goatskin, which is very thin and strong. However goats are small . . . I can usually only make one bag per skin.'

74 Baines (1995), 117 n.

75 Adams (1988), 322–3, 326 and *passim*, offers a number of psychoanalytic perspectives on Marsyas.

76 Discussing mid-fifteenth-century art, Moxey (1980), 131, remarks: 'Traditionally associated with the lower orders of

society, the bagpipe was often used as a literary and visual metaphor of male genitalia.' This topic is discussed further, with visual illustrations, in Colantuono (2010), 136–7.

77 'Case' is noted as bawdy here in Colman (1974), 71. There is no doubt about the sexual meaning of the Nurse's concern for a 'pitiful case', for earlier she told Friar Lawrence that Romeo 'is even in my mistress' case / Just in her case' (3.3.84–5). Likewise, Mistress Quickly in *2H4* says 'since my exion is entered and my case so openly known to the world' (2.1.30–1). Commenting on sexual meanings of 'case' in Shakespeare, Williams (2006), 66, says that 'vaginal applications predominate'.

78 See Williams (1994), I, 59, on bagpipes and the belly, penis and urinary bladder.

79 Boenig (1983) is sceptical about claims that the bagpipe mentioned in the Miller's Prologue in *The Canterbury Tales* (A565–6) is raucous, claiming that some medieval bagpipes were 'indeed loud, but others were not' (4), but admits that by Breughel's time loud bagpipes with multiple drones were the norm (5), which was, of course, before Shakespeare's time.

80 Winternitz (1959), 191. Similarly, while analysing a Ben Jonson masque, Smith (1999), 93, finds that 'blown instruments were proverbial in Platonic lore for their gutsiness, their mindlessness, their distance from *logos*'.

81 The curse is described by Pausanias, quoted in the Theoi Project, and is addressed in Winternitz (1959).

82 Sandys (1632), 225, commenting on Book Six of Ovid's *Metamorphoses* in the tradition of moralizing Ovid which is discussed, for instance, in Wyss (1996), 34–5.

83 Quoted from *Orat.*, lxxii.9 in Baines (1960), 63–4, where Baines seeks the earliest mention of bagpipes. This he thinks may possibly be in Aristophanes, but more likely in Suetonius' *Life of Nero*.

84 Shakespeare repeatedly mentions Nero by as a figure of cruelty, identifying him as a musician once when Talbot says he will 'like thee, Nero, / Play on the lute, beholding the towns burn' (*1H6* 1.6.73–4).

85   *Politics*, VIII, 1341a–b. Just after this Aristotle expresses mild
     anti-hedonism: 'Thus we reject the professional instruments
     and also the professional mode of education in music . . . for in
     this the performer practices the art, not for the sake of his own
     improvement, but in order to give pleasure, and at that a vulgar
     pleasure, to his hearers.'

86   Castiglione (1975), 98.

87   Castiglione (1975), 100.

88   Castiglione (1975), 49.

89   Fantham (2005), 227.

90   From, respectively: Wiseman (1988), 4, 5; Small (1982), 92;
     Kuttner (1999), 357–8. In addition, Small (1982) explains
     (68–92) that over a long time Marsyas' statues came to
     symbolise *libertas* in Etruscan Italy as well as in Rome, and
     Niżyńska (2001), 158–60, and *passim,* discusses political
     aspects of Ovid twice telling Marsyas' story.

91   Winternitz (1959), 186, and Small (1982), 68–9, agree that
     Apollo cheats.

92   Maniates (2000), 123, 126, 140–1.

93   Maniates (2000), 124.

94   Maniates (2000), 124, and see 156 n.17.

95   A formula whereby the contestants agree that the winner of the
     musical contest will do what they please with the loser appears
     in Pseudo-Apollodorus (quoted in the Theoi Project), and in
     Conti (2006), II, 520.

96   According to Masson (1949), 309, 'Plusieurs de nos sources
     déclarent que Babys était un frère de Marsyas'. Armand
     D'Angour informs me that the earliest source of this was
     probably 'the 2nd-century AD collector of proverbs Zenobius
     (i4.81)'.

97   Quoted here from Athenaeus (1927–41), Book 14, 624b.

98   Case (1586), 30–1.

99   Erasmus (1992), 18–19.

100 Austern (2006), 450, supposes 'Othello's indifference to music,
     especially when taken in conjunction with his own description
     of Desdemona as "an admirable musician" . . . may hint at one

of the underlying causes of their tragedy.' But Othello simply may not wish to hear loud badly played music early in the morning.

101 See, for instance, Minear (2011), 17–20, 25–31, and 84, which claims (84) the Clown '*does* evoke the idea of divine harmony … in a context that makes the idea seem alien, even frightening'. King (1987), 155, holds that (through his servant) Othello 'is demanding the music of the spheres which is inaudible to the ears of fallen man but which alone would be a suitable accompaniment to his love for his wife'. King also discusses here the musician's down-to-earth reply to a request for a 'music that may not be heard', which is 'We ha' *none such*, sir' (3.1.18, my italics), noting that '"Nonesuch" was the title of a contemporary popular tune'.

102 Reed-instrument music must be played to motivate the Clown's comment. Cutts (1960) suggests it is a 'delicate aubade', but Ross (1966), 124, more plausibly thinks it raucous. Ortiz (2011), 151–7, especially 151–2, posits that Cassio's raucous music is intended to cover up Desdemona's cries at her deflowering and Othello rejects this music because he rejects her sexuality. Despite finding an analogue in a passage in Puttenham, this interpretation seems far-fetched.

103 *Oth* 3.1.3–4 is quoted from the Folio tln 1521–2, because the modernization might compound the difficulty of finding an adequate reading.

104 Furness (1886), 154.

105 Quoted from Sanders (2012), 121, but the same glosses appear in most editions.

106 When young I often heard the Neapolitan accent spoken, and also have asked many Italians who confirm that it is not known to be particularly nasal. Lessons in the Neapolitan dialect on You Tube confirm this as well. Neither, as far as I can determine, were the Neapolitan dialect or Neapolitan language voiced nasally in the distant past.

107 *OED* speak, *v.* 7.a; Naples, *n.* 1; Neapolitan, *adj.* B. 2.

108 Syphilis (known as a 'great mimicker' on account of the wide range of its symptoms) might damage the sinuses or the nerves controlling the palate, but that would be rare.

109 Ridley (1967), 90 n.

110 Neill (2006), 279 n., says that the two Clown scenes in *Othello* 'are often omitted in performance' because they are 'unusually perfunctory'.

111 Muir (2005), 199. This would accord with Austern (2006), 449: 'The original music probably belonged to the classic and widespread morning genre of the aubade (or hunts-up).' Guinle (2003), 114, discusses an English musical tradition of playing 'The Bride's Good Morrow' and illustrates from Lyly's *Mother Bombie* (190–2). Neill (2006), 279 n., proposes that Cassio calling for music to 'bid "Good morrow, general"' (3.1.2) relates to a 'folk ritual' in which 'songs and music were customarily performed outside the bridal chamber to greet the dawn'.

112 Laroque (1991), 288–9.

113 See Stone (1977), 101, on this tradition.

114 Grennan (1987), 275, claims that 'circumstances' are the motivator of Cassio's 'pliable [styles of] speech'; certainly his downfall seems to change it.

115 Passing notice is taken of Parr's gloss in Neill (2006), 279 n. Draya and Whalen (2010), 132, seem to borrow its contents without attribution in an 'Oxfordian' reading of the play.

116 In Furness, (1886), 154.

117 Parr (1795), 36. Parr argues 'that the scenes of Shakespeare contain so much minute knowledge of local customs that they can only be understood by the people of the country', in order to support a contention that a recent Italian translation of *Othello* surpasses the original. The hautboy-like double reed placed in the mouth of a modern Punch is called a *swazzle*.

118 The *World Shakespeare Bibliography Online* indexes from 1960; the review article Henke (2008) covers studies going back to the early twentieth century; Faherty (1991) treats particularly *Othello*.

119 Thus I think that Cassio shows himself 'unattractive and shallow', as the enlightening essay by Evans (2001), 29, puts it, not for 'the first time in the play' in 4.1.116, as that essay suggests, but rather in 3.1.

120 Iago projects his own misogynistic and paranoiac jealous
    suspicions – 'And it is thought abroad that 'twixt my sheets /
    He has done my office' (1.3.379–80) – into Othello, who at
    first would seem to be the opposite of a jealous type. Indeed,
    according to Renaissance geohumoural theories discussed in
    Sokol (2008), 122–4, 129, 137–8, Moors are constitutionally
    disinclined to jealousy.

Afterword

1 Sidney (1961), 7 and 5.

2 See Wyss (1996), 130–2, and Niżyńska (2001), 157–8, on the
    Renaissance reception of this passage in the *Symposium* via Pico
    della Mirandola, Erasmus and others.

3 Wind (1968), 176, which surrounds this sentence with 'The
    comic mask of the fluting Silenus, which must be opened to
    reveal the perfection of the gods, represented the same mystery
    as Marsyas flayed', and 'Dionysus, the dispenser of copious joy,
    is himself the god of tragic frenzy.'

4 See Wind (1968), 171–6 on Dante (1941), 2–3, *Paradiso* I, 20–1.
    Wyss (1996), especially 160 n.32, contests Wind's view of this.
    In the *House of Fame*, 1229–32, Chaucer misreads Dante and
    identifies Marsyas as female.

5 For instance, King Curtis's saxophone produces brilliantly mixed
    joyous, mocking and sarcastic cadences in The Coasters' 1958
    'Yakety Yak', a song written and produced by Lieber and Stoller.
    A wide range of speech-like articulations is heard from the
    saxophone of Herbert Hardesty, especially when playing with
    Fats Domino in recordings produced by Dave Bartholemew. In
    an extraordinary instance (this one not even involving reed
    instruments), the 1963 song 'Time Is On My Side' was originally
    largely 'spoken' by the trombone of Kai Winding; the next year
    it was given additonal words and recorded first by Irma Thomas
    and then by the Rolling Stones.

6 Mersenne (1637), II, 284 (Book 5, Proposition XXVI) (my
    translation).

7 Cocks and Scot (1952).

8   Marsh (2010), 168–9.

9   Whythorne (1962), 201–2. Whythorne follows this with another story in which an itinerant musician saves his life by dispersing a pack of wolves by playing his bagpipe.

10 Wotton (1624), 88. There may have been partial drafts of Wotton's *Elements* circulating by 1608: see Sokol (1994), 207 n.34.

11 *AYL* 2.7.181–4 and 191–4.

BIBLIOGRAPHY

Adair, Tom. 'Shakespeare's Horatian Poet.' *Notes and Queries* 45 (1998): 353–5.

Adams, Laurie. 'Apollo and Marsyas: a metaphor of creative conflict.' *Psychoanalytic Review* 7 (1988): 319–38.

Adams, Robert M. '"I Porni", review of I Modi, ed. by L. Lawner.' *New York Review of Books* (18 May 1989): 40.

Aelian. *A Registre of Hystories*. Trans. Abraham Fleming from Aelian's Various History. London, 1576.

Alberti, Leon Battista. *On Painting*. Trans. John R. Spencer. New Haven: Yale University Press, 1973.

Ames-Lewis, Francis. *The Intellectual Life of the Early Renaissance Artist*. New Haven: Yale University Press, 2000.

Apollodorus. *The Library*. Trans. Sir James George Frazer, Loeb Classical Library. Cambridge, MA: Harvard University Press, 1921.

Ariosto. *Orlando Furioso*. Venice, 1562.

Aristotle. *The Basic Works*. Ed. Richard McKeon. New York: Random House, 1941.

Astley, John. *The Art of Riding*. London, 1584.

Athenaeus. *The Deipnosphists*. Loeb ed., trans. Charles Burton Gulick. 7 vols. London: William Heinemann Ltd, 1927–41.

Atkins, J.H.W. *English Literary Criticism: The Renaissance*. London: Methuen & Co. Ltd., 1951.

Auden, W.H. 'Music in Shakespeare.' *Shakespeare Criticism, 1935–1960*. Ed. Anne Ridler. London: Oxford University Press, 1963. 306–28.

Auden, W.H. 'Introduction.' *William Shakespeare: The Sonnets*. Ed. William Burton. New York: New American Library, 1964. xvii–xxviii.

Austern, Linda Phyllis. 'Thomas Ravenscroft: Musical Chronicler of an Elizabethan Theater Company.' *Journal of the American Musicological Society* 38 (1985): 238–63.

Austern, Linda Phyllis. '"Alluring the Auditorie to Effeminacie":
    Music and the Idea of the Feminine in Early Modern England.'
    Music and Letters 74 (1993): 343–54.

Austern, Linda Phyllis. 'No Women are Indeed: The Boy Actor as
    Vocal Seductress in English Renaissance Drama.' *Embodied
    Voices: Representing Female Vocality in Western Culture.* Eds
    Leslie C. Dunn and Nancy A. Jones. Cambridge: Cambridge
    University Press, 1994. 83–102.

Austern, Linda Phyllis. 'Nature, Culture, Myth, and the Musician in
    Early Modern England.' *Journal of the American Musicological
    Society* 51 (1998a): 1–47.

Austern, Linda Phyllis. '"For, Love's a Good Musician":
    Performance, Audition, and Erotic Disorders in Early Modern
    Europe.' *Musical Quarterly* 82 (1998b): 614–53.

Austern, Linda Phyllis. 'Music in the Play.' *Othello.* The Oxford
    Shakespeare; Appendix D. Ed. Michael Neill. Oxford: Oxford
    University Press, 2006. 445–54.

Babb, Lawrence. *The Elizabethan Malady: a Study of Melancholia in
    English Literature from 1580 to 1642.* East Lansing: Michigan
    State College Press, 1951.

Baines, Anthony. *Bagpipes.* Oxford: Pitt Rivers Museum, 1960.

Baines, Anthony. *Bagpipes.* Third edition. Oxford: Pitt Rivers
    Museum, 1995.

Barber, C.L. 'Shakespeare in his Sonnets.' *Massachusetts Review* 1
    (1960): 648–72.

Bardelman, Claire. 'Apollo.' *A Dictionary of Shakespeare's Classical
    Mythology* (2009–). Ed. Yves Peyré. http://www.shakmyth.org/
    myth/28/apollo/some+secondary+sources

Barolsky, Paul. 'Dante and the Modern Cult of the Artist.' *Arion:
    A Journal of Humanities and the Classics* 12 (2004): 1–15.

Barton, Anne. *Essays, Mainly Shakespearean.* Cambridge and New
    York: Cambridge University Press, 1994.

Bate, Jonathan. *Shakespeare and Ovid.* Oxford: Clarendon Press,
    1993.

Bates, Ernest Sutherland. 'The Sincerity of Shakespeare's Sonnets.'
    Modern Philology 8 (1910): 87–106.

Bell, Ilona. 'The Circulation of Writings by Lady Mary Wroth.' *The
    Ashgate Research Companion to The Sidneys, 1500–1700.* 2 vols.
    Eds Margaret P. Hannay, Michael G. Brennan and Mary Ellen
    Lamb. Vol. 2. Farnham: Ashgate, 2015. 77–85.

Belsey, Catherine. 'Invocation of the Visual Image: Ekphrasis in "Lucrece" and Beyond.' *Shakespeare Quarterly* 63 (2012): 175–98.

Bender, John B. *Spenser's Literary Pictorialism*. Princeton: Princeton University Press, 1972.

Blunt, A. 'An Echo of the "Paragone" in Shakespeare.' *Journal of the Warburg and Courtauld Institutes* 2 (1939): 260–2.

Boenig, Robert. 'The Miller's Bagpipe: A Note on *The Canterbury Tales* A565–566.' *English Language Notes* 21 (1983): 1–6.

Booth, Stephen. *An Essay on Shakespeare's Sonnets*. New Haven: Yale University Press, 1969.

Booth, Stephen, ed. *Shakespeare's Sonnets: Edited with Analytic Commentary*. New Haven: Yale University Press, 2000.

Brennecke, Ernest. 'Shakespeare's Musical Collaboration with Morley.' *PMLA* 54 (1939): 139–52.

Brennecke, Ernest. 'Shakespeare's "Singing Man of Windsor".' *PMLA* 66 (1951): 1188–92.

Brennecke, Ernest. '"Nay, That's Not Next!": The Significance of Desdemona's "Willow Song".' *Shakespeare Quarterly* 4 (1953): 35–8.

Brereton, Geoffrey, ed. *The Penguin Book of French Verse 2: Sixteenth to Eighteenth Centuries*. Harmondsworth: Penguin Books, 1967.

Brodsky, Vivien. 'Widows in Late Elizabethan London: Remarriage, Economic Opportunity and Family Orientation.' *The World We Have Gained*. Eds Lloyd Bonfield, Richard M. Smith and Keith Wrightson. Oxford: Basil Blackwell, 1986. 122–54.

Brooks, Harold F., ed. *A Midsummer Night's Dream*. Second Arden Edition. London: Routledge, 1989.

Brown, Christopher. 'British Painting and the Low Countries, 1530–1630.' *Dynasties: Painting in Tudor and Jacobean England 1530–1630*. Ed. Karen Hearn. New York: Rizzoli, 1995. 27–31.

Bruster, Douglas. 'Shakespearean Spellings and Handwriting in the Additional Passages Printed in the 1602 Spanish Tragedy.' *Notes and Queries* 60 (2013): 420–4.

Bundy, Murray W. '"Invention" and "Imagination" in the Renaissance.' *Journal of English and Germanic Philology* 29 (1930): 535–45.

Burrow, Colin. 'Life and Work in Shakespeare's Poems.' *Proceedings of the British Academy* 97 (1998): 15–50.

Burrow, Colin, ed. *The Complete Sonnets and Poems*. New York: Oxford University Press, 2002.

Bushnell, Rebecca. 'Review of *Shakespeare's Nature: From Cultivation to Culture* – by Charlotte Scott.' *Shakespeare Quarterly* 66 (2015): 474–6.

Carlson, Raymond. '"Eccellentissimo poeta et amatore divinissimo": Benedetto Varchi and Michelangelo's poetry at the Accademia.' *Italian Studies* 69 (2014): 169–88.

Carpenter, Nan Cooke. 'Shakespeare and Music: Unexplored Areas.' *Renaissance Drama* 7 (1976): 243–55.

Case, John. *The Praise of Musicke*. Oxford, 1586. [Author only probable.]

Castiglione, Baldassare. *The Book of the Courtier*. Trans. Sir Thomas Hoby, 1561. London: J.M. Dent, 1975.

Chambers, E. K. *William Shakespeare: A Study of Facts and Problems*. 2 vols. Oxford: Clarendon Press, 1930.

Cheney, Patrick. *Shakespeare, National Poet-Playwright*. Cambridge: Cambridge University Press, 2004.

Cheney, Patrick. 'Poetry in Shakespeare's Plays.' *The Cambridge Companion to Shakespeare's Poetry*. Ed. Patrick Cheney. Cambridge: Cambridge University Press, 2007. 221–40.

Cheney, Patrick. *Shakespeare's Literary Authorship*. Cambridge: Cambridge University Press, 2008.

Cocks, William A., and F.S.A. Scot. 'James Talbot's Manuscript. (Christ Church Library Music MS 1187). III. Bagpipes.' *The Galpin Society Journal* 5 (1952): 44–7.

Colantuono, Anthony. 'The Penis Possessed: Phallic Birds, Erotic Magic, and Sins of the Body, ca. 1470–1500.' *The Body in Early Modern Italy*. Eds Julia L. Hairston and Walter Stephens. Baltimore, MD: Johns Hopkins University Press, 2010. 92–108.

Collinson, Patrick. *The Birthpangs of Protestant England: Religious and Cultural Change in the Sixteenth and Seventeenth Centuries*. Houndsmills: Macmillan, 1988.

Colman, E.A.M. *The Dramatic Use of Bawdry in Shakespeare*. London: Longman, 1974.

Conti, Natale. *Mythologiae*. Based on 2nd ed. (Frankfurt 1581). Trans. John Mulryan and Steven Brown. 2 vols. (continuous pagination). Tempe, AZ: ACMRS, 2006.

Coombs, Katherine. '"A Kind of Gentle Painting": Limning in 16th-Century England.' *European Visions, American Voices*. Ed. Kim Sloan. London: British Museum, 2009. 77–84.

Cooper, Tarnya. *Citizen Portrait*. New Haven: Yale University Press, 2012.

Cooper, Tarnya. 'Elizabethan Portraiture: Taste, Style and Patronage.' *Elizabeth I & Her People*. Ed. Tarnya Cooper. London: National Portrait Gallery, 2013. 11–19.

Cooper, Tarnya and Andrew Hadfield. 'Edmund Spenser and Elizabethan Portraiture.' *Renaissance Studies* 27 (2013): 407–34.

Cotgrave, Randall. *A Dictionaire of the French and English Tongues*. Reprint of London, 1611, introduction by William S. Woods. Columbia: University of South Carolina Press, 1968.

Crewdson, H.A.F. *The Worshipful Company of Musicians*. London: Charles Knight & Co. Ltd, 1971.

Cutts, John P. 'Pericles' "most heauenly musicke".' *Notes and Queries* 7 (1960): 172–4.

Daniel, David. *Julius Caesar*. Third Arden Edition. London: Thomson Learning, 2006.

Daniel, Samuel. *The poeticall essayes of Sam. Danyel*. London, 1599.

Dante. *The Paradiso of Dante Alighieri*. London: J.M. Dent and Sons, Ltd., 1941.

Dante. *The New Life*. Trans. William Anderson. Harmondsworth: Penguin Books, 1964.

da Vinci, Leonardo. *The Literary Works*. Eds Jean Paul Richter and Irma A. Richter, third edition. 2 vols. London: Phaidon Press, 1970.

De Grazia, Margreta. 'Revolution in Shakes-peares Sonnets.' *A Companion to Shakespeare's Sonnets*. Ed. Michael Schoenfeldt. Oxford: Blackwell, 2007. 57–69.

Deloney, Thomas. *The Gentle Craft*. London, 1690?

Doebler, John. 'Venus and Adonis: Shakespeare's Horses.' *Images of Shakespeare*. Eds Werner Habicht, D.J. Palmer and Roger Pringle. Newark: University of Delaware Press, 1988. 64–72.

Dolan, Frances E. 'Taking the Pencil out of God's Hand: Art, Nature and the Face-Painting Debate in Early Modern England.' *PMLA* 108 (1993): 224–39.

Dolce, Lodovico and Mark W. Roskill. *Dolce's Arentino and Venetian Art Theory of the Cinquecento*. Toronto: University of Toronto Press, 2000.

Donaldson, Ian. 'Adonis and His Horse.' *Notes and Queries* 19 (1972): 123–5.

Draya, Ren and Richard F. Whalen, eds. *Othello the Moor of Venice*. Truro, MA: Horatio Editions, 2010.

Dubrow, Heather. 'Shakespeare's Undramatic Monologues: Toward
    a Reading of the Sonnets.' *Shakespeare Quarterly* 32 (1981):
    55–68.

Dubrow, Heather. *Echoes of Desire: English Petrarchism and its
    Counter Discourses*. Ithaca: Cornell University Press, 1995.

Dubrow, Heather. '"Incertainties now crown themselves assur'd":
    The Politics of Plotting Shakespeare's Sonnets.' *Shakespeare
    Quarterly* 47 (1996): 291–305.

Dubrow, Heather. *The Challenges of Orpheus: Lyric Poetry and
    Early Modern England*. Baltimore: The Johns Hopkins University
    Press, 2011.

Dubrow, Heather. *Deixis in the Early Modern English Lyric:
    Unsettling Spatial Anchors Like 'Here,' 'This,' 'Come'*.
    Houndsmills: Palgrave, 2015.

Duffin, Ross W. 'An Encore for Shakespeare's Rare Italian Master.'
    Elizabethan Review 1 (1994): 21–5.

Duffin, Ross W. 'To Entertain a King: Music for James and Henry at
    the Merchant Taylors Feast of 1607.' *Music and Letters* 83
    (2002): 525–41.

Duffin, Ross W. *Shakespeare's Songbook*. London: Norton, 2004.

Duncan-Jones, Katherine. 'Was the 1609 *Shake-speares Sonnets*
    Really Unauthorized?' *Review of English Studies* 34 (1983):
    151–71.

Duncan-Jones, Katherine, ed. *Shakespeare's Sonnets*. Third Series
    Arden Edition. London: Thomson Learning, 2001.

Dundas, Judith. *Pencils Rhetoric: Renaissance Poets and the Art of
    Painting*. Newark: University of Delaware Press, 1993.

Edwards, Phillip. *Shakespeare and the Confines of Art*. London:
    Methuen & Co., 1968.

Egan, Gabriel. 'Hearing or seeing a play?: Evidence of early modern
    theatrical terminology.' *Ben Jonson Journal* 8 (2001): 327–47.

Elam, Keir. 'The Fertile Eunuch: *Twelfth Night*, Early Modern
    Intercourse, and the Fruits of Castration.' *Shakespeare Quarterly*
    47 (1996): 1–36.

Elam, Keir. '"Wanton Pictures": The Baffling of Christopher Sly and
    the Visual-Verbal Intercourse of Early Modern Erotic Arts.'
    Shakespeare and the Italian Renaissance. Ed. Michele Marrapodi.
    Farnham: Ashgate, 2014. 123–46.

Eliot, T.S. 'Poetry and Drama.' *On Poetry and Poets*. Lecture given in
    1951. London: Faber & Faber Ltd, 1957a. 72–88.

Eliot, T.S. 'The Tree Voices of Poetry.' *On Poetry and Poets*. Lecture given in 1953. London: Faber & Faber Ltd, 1957b. 89–102.

Eliot, T.S. *The Sacred Wood: Essays on Poetry and Criticism*. New York: Barnes and Noble Inc., 1964.

Elliott, Jack and Brett Greatley-Hirsch. 'Arden of Faversham, Shakespearean Authorship, and "The Print of Many".' *The New Oxford Shakespeare Authorship Companion*. Eds Gary Taylor and Gabriel Egan. Oxford: Oxford University Press, 2017. 139–81.

Erasmus, Desiderius. *Adages*. Vol. 72. Trans. Sir R.A.B. Mynors. Toronto: University of Toronto Press, 1992.

Erne, Lukas. *Shakespeare as Literary Dramatist*. Cambridge: Cambridge University Press, 2003.

Erne, Lukas. 'Print and Manuscript.' *The Cambridge Companion to Shakespeare's Poetry*. Ed. Patrick Cheney. Cambridge: Cambridge University Press, 2007. 54–71.

Esdaile, Arundell, ed. *Daniel's Delia and Drayton's Idea*. London: Chatto & Windus, 1908.

Evans, G. Blakemore, ed. *Romeo and Juliet*. New Cambridge Shakespeare. Cambridge: Cambridge University Press, 2003.

Evans, G. Blakemore, ed. *The Sonnets*. New Cambridge Shakespeare. Cambridge: Cambridge University Press, 2006.

Evans, Maurice. *Elizabethan Sonnets*. London: Dent, 1977.

Evans, Robert C., 'Flattery in Shakespeare's "Othello": The Relevance of Plutarch and Sir Thomas Elyot.' *Comparative Drama* 35 (2001): 1–41.

Ewbank, Inga-Stina. 'Shakespeare's Poetry.' *A New Companion to Shakespeare Studies*. Eds Kenneth Muir and S. Schoenbaum. Cambridge: Cambridge University Press, 1971. 99–115.

Ewbank, Inga-Stina. 'Sincerity and the Sonnet.' *Essays and Studies* 34 (1981): 19–44.

Ewbank, Inga-Stina. 'Self and Shakespeare's Sonnets.' *Self-Fashioning and Metamorphosis in Early Modern English Literature*. Eds Olav Lausund and Stein Haugom Olsen. Oslo: Novus, 2003. 1–14.

Faas, Ekbert. *Shakespeare's Poetics*. Cambridge: Cambridge University Press, 1986.

Fabry, Frank. 'Shakespeare's Witty Musician: Romeo and Juliet, IV.v.114–17.' *Shakespeare Quarterly* 33 (1982): 182–3.

Faherty, Teresa J. '"Othello dell'Arte": The Presence of "Commedia" in Shakespeare's Tragedy.' *Theatre Journal* 43 (1991): 179–94.

Fantham, Elaine. 'Liberty and the People in Republican Rome.'
    Transactions of the American Philological Association 135
    (2005): 209–29.
Farago, Claire J. *Leonardo Da Vinci's Paragone*. Leiden: E.J. Brill,
    1992.
Ferne, John. *The Blazon of Gentrie*. London, 1586.
Ferry, Anne. *All in War with Time: Love Poetry of Shakespeare,
    Donne, Jonson, Marvell*. Cambridge, MA: Harvard University
    Press, 1975.
Finney, Gretchen L. 'A World of Instruments.' *ELH* 20 (1953): 87–120.
Finney, Gretchen L. 'Music: A Book of Knowledge in Renaissance
    England.' *Studies in the Renaissance* 6 (1959): 36–63.
Finney, Gretchen L. *Musical Backgrounds for English Literature:
    1580–1650*. New Brunswick, NJ: Rutgers University Press,
    1962.
Fischlin, Daniel. *In Small Proportions: Poetics of the English Ayre,
    1596–1622*. Detroit, MI: Wayne State University Press, 1997.
Folkerth, Wes. *The Sound of Shakespeare (Accents on Shakespeare)*.
    London: Routledge, 2002.
Foster, Donald W. 'Master W. H., P. I. P.' *PMLA* 102 (1987): 42–54.
Fowler, Alastair. *Triumphal Forms: Structural Patterns in
    Elizabethan Poetry*. London: Cambridge University Press, 1970.
Freud, Sigmund. 'The Antithetical Sense of Primal Words.' *On
    Creativity and The Unconscious*. 1910. Ed. Benjamin Nelson.
    New York: Harper & Row, 1958a. 55–62.
Freud, Sigmund. 'The Theme of the Three Caskets.' *On Creativity
    and The Unconscious*. 1913. Ed. Benjamin Nelson. New York:
    Harper & Row, 1958b. 63–75.
Freud, Sigmund. *Jokes and their Relation to the Unconscious*. 1905.
    Trans. and ed. James Strachey. New York: W.W. Norton and
    Company, 1963.
Freud, Sigmund. 'Three Essays on the Theory of Sexuality.' *Pelican
    Freud Library*. 1905. Ed. Angela Richards. Vol. 7. London:
    Penguin, 1977. 45–169.
Freud, Sigmund. 'Psychoanalytic notes on an autobiographical
    account of a case of paranoia.' *Pelican Freud Library*. 1911. Ed.
    Angela Richards. Vol. 9. London: Penguin, 1984. 138–223.
Frye, Northrop. 'How True a Twain.' *The Riddle of Shakespeare's
    Sonnets*. New York: Basic Books, 1962. 23–53.
Fuller, John. *The Sonnet*. London: Methuen & Co., 1978.

Furness, H.H., ed. *Othello*. A New Variorum Edition of Shakespeare. Philadelphia: Lippincott, 1886.

Furness, H.H., ed. *Romeo and Juliet*. A New Variorum Edition of Shakespeare. London: J.M. Dent & Co., 1898.

Gardner, Helen, ed. *John Donne: The Divine Poems*. Second ed. Oxford: Oxford University Press, 1978.

Gascoigne, George. 'Certayne Notes of Instruction Concerning the Making of Verse or Ryme in English.' *Elizabehan Critical Essays*. Ed. G. Gregory Smith. Vol. 1. Oxford: Clarendon Press, 1904. 46–57.

Gaunt, D. M. 'Hamlet and Hecuba.' *Notes and Queries* 16 (1969): 136–7.

Gellert, Bridget. 'Note on Hamlet, II.ii.356–357.' *Notes and Queries* 15 (1968): 139–40.

Gibbons, Brian, ed. *Romeo and Juliet*. Second Arden Edition. London: Methuen, 1980.

Gillespie, Stuart. *Shakespeare's Books: A Dictionary of Shakespeare Sources*. London: Continuum, 2004.

Girard, René. *A Theatre of Envy*. Oxford: Oxford University Press, 1991.

Gombrich, E.H. *Meditations on a Hobby Horse*. London: Phaidon, 1963.

Gombrich, E.H. *Art and Illusion: A study in the psychology of pictorial representation*. Oxford: Phaidon, 1977.

Gordon, D. J. 'Poet and Architect: The Intellectual Setting of the Quarrel between Ben Jonson and Inigo Jones.' *Journal of the Warburg and Courtauld Institutes* 12 (1949): 152–78.

Grennan, Eamon. 'The Women's Voices in Othello: Speech, Song, Silence.' *Shakespeare Quarterly* 38 (1987): 275–92.

Greville, Fulke. *Certaine Learned and Elegant Works*. London, 1633.

Greville, Fulke. *Sir Fulke Greville's Life of Sir Philip Sidney*. Oxford: Clarendon Press, 1907.

Greville, Fulke. *Poems and Dramas*. Ed. Geoffrey Bullough. 2 vols. New York: Oxford University Press, 1945.

Greville, Fulke. *The Complete Poems and Plays of Fulke Greville, Lord Brooke (1554–1628), in Two Volumes*. Lampeter: Edward Mellen, 2006.

Guilpin, Edward. *Skialetheia or A Shadow of Truth in certaine Epigrams or Satyres*. London: Nicholas Ling, 1592.

Guinle, Francis. *The concord of this discord: La structure musicale du Songe d'une nuit d'été de William Shakespeare*. Saint-Etienne: Publications Universitaires de Saint-Etienne, 2003.

Gurr, Andrew. 'Shakespeare's First Poem: Sonnet 145.' *Essays in Criticism* 21 (1971): 221–6.

Gurr, Andrew. 'Shakespeare's Many-headed Audience.' *Essays in Theatre* 1 (1982): 52–62.

Gurr, Andrew. 'In-Jokes about Spear-Shakers.' *Notes and Queries* 58 (2011): 37–41.

Hagerman, Anita M. ' "But Worth pretends": Discovering Jonsonian Masque in Lady Mary Wroth's Pamphilia to Amphilanthus.' *Early Modern Literary Studies* 6 (2001) at http://extra.shu.ac.uk/emls/06-3/hagewrot.htm

Harbage, Alfred. 'Shakespeare and the Professions.' *Shakespeare's Art: Seven Essays*. Ed. Milton Crane. Chicago: University of Chicago Press, 1973. 11–28.

Hearn, Karen, ed. *Dynasties: Painting in Tudor and Jacobean England 1530–1630*. New York: Rizzoli, 1995.

Henke, Robert. 'Back to the Future: A Review of Comparative Studies in Shakespeare and the Commedia dell'Arte.' *Early Theatre* 11 (2008): 227–40.

Hieatt, A. Kent. *Short Time's Endless Monument: The Symbolism of the Numbers in Edmund Spenser's Epithalamion*. New York: Columbia University Press, 1960.

Hilliard, Nicholas. 'A Treatise Concerning the Arte of Limning.' *The Volume of the Walpole Society* 1 (1911–1912): 1–54.

Hollander, John. *The Untuning of the Sky: Ideas of Music in English Poetry, 1500–1700*. Princeton: Princeton University Press, 1961.

Holman, Peter. *Dowland: Lachrimae (1604) (Cambridge Music Handbooks)*. Cambridge: Cambridge University Press, 1999.

Holman, Peter and Paul O'Dette. 'John Dowland'. *Grove Music Online*. Revised 2009. http:// www.oxfordmusiconline.com/subscriber/article/grove/music/08103

Hopkins, Lisa. ' "What did thy song bode, lady?": *Othello* as Operatic Text.' *Shakespeare Yearbook* 4 (1994): 61–70.

Horace. 'The Art of Poetry.' *Classical Literary Criticism*. Eds T.S. Dorsch and Penelope Murray. London: Penguin Classics, 2000. 98–112, 180–3.

Hosley, Richard. 'Oberon, the Fairy Prince, by Ben Jonson.' *A Book of Masques*. Eds Stanley Wells, T.J.B. Spencer and Allardyce Nicoll. Cambridge: Cambridge University Press, 1980. 45–64.

Hubbard, Frank. *Three Centuries of Harpsichord Making*. Cambridge, MA: Harvard University Press, 1965.

Hulse, Clark. 'Shakespeare's Sonnets and the Art of the Face.' *John Donne Journal* 5 (1986): 3–26.

Hunt, John Dixon. 'Shakespeare and the Paragone: A Reading of *Timon of Athens*.' *Images of Shakespeare*. Eds Werner Habicht, D.J. Palmer and Roger Pringle. Newark: University of Delaware Press, 1988. 47–63.

Hunt, Maurice A. *Shakespeare's Religious Allusiveness: Its Play and Tolerance*. Aldershot: Ashgate, 2004.

Hunt, Maurice A. *Shakespeare's Speculative Art*. Basingstoke: Palgrave Macmillan, 2011.

Ingram, W.G. and Theodore Redpath, eds. *Shakespeare's Sonnets*. London: University of London Press, 1964.

Iselin, Pierre. 'Le musicien professionnel et sa représentation dans le drame élisabéthain.' *La représentation du monde du travail britannique dans la littérature et les arts*. 3 vols. Eds Michel Jouve and Marie-Claire Rouyer. Talence: MSHA, Université de Bordeaux III, 1988. 3:7–4.

Iselin, Pierre. '"My Music for Nothing": Musical Negotiations in *The Tempest*.' *Shakespeare Survey* 48 (1996): 135–45.

Jakobson, Roman. 'On Linguistic Aspects of Translation.' *The Translation Studies Reader*. 1959. Ed. Lawrence Venuti. London: Routledge, 2000 [1959]. 113–18.

Jankowski, Andrzej. *Shakespeare's Idea of Art*. Poznan: Adam Mickiewicz University Press, 1989.

Jonson, Ben. *Every Man In his Humor*. London, 1601.

Jonson, Ben. *The Cambridge Edition of the Works Online*. Ed. Martin Butler. Cambridge: Cambridge University Press, 2015.

Jonson, Ben. *The Complete Poems*. Ed. George Parfitt. London: Penguin, 1980.

Karim-Cooper, Farah. *Cosmetics in Shakespearean and Renaissance Drama*. Edinburgh: Edinburgh University Press, 2006.

Kelleher, Richard. '"Gold is the strength, the sinnewes of the world": continental gold and Tudor England.' *British Numismatic Journal* 77 (2007): 210–25.

Kellogg, Amanda Ogden. 'Pyrrhonist Uncertainty in Shakespeare's Sonnets.' *Shakespeare* 11 (2015): 408–24.

Kemp, Martin. 'Equal excellences': Lomazzo and the explanation of individual style in the visual arts.' *Renaissance Studies* 1 (1987): 1–26.

Kerrigan, John, ed. *The Sonnets and A Lover's Complaint*. New Penguin Shakespeare. New York: Penguin, 1968.

Kerrigan, John, 'Between Michelangelo and Petrarch: Shakespeare's sonnets of Art.' *On Shakespeare and Early Modern Literature*. Ed. John Kerrigan. Oxford: Oxford University Press, 2001. 23–40.

King, Rosalind. '"Then murder's out of tune": The Music and Structure of *Othello*.' *Shakespeare Survey* 39 (1987): 149–58.

King, Rosalind. '*Arden of Faversham*: The Moral History and the Thrill of Performance.' *The Oxford Handbook of Tudor Drama*. Eds Thomas Betteridge and Gregg Walker. Oxford: Oxford University Press, 2012. 635–52.

Kingsley-Smith, Jane. 'Mythology.' *A New Companion to English Renaissance Culture*. Ed. Michael Hattaway. Oxford: Wiley-Blackwell, 2010. 134–49.

Kingsley-Smith, Jane. '"Let me not to the Marriage of True Minds": Shakespeare's sonnet for Lady Mary Wroth.' *Shakespeare Survey* 69 (2016): 277–91.

Kitson, P.R. 'Virginal Jacks.' *Notes and Queries* 34 (1987): 204–5.

Klibansky, Raymond, Erwin Panofsky and Fritz Saxl. *Saturn and Melancholy*. London: Thomas Nelson, 1964.

Koskimies, Rafael. 'The Question of Platonism in Shakespeare's Sonnets.' *Neuphilologische Mitteilungen* 71 (1970): 260–70.

Koster, John. 'The Importance of the Early English Harpsichord.' *The Galpin Society Journal* 33 (1980): 45–73.

Kreps, Barbara. 'Elizabeth Pickering: The First Woman to Print Law Books in England and Relations within the Community of Tudor London's Printers and Lawyers.' *Renaissance Quarterly* 56 (2003): 1053–88.

Kristeller, Paul Oskar. 'The Modern System of the Arts: A Study in the History of Aesthetics (I).' *The Journal of the History of Ideas* 12 (1951): 496–527.

Kristeller, Paul Oskar. *Renaissance Concepts of Man*. New York: Harper & Row, 1972.

Kuttner, Ann L. 'Culture and History at Pompey's Museum.' *Transactions of the American Philological Association* 129 (1999): 343–73.

Kyd, Thomas. *The Spanish Tragedy*. Eds Clara Calvo and Jesus Tronch. London: Bloomsbury Publishing, 2013.

Langer, Ullrich. 'Invention.' *Cambridge History of Literary Criticism: The Renaissance*. Ed. Glyn P. Norton. Vol. 3. Cambridge: Cambridge University Press, 1999. 136–44.

Laroque, François. *Shakespeare's Festive World*. Cambridge: Cambridge University Press, 1991.

Latham, Agnes, ed. *As You Like It*. Second Arden Edition. London: Methuen & Co., 1975.

Lathrop, H. B. 'Shakespeare's Dramatic Use of Songs.' *Modern Language Notes* 23 (1908): 1–5.

Laurence, Anne. *Women in England 1500–1760*. London: Weidenfeld and Nicolson, 1994.

Lawner, Lynne, ed. *I Modi: The Sixteen Pleasures, An Erotic Album of the Italian Renaissance*. Evanston, IL: Northwestern University Press, 1988.

Leishman, J.B. *Themes and Variations in Shakespeare's Sonnets*. London: Hutchinson, 1961.

Leland, John and Alan Baragona. *Shakespeare's Prop Room: An Inventory*. Jefferson: McFarland & Company, 2016.

Leslie, Michael. 'The dialogue between bodies and souls: pictures and poesy in the English Renaissance.' *Word and Image* 1 (1985): 17–30.

Lever, J.W., ed. *Measure for Measure*. Second Arden Edition. New York: Vintage Books, 1966.

Lévi-Strauss, Claude. *The Raw and the Cooked*. Chicago: University of Chicago Press, 1983.

Levith, Murray J. *Shakespeare's Cues and Prompts*. London and New York: Continuum, 2007.

Lindley, David. *Shakespeare and Music*. London: Arden Shakespeare, 2006.

Lomazzo, Giovanni. *A Tracte Containing the Artes of Curious Painting, Carvinge, and Building*. Trans. and ed. Richard Haydocke. Oxford, 1598.

Lord, Suzanne. *Music from the Age of Shakespeare: A Cultural History*. Westport: Greenwood Press, 2003.

Mackinnon, Lachlan. *Shakespeare the Aesthete*. Basingstoke: Macmillan, 1988.

Mander, Karel van. *Principe et fondement de l'art noble et libre de la peinture*. Traduit et présenté par Jan Willem Noldus. Paris: Les Belles Lettres, 2008.

Maniates, Maria Rika. 'Marsyas Agonistes.' *Current Musicology* 69 (2000): 118–63.

Marcus, Steven. *The Other Victorians*. London: Weidenfeld and Nicholson, 1966.

Markham, Gervaise. *The Famous Whore or Noble Curtizan*. London: John Budge, 1609.

Marlowe, Christopher. *The Complete Plays*. Ed. J.B. Steane. Harmondsworth: Penguin Books, 1973.

Marsh, Christopher. *Music and Society in Early Modern England*. Cambridge: Cambridge University Press, 2010.

Marshall, Gail and Anne Thompson. 'Mary Cowden Clarke.' *Great Shakespeareans*. Ed. Gail Marshall. Vol. 7. London: Continuum, 2011. 58–91.

Marston, John. *The Metamorphosis of Pigmalions Image And Certain Satyres*. London, 1598.

Martinet, Marie-Madeleine. '*The Winter's Tale* et "Julio Romano".' *Etudes Anglaises* 28 (1975): 257–68.

Masson, Olivier. 'Sur un papyrus contenant des fragments d'Hipponax (P. Oxy XVIII. 2176).' *Revue des Études Grecques* 62 (1949): 300–19.

Maynard, Winifred. *Elizabethan Lyric Poetry and Its Music*. London and New York: Oxford University Press, 1986.

McCarthy, Dennis. 'Shakespeare and *Arden of Faversham*.' *Notes and Queries* 60 (2013): 391–7.

McClumpha, C.F. 'Parallels between Shakespeare's Sonnets and *Love's Labour's Lost*.' *Modern Language Notes* 15 (1900): 168–74.

McGee, Timothy J. 'The Fall of the Noble Minstrel: The Sixteenth-Century Minstrel in a Musical Context.' *Medieval and Renaissance Drama in England* 7 (1995): 98–120.

Meek, Richard. *Narrating the Visual in Shakespeare*. Farnham: Ashgate, 2009.

Melion, Walter S. *Shaping the Netherlandish Canon: Karel van Mander's Schilder-boeck*. Chicago: University of Chicago Press, 1991.

Mendelsohn, Leatrice. *Paragoni: Benedetto Varchi's Due Lezzioni and Cinquecento Art Theory*. Ann Arbor: University of Michigan Press, 1982.

Mercer, Eric. *English Art 1553–1625*. Oxford: Clarendon Press, 1962.

Merchant, W. Moelwyn. *Shakespeare and the Artist*. Oxford: Oxford University Press, 1959.

Mersenne, Marin. *De L'Harmonie Universelle*. 2 vols. Paris, 1637.

Michelangelo. *The Complete Poems*. Trans. Joseph Tusiani. London: Peter Owen, 1986.

Minear, Erin. *Reverberating Song in Shakespeare and Milton: Language, Memory, and Musical Representation*. Farnham, Surrey, and Burlington, VT: Ashgate, 2011.

Montaigne, Michel. *Essays*. Trans. John Florio. 3 vols. London: J.M. Dent & Sons Ltd, 1942.

Moore, Gene M. 'Virginal Jacks.' *Notes and Queries* 32 (1985): 31–2.

Morley, Thomas. *A plaine and easie introduction to practicall musicke set downe in forme of a dialogue*. London, 1597.

Moxey, Keith P.F. 'Master E.S. and the Folly of Love.' *Simiolus: Netherlands Quarterly for the History of Art* 11 (1980): 125–48.

Muir, Kenneth. 'In Defense of Timon's Poet.' *Essays in Criticism* 3 (1953): 120–1.

Muir, Kenneth. 'Shakespeare's Poets.' *Shakespeare Survey* 3 (1970): 91–100.

Muir, Kenneth. *Shakespeare's Sonnets*. London: George Allen & Unwin, 1979.

Muir, Kenneth, ed. *Othello*. Penguin Shakespeare. London: Penguin Books Ltd, 2005.

Mulcaster, Richard. *Positions for the Training up of Children*. London: 1581.

Nance, John V. 'Shakespeare and the Painter's Part.' *The New Oxford Shakespeare Authorship Companion*. Eds Gary Taylor and Gabriel Egan. Oxford: Oxford University Press, 2017. 261–77.

Naylor, Edward Woodhall. 'Music and Shakespeare.' *The Musical Antiquary* 1 (1910): 129–48.

Naylor, Edward Woodhall. *The Poets and Music*. London: J.M. Dent & Sons Ltd., 1928.

Naylor, Edward Woodhall. *Shakespeare and Music: With Illustrations from the Music of the 16th and 17th Centuries*. Second edition, first published 1896. London: J. M. Dent & Sons Ltd., 1931.

Neill, Michael, ed. *Othello*. The Oxford Shakespeare. Oxford: Oxford University Press, 2006.

Nelson, Katie. 'Love in the music room: Thomas Whythorne and the private affairs of Tudor music tutors.' *Early Music* 40 (2012): 15–26.

Niżyńska, Joanna. 'Marsyas's Howl: The Myth of Marsyas in Ovid's Metamorphoses and Zbigniew Herbert's "Apollo and Marsyas".' *Comparative Literature* 53 (2001): 151–69.

Nonnos. *Dionysiaca*. Trans. W.H.D. Rouse, Loeb Library. 3 vols. London: William Heinemann Ltd, 1940–2.

Nuttall, A.D. *Timon of Athens*. Hemel Hempstead: Harvester Wheatsheaf, 1989.

O'Neill, David G. 'The Influence of Music in the Works of John Marston, III.' *Music and Letters* 53 (1972): 400–10.

Ortiz, Joseph M. *Broken Harmony: Shakespeare and the Politics of Music*. Ithaca: Cornell University Press, 2011.

Overbury, Sir Thomas. *Characters*. London, 1614.

Overbury, Sir Thomas. *Characters*. London, 1616.

Ovid. *Fasti*. Trans. James George Frazer, Loeb Library. London: William Heinemann Ltd, 1959.

Ovid. *Metamorphoses*. Trans. Frank Justus Miller. Loeb Library. 2 vols. London: William Heinemann Ltd, 1971.

Ovid. *Metamorphoses*. Trans. Arthur Golding. Ed. Madeline Forey. London: Penguin Books, 2002.

Ovid. *Metamorphoses*. Trans. David Raeburn. London: Penguin Books, 2004.

Parr, Wolstenholme. *The Story of the Moor of Venice: Translated from the Italian. With Two Essays on Shakespeare, and Preliminary Observations*. London, 1795.

Pattison, Bruce. *Music and Poetry of the English Renaissance*. London: Methuen & Co. Ltd, 1970.

Pedretti, Carlo. *The Literary Works of Leonardo da Vinci, Commentary*. 2 vols. Oxford: Phaidon, 1977.

Petronella, Vincent F. 'The Musicians' Scene in *Romeo and Juliet*.' *Humanities Association Review/La Revue de l'Association des Humanites* 23 (1972): 54–6.

Pettet, E.C. 'Shakespeare's Conception of Poetry.' *Essays and Studies* 3 (1950): 29–46.

Pitcher, John, ed. *The Winter's Tale*. Third Arden Shakespeare. London: Methuen Drama, 2010.

Plato. *Collected Dialogues*. Ed. Francis Macdonald Cornford. Oxford: Clarendon Press, 1948.

Plutarch. *The lives of the noble Grecians and Romanes*. Trans. Thomas North. London, 1579.

Plutarch. *Moralia*. Trans. Philemon Holland. London, 1603.

Poisson, Rodney. 'Coriolanus I.vi.21–24.' *Shakespeare Quarterly* 15 (1964): 449–50.

Pollard, Tanya. 'Beauty's poisonous properties.' *Shakespeare Studies* 27 (1999): 187–210.

Poulton, Diana. *John Dowland*. Revised ed. Berkeley and Los Angeles: University of California Press, 1982.

Poulton, Diana. 'Dowland's Darkness.' *Early Music* 11 (1983): 517–19.

Price, David C. *Patrons and Musicians of the English Renaissance*. Cambridge: Cambridge University Press, 1981.

Prince, F.T., ed. *The Poems*. Arden Shakespeare. London: Routledge, 1992.

Prynne, William. *Histrio-Mastix: The players scourge, or, Actors Tragaedie*. London, 1632.

Puttenham, George. *The arte of English poesie*. London, 1589.

Quinn, Kelly A. 'Ecphrasis and Reading Practices in Elizabethan Narrative Verse.' *SEL: Studies in English Literature, 1500–1900* 44 (2004): 19–35.

Radden, Jennifer, ed. *The Nature of Melancholy: From Aristotle to Kristeva*. Oxford: Oxford University Press, 2000.

Rancière, Jacques. *The Aesthetic Unconscious*. Trans. Debra Keates and James Swenson. Cambridge: Polity Press, 2009.

Reynolds, Graham. '"The painter plays the spider".' *Apollo* 79 (1964): 279–84.

Reynolds, Simon. 'The Spider in the Cup: an echo of Plutarch's *Moralia* in *The Winter's Tale*.' *Notes and Queries* 257 (2012): 544–5.

Richmond, Hugh M. 'Ronsard and the English Renaissance.' *Comparative Literature Studies* 7 (1970): 141–60.

Ridley, M.R., ed. *Othello*. Second Arden Edition. London: Methuen & Co Ltd, 1967.

Ripin, Edwin M. 'Virginal'. *Grove Music Online*. http://www.oxfordmusiconline.com/subscriber/article/grove/music/43136

Robinson, P. 'Pretended Speech Acts in Shakespeare's Sonnets.' *Essays in Criticism* 51 (2001): 283–307.

Rollins, Hyder Edward, ed. *The Sonnets*. A New Variorun Edition of Shakespeare. 2 vols. Philadelphia, PA: J.B. Lippincott Company, 1944.

Rooley, Anthony. 'New Light on John Dowland's Songs of Darkness.' *Early Music* 11 (1983): 6–21.

Rooley, Anthony. *Performance: Revealing the Orpheus Within*. Shaftesbury, Dorset: Element, 1990.

Rosenberg, Raphael and Christoph Klein. 'The moving eye of the beholder: Eye tracking and the perception of paintings.' *Art, Aesthetics, and the Brain*. Eds Joseph P. Huston et al. Oxford: Oxford University Press, 2015. 79–110.

Ross, Lawrence J. 'Shakespeare's 'Dull Clown' and Symbolic Music.' *Shakespeare Quarterly* 17 (1966): 107–28.

Russell, Raymond. *The Harpsichord and Clavichord*. Second ed., revised by Howard Schott. London: Faber & Faber, 1973.

Sabatier, Armelle. *Shakespeare and Visual Culture*. Arden Shakespeare Dictionaries. London: Bloomsbury Arden Shakespeare, 2016.

Sanders, Norman, ed. *Othello*. The New Cambridge Shakespeare. Cambridge: Cambridge University Press, 2012.

S[andys], G[eorge]. *Ovid's Metamorphoses Englished, Mythologiz'd, and Represented in Figures, an Essay to the Translation of Virgil's Aeneis*. Oxford, 1632.

Schmidgall, Gary. *Shakespeare and the Poet's Life*. Lexington: University Press of Kentucky, 1990.

Schoenbaum, S. 'Shakespeare's Dark Lady: a question of identity.' *Shakespeare's Styles*. Eds Inga-Stina Ewbank, P. Edwards and G.K. Hunter. London: Cambridge University Press, 1980. 221–39.

The Second Maiden's Tragedy. Reprint of 1909. Ed. W.W. Gregg. Oxford: The Malone Society, 1964.

Seng, Peter J. *The Vocal Songs in the Plays of Shakespeare*. Cambridge, MA: Harvard University Press, 1967.

Shakespeare, William. *The First Folio*. Facsimile of 1623 prepared by Charlton Hinman. New York: W.W. Norton, 1968.

Shakespeare, William. *Pericles*. Ed. Suzanne Gosset. Third Arden Edition. London: Methuen Drama, 2004.

Shakespeare, William and John Fletcher. *The Two Noble Kinsmen, 1634*. Facsimile of first edition. Oxford: The Malone Society, 2005.

Shiner, Larry. *The Invention of Art: A Cultural History*. Chicago: University of Chicago Press, 2001.

Sidney, Philip. *Apology for Poetrie*. Ed. J.C. Collins. Oxford: Clarendon Press, 1961.

Sidney, Philip. *The Poems of Sir Philip Sidney*. Ed. William A. Ringler. Oxford: Clarendon Press, 1962.

Sillars, Stuart. *Shakespeare and the Visual Imagination*. Cambridge: Cambridge University Press, 2015.

Silvayn, Alexander. 'Declamation 95 of *The Orator*.' *Shakespeare, The Merchant of Venice*. 1596, 'Written in French and Englished by L. P[iot]'. Ed. John Russell Brown. London: Methuen & Co. Ltd, 1977. 168–72.

Skeaping, Lucie and Roger Clegg. *Singing Simpkin and Other Bawdy Jigs*. Exeter: University of Exeter Press, 2014.

Skinner, Quentin. *Forensic Shakespeare*. Oxford: Oxford University Press, 2014.

Sloane, Thomas O. 'Schoolbooks and Rhetoric: Erasmus's *Copia*.' *Rhetorica* 9 (1991): 113–29.

Small, Jocelyn Penny. *Cacus and Marsyas in Etrusco-Roman Legend*. Princeton, NJ: Princeton University Press, 1982.

Smith, Bruce R. 'The Contest of Apollo and Marsyas: Ideas about Music in the Middle Ages.' *By Things Seen: Reference and Recognition in Medieval Thought*. Ed. David L. Jeffrey. Ottawa: University of Ottawa Press, 1979. 81–107.

Smith, Bruce R. *The Acoustic World of Early Modern England: Attending to the O-Factor*. Chicago: University of Chicago Press, 1999.

Smith, Rochelle. 'Admirable Musicians: Women's Songs in *Othello* and *The Maid's Tragedy*.' *Comparative Drama* 28 (1994): 311–23.

Smith, Rosalind. 'Reading Mary Stuart's Casket Sonnets: Reception, Authorship, and Early Modern Women's Writing.' *Parergon* 29 (2012): 149–73.

Sokol, B.J. 'Numerology in Fulke Greville's *Caelica*.' *Notes and Queries* 27 (1980): 327–9.

Sokol, B.J. 'A Spenserian Idea in *The Taming of the Shrew*.' *English Studies* 66 (1985): 310–16.

Sokol, B.J. 'Painted Statues, Ben Jonson and Shakespeare.' *Journal of the Warburg and Courtauld Institutes* 52 (1989): 250–3.

Sokol, B.J. 'Holofernes in Rabelais and Shakespeare and Some Manuscript Verses of Thomas Harriot.' *Etudes Rabelaisiennes* 25 (1991a): 131–5.

Sokol, B.J. 'Figures of Repetition in Sidney's *Astrophil and Stella* and in the Scenic Form of *Measure for Measure.*' *Rhetorica* 9 (1991b): 131–46.

Sokol, B.J. '*The Merchant of Venice* and the Law Merchant.' *Renaissance Studies* 6 (1992): 60–7.

Sokol, B.J. *Art and Illusion in The Winter's Tale.* Manchester: Manchester University Press, 1994.

Sokol, B.J. 'Constitutive Signifiers or Fetishes in *The Merchant of Venice*?' *International Journal of Psycho-Analysis* 76 (1995): 373–87.

Sokol, B.J. 'Prejudice and Law in *The Merchant of Venice.*' *Shakespeare Survey 51.* Ed. Stanley Wells. Cambridge: Cambridge University Press, 1998. 159–73.

Sokol, B.J. *A Brave New World of Knowledge: Shakespeare's The Tempest and Early Modern Epistemology.* London: Associated University Presses, 2003.

Sokol, B.J. *Shakespeare and Tolerance.* Cambridge: Cambridge University Press, 2008.

Sokol, B.J. 'Shakespeare's Weak Signature in Sonnet 76.' *Notes and Queries* 58 (2011): 236–7.

Sokol, B.J. 'Cerimon's "rough and woeful music" in *Pericles.*' *Shakespeare* 10 (2014): 46–55.

Sokol, B.J. and Mary Sokol. *Shakespeare, Law and Marriage.* Cambridge: Cambridge University Press, 2003.

Spenser, Edmund. *The Faerie Queene.* Ed. J.C. Smith, 1909–10. 2 vols. Oxford: Oxford University Press, 1961.

Spenser, Edmund. *Minor Poems.* Ed. E. de Selincourt, 1910. Oxford: Clarendon Press, 1966.

Starr, Pamela F. 'Music Education and the Conduct of Life in Early Modern England: A Review of the Sources.' *Music Education in the Middle Ages and the Renaissance.* Eds Russell E Murray, Jr, Cynthia J. Cyrus and Susan Forscher Weiss. Bloomington: Indiana University Press, 2010. 193–206.

Stern, Tiffany. *Making Shakespeare: From Stage to Page: The Pressures of Stage and Page.* London: Routledge, 2004.

Stern, Tiffany. *Documents of Performance in Early Modern England.* Cambridge: Cambridge University Press, 2009.

Stern, Tiffany. '"I Have Both the Note, and Dittie About Me": Songs on the Early Modern Page and Stage.' *Common Knowledge* 17 (2011): 306–20.

Sternfeld, F.W. 'The Use of Song in Shakespeare's Tragedies.' *Proceedings of the Royal Musical Association* 86 (1959): 45–59.

Sternfeld, Frederick W. and Mary Joiner Chan. 'Come Live with Me and Be My Love.' *Comparative Literature* 22 (1970): 173–87.

Stevens, John. *Music & Poetry in the Early Tudor Court.* Cambridge: Cambridge University Press, 1979.

Stevenson, Warren. 'Shakespeare's Hand in The Spanish Tragedy 1602.' *SEL: Studies in English Literature, 1500–1900* 8 (1968): 307–21.

Stewart, J.I.M. *Character and Motive in Shakespeare.* London: Longman Green & Co., 1949.

Stone, Lawrence. *The Family, Sex and Marriage in England 1500–1800.* London: Weidenfeld and Nicolson, 1977.

Stone, Lawrence. *The Crisis of the Aristocracy, 1558–1641.* Revised, originally 1965. Oxford: Clarendon Press, 1979.

Strong, Roy. *The English Icon: Elizabethan & Jacobean Portraiture.* New Haven: Yale University Press, 1970.

Strong, Roy. *The English Renaissance Miniature.* London: Thames & Hudson, 1983.

Talvacchia, Bette. 'The Rare Italian Master and the Posture of Hermione in *The Winter's Tale*.' *LIT: Literature, Interpretation, Theory* 3 (1992): 163–74.

Talvacchia, Bette. 'Classical Paradigms and Renaissance Antiquarianism in Giulio Romano's "I Modi".' *I Tatti Studies in the Italian Renaissance* 7 (1997): 81–118.

Talvacchia, Bette. *Taking Positions: On the Erotic in Renaissance Culture.* Princeton: Princeton University Press, 1999.

Tassi, Marguerite A. *The Scandal of Images: Iconoclasm, Eroticism, and Painting in Early Modern English Drama.* Selinsgrove: Susquehanna University Press, 2005.

Tayler, E.W. *Nature and Art in Renaissance Literature.* New York: Columbia University Press, 1964.

Taylor, Gary. *Castration: An Abbreviated History of Western Manhood.* New York: Routledge, 2000.

Taylor, Gary. 'Did Shakespeare Write *The Spanish Tragedy* Additions?' *The New Oxford Shakespeare Authorship Companion.* Eds Gary Taylor and Gabriel Egan. Oxford: Oxford University Press, 2017. 246–60.

Thomas, Keith. *Man and the Natural World: Changing Attitudes in England 1500–1800.* London: Allen Lane, 1983.

Thompson, Ann and Gail Marshall. 'Mary Cowden Clarke.' *The Great Shakespeareans Vol VII*. Ed. Gail Marshall. London: Continuum, 2011. 58–91.

Thompson, Ann and Neil Taylor, eds. *Hamlet, Revised Edition*. Second Quarto, Arden Third Series. London: Bloomsbury, 2016.

Thomson, Patricia. 'The Literature of Patronage 1580–1630'. *Essays in Criticism* 2 (1952): 267–84.

Thurman, Christopher. 'Fine Frenzies: Theseus, Shakespeare, and the Politics of Their Poets.' *Shakespeare* 11 (2015): 115–34.

Tilley, Morris Palmer. *A Dictionary of the Proverbs in England in the Sixteenth and Seventeenth Centuries*. Ann Arbor: University of Michigan Press, 1950.

Tittler, Robert. *Portraits, Painters, and Publics in Provincial England 1540–1640*. Oxford: Oxford University Press, 2013.

Trevor, Douglas. *The Poetics of Melancholy in Early Modern England*. Cambridge: Cambridge University Press, 2004.

Trillini, Regula Hohl. 'The Gaze of the Listener: Shakespeare's Sonnet 128 and Early Modern Discourses of Music and Gender.' *Music and Letters* 89 (2008): 1–17.

Trudell, Scott A. 'Performing Women in English Books of Ayres.' *Gender and Song in Early Modern England*. Eds Katherine R. Larson and Leslie C. Dunn. Farnham: Ashgate, 2014. 15–30.

Tudeau-Clayton, Margaret. 'Stepping Out of Narrative Line: A Bit of Word, and Horse, Play in Venus and Adonis.' *Shakespeare Survey* 53 (2000): 12–24.

Valery, Paul. *The Art of Poetry*. Trans. Denise Folliot. New York: Bollingen Foundation, 1958.

Van Mander, Karel. *De l'Art Noble et Libre de la Peinture*. Paris: Les Belles Lettres, 2008.

Varchi, Benedetto. *Due Lezzioni*. Fiorenza, 1549. https://archive.org/details/dvelezzionidimbe00varc.

Vasari, Giorgio. *Lives of the Artists*. Trans. George Bull. 2 vols. London: Penguin, 1987.

Vasari, Giorgio. *Lives of the Most Eminent Painters Sculptors and Architects*. Trans. Gaston Du C. de Vere 1912. 2 vols. London: David Campbell Publishers, 1996.

Vendler, Helen. *The Art of Shakespeare's Sonnets*. Cambridge, MA: Harvard University Press, 1999.

Walton, Izaak. *The Lives of Doctor John Donne, Sir Henry Wotton, etc*. Introduction by George Saintsbury. London: Oxford University Press, 1966.

Watkins, Glen. *The Gesulado Hex: Music, Myth and Memory*. New York: W.W. Norton & Co., Inc., 2010.

Weis, René, ed. *Romeo and Juliet*. Third Arden Edition. London: Bloomsbury, 2012.

Welch, R. D. 'Shakespeare–Musician.' *Musical Quarterly* 8 (1922): 510–27.

Wells, Robin Headlam. 'John Dowland and Elizabethan Melancholy.' *Early Music* 13 (1985): 514–28.

Wells, Robin Headlam. *Elizabethan Mythologies*. Cambridge: Cambridge University Press, 1994.

Wells, Stanley. *An A-Z Guide to Shakespeare*. Oxford: Oxford University Press, 2016. www.oxfordreference.com/view/10.1093/acref/9780191740763.001.0001/acref-9780191740763-miscMatter-0006

Wells, Stanley and Gary Taylor, eds. *Oxford Electronic Shakespeare*. Oxford: Oxford University Press, 1989.

Wells, Stanley and Gary Taylor. *William Shakespeare, a Textual Companion*. Oxford: Oxford University Press, 1997.

Wells, Stanley and Paul Edmondson. 'The Plurality of Shakespeare's Sonnets.' *Shakespeare Survey* 65 (2012): 211–20.

Whall, Helen M. 'Hamlet and the Manner of the Miniature.' *Interfaces* 5 (1994): 295–315.

White, Martin, ed. *Arden of Faversham*. London: A&C Black, 2000.

Whythorne, Thomas. *Autobiography*. Old spelling edition. London: Clarendon Press, 1961.

Whythorne, Thomas. *Autobiography*. London: Oxford University Press, 1962.

Wilkes, G.A. 'The Sequence of the Writings of Fulke Greville, Lord Brooke.' *Studies in Philology* 56 (1959): 489–503.

Wilkes, G.A. '"Left . . . to Play the Ill Poet in My Own Part": The Literary Relationship of Sidney and Fulke Greville.' *Review of English Studies* 57 (2006): 291–309.

Williams, Gordon. *A Dictionary of Sexual Language and Imagery in Shakespeare and Stuart Literature*. 3 vols. London: Athlone Press, 1994.

Williams, Gordon. *Shakespeare's Sexual Language: a Glossary*. London: Continuum, 2006.

Wilson, Christopher R. 'Shakespeare's "Fair viols, sweet lutes, and rude pipes" as Symbolic Musics.' *Lute News: The Lute Society Magazine* 48 (1998): 7–12.

Wilson, Christopher R. 'Shakespeare and Early Modern Music.' *The Edinburgh Companion to Shakespeare and the Arts*. Eds Mark Thornton Burnett, Adrian Streete and Ramona Wray. Edinburgh: Edinburgh University Press, 2011a. 119–41.

Wilson, Christopher R. *Shakespeare's Musical Imagery*. London: Continuum, 2011b.

Wilson, Christopher R. and Michela Calore. *Music in Shakespeare: A Dictionary*. Athlone Shakespeare Dictionary Series. London: Thoemmes, 2005.

Wilson, Miranda. 'Watching flesh: poison and the fantasy of temporal control in Renaissance England.' *Renaissance Studies* 27 (2013): 97–113.

Wilson, Richard. '"A stringless instrument": Richard II and the Defeat of Poetry.' *Autour de Richard II de William Shakespeare*. Ed. Guillaume Winter. Paris: Artois Presses Université, 2005. 13–26.

Wind, Edgar. *Pagan Mysteries of the Renaissance*. London: Faber & Faber, 1968.

Winternitz, Emanuel. 'The Curse of Pallas Athena: Notes on a "Contest Between Apollo and Marsyas" in the Kress Collection.' *Studies in the History of Art, Dedicated to William E. Suida on his 80th Birthday*. Ed. Samuel H. Kress Foundation. London: Phaidon Press, 1959. 186–95.

Wiseman, T. P. 'Satyrs in Rome? The Background to Horace's Ars Poetica.' *The Journal of Roman Studies* 78 (1988): 1–13.

Wittkower, Rudolf and Margot Wittkower. *Born Under Saturn*. London: Weidenfeld and Nicolson, 1963.

Wollheim, Richard. *Art and its Objects*. New York: Harper & Row, 1971.

Wong, Katrine K. *Music and Gender in English Renaissance Drama*. New York: Routledge, 2013.

Woodfill, Walter L. *Musicians in English Society from Elizabeth to Charles I*. Princeton and London: Princeton University Press and Oxford University Press, 1953.

Wotton, Sir Henry. Letters from Venice. PRO SP 99/5.

Wotton, Sir Henry. *The Elements of Architecture*. London, 1624.

Wyatt, Sir Thomas. *Collected Poems*. Oxford: Oxford University Press, 1975.

Wyss, Edith. *The Myth of Apollo and Marsyas in the Art of the Italian Renaissance*. London: Associated University Presses, 1996.

Young, Alan R. 'A Note on the Tournament Impresas in *Pericles*.' *Shakespeare Quarterly* 36 (1985): 453–56.

Young, Wayland. *Eros Denied*. London: Weidenfeld and Nicholson, 1964.

Younge, Nicholas. *Musica Transalpina*. London, 1588.

Zecher, Carla. *Sounding Objects: Musical Instruments, Poetry, and Art in Renaissance France*. Toronto: University of Toronto Press, 2007.

INDEX

Note: pages containing images are listed in italics.